Until My Freedom Has Come

The New Intifada in Kashmir

Until My Freedom Has Come

The New Intifada in Kashmir

Edited by
SANJAY KAK

Haymarket Books
Chicago, IL

First published in 2011 by Penguin Books India.
This edition published in 2013 by Haymarket Books.

Published by:
Haymarket Books
P.O. Box 180165
Chicago, IL 60618
773-583-7884
info@haymarketbooks.org
www.haymarketbooks.org

Cover photos:
Bottom: An Indian paramilitary solider stands guard outside a closed market during a shutdown in Srinagar, India, Friday, Jan. 6, 2012. A general strike against the killing of a student by paramilitary soldiers earlier that week during a demonstration over frequent power cuts had shut most of Indian-controlled Kashmir. (AP Photo/Dar Yasin)
Top: Srinagar protest, August 18, 2008, by Javed Dar.

ISBN: 978-1-60846-252-0

Trade distribution:
In the U.S. through Consortium Book Sales and Distribution, www.cbsd.com
In the UK, Turnaround Publisher Services, www.turnaround-uk.com
In Canada, Publishers Group Canada, www.pgcbooks.ca
In Australia, Palgrave Macmillan, www.palgravemacmillan.com.au
All other countries, Publishers Group Worldwide, www.pgw.com

Special discounts are available for bulk purchases by organizations
and institutions. Please contact Haymarket Books for more information
at 773-583-7884 or info@haymarketbooks.org.

This book was published with the generous support of
the Wallace Global Fund and Lannan Foundation.

Printed in Canada by union labor on recycled paper containing 100 percent
postconsumer waste in accordance with the Green Press Initiative,
www.greenpressinitiative.org.

Library of Congress CIP Data is available.

10 9 8 7 6 5 4 3 2 1

RECYCLED
Paper made from
recycled material
FSC® C103567

Contents

Captive City

A Place of Blood and Memory

Tsaalun chu vuzmall ti tratay
Tsaalun chu mandanis gatakar
Tsaalun chu parbatas karun attey
Tsaalun chu manz athas hyon naar
Tsaalun chu paan kadun grattay
Tsaalun chu khyon ekvat zahar khar

We must bear the lightning and thunder
We must bear the darkness at noon
We must bear the mountain on our shoulders
We must bear the fire we place on our palms
We must bear our bodies milled to dust
We must bear to swallow the poison load together

—Sheikh Nuruddin
Nund Rishi | Sheikh-ul-Alam | Alamdar-e-Kashmir
1377–1440

The Fire Is at My Heart
An Introduction

Away from the tumult of its streets, away from the heady slogans, from the explosive whoosh and clatter of tear-gas shells, and the deadly crackle of live ammunition, one moment returns from Kashmir's turbulent summer of 2010. It insinuates a place for itself, a whispered observation of oddly unsettling precision. *Mummy, mae-ae aav heartas fire*. Mummy, the fire is at my heart.

These were the last words spoken by twenty-four-year-old Fancy Jan as she turned away from the first-floor window of her working-class home in downtown Srinagar that July morning. She was reaching for the curtain, her family said, to keep out the acrid tear-gas smoke floating in from the streets of her volatile Batmaloo neighbourhood. (The window lacked glass-panes; the room was still being built.) The 'fire' she had drawn into the privacy of her home was a bullet, and she dropped dead soon after, a victim of a casual brutality, of a weapon fired carelessly by one of the hundreds of police and paramilitary soldiers on the streets outside.

Fancy Jan was one of a handful of women killed in the summer, in this most recent upsurge in Kashmir's tortuous history. The rest were young men in their twenties, but many were just teenagers—boys, really. That grisly calendar had been quietly unveiled early in January 2010, when sixteen-year-old Inayat Ahmad was shot dead by paramilitary soldiers in the heart of Srinagar. On 31 January, a thirteen-year-old was killed when a tear-gas shell fired by the Jammu and Kashmir police hit Wamiq Farooq on the head. Less than a week later, as sixteen-year-old Zahid Farooq returned from an evening's cricket with his friends, he was shot dead by a passing Border Security Force patrol. His killing may have been provoked, we are told, because the boys had jeered at the passing vehicle of a senior officer.

The years since 1989, when the uprising against Indian rule first began, have been bloody for Kashmiris. The militancy, initially armed and supported by Pakistan, was quick to draw the full weight of the Indian sledgehammer. For Kashmiris, the insurgency, and the counter-insurgency that was unleashed to flatten it, ended up shredding the everyday fabric of life. The sheer force of India's massive military commitment may appear to have overwhelmed the armed militancy, but twenty years of this presence has resulted in a deeply militarized society. With well over 6,00,000 army, police and paramilitary personnel already deployed in Kashmir, the numbers that go into holding down a rebellious population are clearly at saturation point. Today the Kashmir Valley has the highest concentration of soldiers in the world—more than Afghanistan, Iraq or Burma. It is only in the last five years that the shape of this intervention has been dragged out of the guarded penumbra of Indian 'national interest'. Away from that shadowy protection, it now stands increasingly exposed as a clumsy attempt to overwhelm, with sheer force, that obstinate, often inchoate, but in the end, very political desire for *Azadi*—freedom.

These decades of a silent, undeclared war have extracted an enormous price: seventy thousand Kashmiris have been killed since 1989, and eight thousand have gone 'missing'. To this must be added the less visible costs of torture, rape, life-long physical incapacities and grievous economic, social, and psychological damage. The extent of this devastation will probably never be fully estimated, but its restive contours are beginning to stir under the blanket silence that has enveloped Kashmir for most of this recent past. The long-whispered murmurs about the existence of mass graves, for example, found confirmation only in 2009, when a civil society group patiently assembled a list of their locations. (The

International People's Tribunal on Human Rights and Justice in Kashmir has recorded nearly 3,000 such unknown and unrecorded graves.)[1]

Word of one such unmarked grave, in the faraway forests of Machil, in Kupwara, north Kashmir, arrived in the month of May 2010. It was news because it was still a fresh site: three unarmed civilians had been killed, shot in cold blood by soldiers of a Rashtriya Rifles unit, the specialized counter-insurgency force of the Indian Army. The bodies had been buried anonymously, and then announced as those of militants killed in an 'encounter'. Such calculated venality is not unusual, except that it had become public in time, and news of it had reached the already volatile streets of Srinagar.

It was on the fringes of one of these protests that another lethally aimed police tear-gas canister took apart the skull of seventeen-year old Tufail Matoo, as he walked home from his tuition class. This was already June. Tufail's killing set off huge, emotionally surcharged demonstrations, unprecedented even by Kashmir's overwrought standards. A civilian killed inevitably led to other killings by the police and paramilitary soldiers. Sometimes there were several in a day. Then more protests, and more killing. In four months of this bloody oscillation 112 people had been shot dead on the streets of Kashmir.

Summer has gradually emerged as the season for a face-off, played out almost ritually in the Valley. India comes wearing the mask of what it calls its 'security' forces—the army, paramilitary and police personnel it deploys. And confronting this well-entrenched military machinery have been thousands of young men who have taken on the soldiers in a *kani jang*—a war with stones.

---

[1]Buried Evidence: Unknown, Unmarked, and Mass Graves in Indian-administered Kashmir, 2009 [http://www.kashmirprocess.org/reports/graves/toc.html].

Perhaps it is the extraordinary duration of its troubles that's given Kashmir's summer this sharp edge. You could date its origins to the anti-feudal struggle against its autocratic maharaja in the 1930s. Or say that Kashmir is the unfinished business of the end of Empire, of the Partition of British India, carved up into India and Pakistan in 1947. Either way, that still makes it one of the oldest unresolved disputes in the world. Or maybe it's just the skin of its people that has worn thin over the long years of this uprising. The gentle warmth of its June sun now seems enough to stoke up a volatile impulse, and provoke people to take their places outside of their homes, in the streets, in protest.

So every year since 2008, just when Indian security forces think they have a firm grip on the situation, the incendiary arrival of summer reduces the patrolling police and paramilitary forces to puzzled bystanders. Then they can only watch, as people reclaim the streets, coming out in massive demonstrations, sometimes hundreds of thousands strong, and noisily destroy the silence imposed on them. Several decades after the idea of Azadi was first voiced openly in the towns and villages of the Valley, one slogan, chanted endlessly, continues to dominate this tumult.

Hum kya chahte? What do we want? *Azadi!* Freedom.

Sceptics in India, eager to contain Kashmir within the beleaguered imagination of the Indian nation-state, will continue to tirelessly interrogate the many uncertainties packed into that fraught word: freedom. But in the summer of 2010, protesters in Kashmir unambiguously spelt out at least one of its oldest meanings. On a blackboard of macadam, they scrawled in large white letters: Go India. Go back.

This is no ordinary rejection, for it comes at a time when India has ambitiously invited itself to the select ring of global superpowers, parlaying its potential for economic growth, and the lure of its huge markets, into greater international clout. With a standing army that is more than 1.3 million strong, India does appear ready to be part of this club of the powerful: there are ambitious whispers of a seat in the United Nations Security Council.

Yet, in 2010, with at least half of its huge army deployed in 'securing' Kashmir, India's fierce grip was frequently beginning to look slippery. A vast and often brutal counter-insurgency grid, an all-pervasive system of surveillance and intelligence-gathering, tight control over the media—yet nothing seemed to be giving India traction. With the place of the gun-wielding *mujahid* rebels of an earlier generation now taken up by these unarmed civilians, you couldn't help notice that the very long embrace with militarization had seriously dulled the government's reflexes.

India has historically—and systematically—circumscribed the political space for the 'separatist' sentiment in Kashmir. Having driven it underground in the 1970s, and into armed rebellion by the end of the 1980s, a long and humiliating history of rigged elections followed. A cynically imposed superstructure of what are locally called 'pro-India' parties, but are really disempowered proxies, now play out an elaborate charade of democracy. Faced with a massive upsurge in 2010, the Indian state seems to have reacted in the only way it knew. It ratcheted up the mechanisms of coercion.

Two recent images reflected this response. The first was a cosmetic makeover for the patrolling soldiers, as the paramilitary were deployed on the streets in futuristic new protective body-gear. This brittle air of menace, 'Darth Vader in cheap black plastic', as one acidic commentator in Srinagar called them, was shored up by new 'non-lethal' measures of crowd control. Proudly announced by the mandarins of the home ministry in New Delhi, they included a pressure-pump pellet-gun that shoots out hundreds of high-velocity plastic pellets simultaneously. (On the very first day it was used, in Sopore town in north Kashmir, a paramilitary soldier fired the 'non-lethal' gun at close range, and killed a man.)

More telling evidence of this battlefront panic was another, less obvious weapon that the paramilitary soldiers took to. Unable to stem the tide of protesters, and with a kill rate beginning to average one civilian a day, the soldiers began to aggressively use slingshots. They were loading catapults with a vicious charge of glass marbles and sharp pebbles, and this abomination led to permanent damage to the eyes—and sometimes even blindness—for scores of young protesters. But it didn't kill them, which would have been bad for public relations.

In the full glare of the public eye, the contrast could not have been more stark and, in the end, more damaging for India's image as a showpiece of Democracy at Work. Though padded up in their black armour, the soldiers appeared daunted by the raw courage of the young men. The stone-throwing *sang-baz*, in turn, with their faces covered, and their chests often bared, were seen as taunting and provoking the soldiers. A few hundred people on street corners in Kashmir were suddenly able to show up the emerging superpower.

It is these images of naked courage that allowed people in Kashmir to tremulously make a connection with the long and heroic resistance of the people of Palestine. And refer to the summer of 2010 as their intifada, the 'shaking off' of the chains of occupation.

Hindsight has made a prophecy of a dying whisper.

Mummy, mae-ae aav heartas fire. When that bullet tore through Fancy Jan in July 2010, the fire had indeed reached the heart. Something massive had been breached, and this may well have been the tightly controlled knot of memory of a new generation of Kashmiris. Unlike many others in the last twenty years, the brutal deaths of Inayat, Wamiq, and Zahid, and the meaning of their killing, were not easily interred at *mazar-e-shouhda*, the martyr's graveyard. These were taken note of, and written about extensively; word was passed on and debated, and memories of struggle revived in very distinct ways.

Young people were dying, and it was other young people who ardently remembered them. This was a generation that had grown up within the searing conflict of the past two decades, but even amongst Kashmiris they had been frequently (although inexplicably) represented as apolitical, as disconnected, as innocent victims. Young Kashmiris, we had been told, had moved on, distracted by beauty parlours, coffee shops, pool tables and Internet cafes. The furious footfalls of the last three summers quickly rubbed away that spurious patina, making it clear that the young protesters refused to see themselves as outside of the events around them. The almost daily killings did little to subdue them, making them only more eager to be part of the confrontation.

This stepping out of young people on the streets was a major consequence of the recent transformation in the nature of the uprising in Kashmir. The strategic shift from the militant's gun to unarmed—if stone-pelting—protest was nothing short of tectonic. Yet every attempt was made to disregard this reality, and the government and the media tried to run every possible spin on it. The crowds were mobilized by the Lashkar-e-Toiba, they said; these were hired goons paid for by Pakistan; they were drug-addicts who pelted stones only because they were on a high; they were social malcontents; urban detritus. The attempt to tarnish a reality that was quite evident to everybody may even have succeeded, but sometime in the middle of the summer of 2010 someone in the security establishment inadvertently pressed the wrong switch. With stifling curbs on the local print and television media already in place, a panicked government blocked the popular text messaging service on the cellphone network, a critical artery through which news—and rumour—circulates within Kashmir. For the next six months, subscribers could only receive commercial messages on their cellphones. (In the midst of adversity, a bonanza for advertisers!)

Choked at one place, news in Kashmir quickly found another way to move—travelling like quicksilver through the newly arrived phenomenon of Internet-based social networking sites. Facebook, Twitter, and YouTube had emerged as a critical arena of contestation in Kashmir. Instead of only speaking to each other, Kashmiris were suddenly speaking to the world.

Daily, and sometimes hourly, updates on the protests began to appear. Within days the response to the Aalaw (the Call) group had clocked up thousands on Facebook. (Today it has 17,500.) Bekar Jamat (Union of Idlers) signed up nearly 12,000, offering methods of dealing with the effects of tear gas, and even first-aid tips for shooting victims. When Bekar Jamat was mysteriously hacked, it cheekily reappeared as Hoshiar Jamat (Union of the Vigilant). Like the covered faces and the bared chests of the young stone-pelters on the streets, the identities were a message in themselves: Aam Nafar (Ordinary Guy), Dodmut Koshur (Burnt Kashmiri) and Karim Nannavor (Barefoot Karim) joined other proletarians, like Khinna Mott (Snot Crazy), Nanga Mott (Naked Crazy) and Kale Kharab (Hot-head). Meanwhile 'Oppressedkashmir1' was recording video images of the street protests, probably on his cellphone, and joining dozens of others in uploading them on YouTube.

Through the summer, as the stones pelted on the streets held down the police and paramilitary forces, a simultaneous barrage of news and commentary on the Internet had equally serious consequences for the mainstream Indian media. Unused to any sort of scrutiny, comfortable and unchallenged in their representations of the unfolding situation, the protection of the newsrooms was suddenly not swaddled enough for the journalists and television anchors of New Delhi. They found themselves inundated with alerts and corrections, and inevitably, some abuse. International observers had the equivalent of a ball-by-ball commentary of street battles, with a rich context that was impossible to ignore. Watchful young people from small towns across Kashmir were reminding the Indian establishment that communication on Twitter was two-way, and that Facebook was, after all, available to millions on the worldwide web.

A deluge of well-argued commentary and analyses began drawing in the intellectual resources of a virtual community from across the world, and these were not all Kashmiris either. Suddenly there were vibrant alternatives to the stale shibboleths of the official Indian line, challenging it at every step. The protests on the ground were also able to provoke the international community into a new appreciation of events in Kashmir. Where not so long ago masked gunmen had read out old-fashioned press releases from one or the other militant tanzeem, there was now a massive opening out of the language in which Kashmir was being spoken about. On the Internet, there was news, and analyses, but there was also a spate of music videos, which cut images from this week's protests (usually shot on cellphones) into next week's rousing protest anthem. 'Stone in My Hand', by the radical Irish American rap singer Everlast, was an early, and unexpected, hit. Young stone-pelters were known to cruise the streets listening to the song (naturally on their cellphones). There were stories, often elliptical, yet highly political, including a short graphic novel exquisitely drawn in black and white, about the Kashmir 'Intifada'. And it was the Internet again that would soon carry out the words of teenaged Kashmiri rap artists, like the nineteen-year-old MC Kash, 'Coming to You Live from Srinagar Kashmir', as he promised. As the summer slowly wound down, it was impossible not to be snagged by the closing lines of his runaway hit, 'I Protest':

I Protest, Fo' My Brother Who's Dead!
I Protest, Against The Bullet In his Head!
I Protest, I Will Throw Stones An' Neva Run!
I Protest, Until My Freedom Has Come!

A recitation of names followed, a flat monotone for the summer that was going past. 'Let's remember all those who were martyred this year—Inayat Khan, Wamiq Farooq, Zahid Farooq, Zubair Ahmed Bhat, Tufail Ahmed Matoo, Rafiq Ahmed Bangroo, Javaid Ahmed Malla, Shakeel Ganai . . .' (Halfway through that seemingly endless litany and I had almost missed the name I was listening for—Fancy Jan, under her formal name, Yasmeen Jan.)

These were young people born into this conflict, and they seemed to have absorbed everything that history and circumstance had thrown their way. When the sixteen-year-old 'Renegade' rapped out a 'Resistance Anthem', speaking of 'lyrical guerilla warfare', and fighting with 'knowledge and wisdom', it was a clear signal that something had changed. This new generation was taking up its place on the streets, and these were the sites for the new battle—some filled with stones and tear gas, others with words and ideas. But these two struggles did intersect in some unusual places, and the handshake was unexpectedly warm.

Amidst all the bloodshed, the summer of 2010 was an oddly hopeful time, and much that was repressed was finally beginning to come out in the open.

'I can hear birds,' a friend called in to say that morning in September. Unusual, because you don't often hear birds in Srinagar. Not for the roar of its chaotic traffic, and for the past several months of the summer of 2010, not for the tumult of the streets.

'But nothing else,' he added in a brittle voice, 'I hear nothing else.'

It was the day after Eid, usually a day of continuing celebration, for it marked the end of the month of Ramzan. In the past two years it was the physical rigours of just this month of fasting that had finally leached the flagging energy from those immense agitations. This year was different though: after nearly four months of protests, and with 112 people killed, the onset of autumn gave no indication of a slowdown in the tempo. The visible faces of the 'separatist' sentiment were all in custody. But from somewhere far underground other anonymous organizers were still able to issue the 'timetable', as the relentless calendar of the hartal protests were locally known. By supporting these, despite the enormous dislocation and deprivation that the shutdowns caused, people were continuing to signal their fierce support to the revolt.

Retribution for such insolence was inevitable, and when it came, it was as fierce. The government began to impose its own calendar of harshly enforced shutdowns. These were usually timed for the days of relief in the carefully calibrated 'timetable'. Curfew was rarely declared though, but enforced through its extra-legal local variant, the 'undeclared' curfew. Put together—people's curfew and police curfew, end-to-end—it meant that people in the cities and towns of Kashmir were often unable to step out of their homes for most of a week. No milk, no bread, no vegetables; no infant food, no doctors, no medicines—nothing.

When the friend called the day after Eid, there was no food in the house, and little to celebrate with. The paramilitary forces were smarting from events of the previous day, when a relaxation in the curfew had seen massive protests erupt in the very heart of Srinagar, in Lal Chowk. When he tried stepping out of his home, the soldiers in the sandbagged bunker outside had threatened to shoot him. 'You can stuff that pass up your arse,' they had said firmly when he walked up, holding his journalist's curfew pass like a white flag. He called their superior, the Central Reserve Police Force (CRPF) Public Relations Officer, to describe what was going on, conspicuously holding his cellphone up, speakers on. The men were even more emphatic now. 'Call him too,' they said of their officer, confidently. 'Call him here, now. We'll stuff it up his arse too . . .'

This quick tightening of the tourniquet was carefully timed. In the nerve centres of the uprising—in Sopore in the north, and Shopian in the south—late September was also the time to bring in the abundant apple crop. To turn their backs on it, or do it badly, would spell ruin. This is what makes autumn critical in the predominantly agricultural economy of rural Kashmir, with its anxious prospect of being unprepared for the difficult winter ahead. An unspoken tactical withdrawal was materializing.

The silence surrounding the birdsong presaged the most severe repression that Kashmiris have experienced in a decade. And once again it was in the countryside, away from even the minimal scrutiny of the media, that the brunt of the renewed aggression would be borne. Only thirty kilometres north of Srinagar, the rebellious village of Palhalan had its phone lines snapped, its mobile phone services disabled, and physical access to it made nearly impossible for outsiders. At a highway checkpoint, if your identity card carried the name Palhalan on it, you were likely to be pulled out of a public bus, and made to walk. Students from the village were summarily ejected from examination halls, and taken straight to detention. Before the year was out, Palhalan had endured almost two-and-a-half months of curfew, including one straight stretch of thirty-nine days.

No defiance was too small to be ignored. In the remote fastness of Kulgam, paramilitary soldiers surrounded Kujar village, and asked everyone to step out of their homes. They then stood guard as the police moved in, first smashing all the precious windowpane glass, and after that, with pointed cruelty, systematically destroying the kitchen. There was no media on hand to report any of this at the time, but even if they were, what would they be saying? 'Police smash windowpanes'? 'Paramilitary destroy kitchen'? No one had been killed, or even seriously injured. Who would care to understand the significance of this brutalization? Meanwhile in Srinagar and other towns, Facebook groups had begun to be infiltrated, and outspoken members tracked down through their IP addresses. The mostly teenaged net warriors were systematically called in to the local police station for questioning, and the threat of worse to come.

As *chila-e-kalan*, traditionally the coldest part of Kashmir's winter, placed its freezing hands on life in the Valley, the police seemed to be slowly coming into their own. Increasingly triumphant stories were being released to the press: Irfan Ahmed Bhat, a seventeen-year-old from Nagin, Srinagar, had been detained for questioning, they said, suspected of being the dreaded Kale Kharab of Facebook[2]. Records were being created, a police spokesman said, depending on the 'level' of involvement. 'In Group A habitual protesters and stone-pelters would be inducted,' we were informed. 'In Group B only those people who have fervently participated in

---

[2]http://kafila.org/2011/01/18/these-are-not-stones-these-are-my-feelings-kashmir/

protests and initiated stone pelting will be listed; and Group C includes those persons who have been once lodged in the jail for any unlawful activity.'[3] Stone-pelters were being hunted down with the dogged tenacity that not long ago had been reserved for armed militants. The politics of the summer upsurge were being drowned under an endless series of stories that tried to represent the protesters as delinquents, even criminals.

As the smug triumphalism of government propaganda readied to fill the media space, and claim yet another spectacular success against the separatists, a warning wafted off the streets, like a sullen fog.

Khoon ka badla June mein lenge, it said.

Blood will be avenged, in June.

In the new year, with the snow still thick on the ground, Kashmiris drew warmth from faraway Egypt, from the gossamer hope that the masses of people in Tahrir Square—ranged against tanks and soldiers, and the faraway machinations of powerful empires—might still bring about change for Egyptians (and eventually, for the interlinked fortunes of Palestine, and the entire Middle East). The Internet had proved to be a valuable resource in Egypt, threading together the gathering forces of change. And it was on Facebook that many young Kashmiris noted the Western world's embrace of the revolt in Egypt, wondering why it was so much more circumspect about the 112 young people killed in Kashmir.

But hope had already been put on notice. Imperceptible at first, but palpable when you put your ear quietly to the ground, we watched the euphoria of the summer, and its openness, in retreat. With the revolt in the street having exhausted itself, and the young

---

[3]http://www.greaterkashmir.com/news/2011/Feb/10/protesters-had-personal-problems-claims-ssp-50.asp

people made to cede that space, the pressure on the Indian state was missing. Even the political resistance of the Kashmiri 'separatists' seemed unmoored now. In the summer they had seemed to be out there, in touch with the people, but now found themselves forced right back into the corner painted for them.

The highest ranking Indian Army general in Kashmir took the time to step outside his brief and accuse social networking sites of being 'used as a tool of propaganda against the army and other security agencies, by elements hell-bent on disturbing peace in the Valley.'[4] When the press asked for an update on the army's fake 'encounter' of three civilians in Machil, the incident which first triggered the avalanche of protests, he was more taciturn, saying he had no comment, and the matter was 'sub judice'.

A top-ranking police officer told the press in Srinagar that of the 1,000 young men they had detained, 72 per cent were social misfits, either drug addicts, or people with problems at home. Waving a picture of a young man attacking a police jeep with a stone, he said 'They do such acts of heroism only under the influence of drugs.'

Meanwhile, from an exhibition of defence products in faraway Bengaluru came news of a new toy on offer to security forces in Kashmir—a US-made 'pain gun', which sends out beams of radiation that stimulate human nerve endings, causing extreme pain. It 'barely' penetrates the skin, Raytheon, the global weapons giant, promised, so the 'ray gun' cannot cause visible or permanent injury.[5] A step ahead then, from last year's catapults, which blinded so many young men on the streets of Srinagar. (The US military first used this Silent Guardian Protection System in war-torn Afghanistan, but withdrew it last year, amidst opposition from human rights activists.)

---

[4]http://www.indianexpress.com/news/facebook-used-to-fuel-unrest-in-kashmir-army/745010/

[5]http://www.risingkashmir.com/news/us-made-pain-gun-to-tackle-kashmir-protests-6371.aspx

Khoon ka badla June mein lenge. Blood will be avenged, they had said.

Who will retaliate, I wonder, and what will be avenged, this coming June, and in the summers to come?

From Sopore, heartland of the pro-Azadi movement, comes news of the killing of two young women, seventeen-year-old Arifa and nineteen-year-old Akhtara. They had been warned twice, neighbours said, explicitly told to break links with security forces. Sopore had seen handbills recently, warning people not to consort with police, military or intelligence people. On the day of their cold-blooded execution, bystanders confirmed that more than a dozen men brazenly walked into the neighbourhood, a few went in to meet the girls, while the rest stood guard on the street. Arifa and Akhtara were later taken away, and killed a bare twenty minutes away from their dingy one-room home. All evidence pointed to the Lashkar-e-Toiba.

So there they were, the Lashkar, that ruthless Army of the Faithful, trained to destroy and dislodge, back after several years of lying low. The quiet rumble of public opinion had discreetly made them concede the resistance to the mass of people, to the stone-pelters, to the open street. As the police hunt down the sang-baz, grade them in categories A, B, and C, and put them in jail; as they take in the hot-headed Kale Kharab, and smash windowpanes in town and village, people are once again being forced to step back. The tired, sullen silence of the street will inevitably create a vacuum, and make space for the old fighters to return. It will be an invitation to the earlier ways, of armed resistance, of the Hizb-ul-Mujahidin, and heaven forbid, the Lashkar-e-Toiba.

In the 1990s, this valley was also drawn into the cauldron of war by its neighbours, as the defeat of the Soviet Union in the mountains of Afghanistan redirected the energies of the mujahidin into Kashmir. That neighbourhood is teetering dangerously again. Preparing for defeat this time is the United States, shadowy victors of that earlier war, even as they try to dress it up as a strategic withdrawal.

There is an ominously familiar feeling in the air.
The fire is indeed at the heart.

~

This collection brings together a diverse set of responses to the events of 2010, a time of great upheaval in Kashmir. It seemed as if the events and ideas that have animated the struggle of its people had, after almost twenty years of a muted, subterranean existence, entered a new phase. A time marked—we imagine—by openness and candour, and by a diversity of opinion.

Most of what appears here came in a furious rush in the summer itself, and reflects the intensity of what people were responding to. The chill of winter was yet to settle in. It is left to the readers to discover what runs common through the range of ideas in *Until My Freedom Has Come*. But attention can—and must—be drawn to the hope that attends this volume. As always, we know we can trust Agha Shahid Ali, Kashmiri poet, to make eloquent our present hopes—and ever-present fears.

We shall meet again, in Srinagar
by the gates of the Villa of Peace,
our hands blossoming into fists
till the soldiers return the keys
and disappear. Again we'll enter
our last world, the first that vanished

in our absence from the broken city.

New Delhi   SANJAY KAK
March 2011

Summers of Unrest

Azadi is our birthright
and we will leave no stone unturned to get it.

Yirvun Kreel

Summers of Unrest
Challenging India

Parvaiz Bukhari

The summer of 2010 witnessed a convulsion in the world's most militarized zone, the Indian-controlled part of Kashmir, an unprecedented and deadly civil unrest that is beginning to change a few things on the ground. The vast state intelligence establishment, backbone of the region's government, almost lost its grip over a rebelling population. Little-known and relatively anonymous resistance activists emerged, organizing an unarmed agitation more fierce than the armed rebellion against Indian rule two decades earlier. And apparently aware of the post-9/11 world, young Kashmiris, children of the conflict, made stones and rocks a weapon of choice against government armed forces, side-stepping the tag of a terrorist movement linked with Pakistan. The unrest represents a conscious transition to an unarmed mass movement, one that poses a moral challenge to New Delhi's military domination over the region.

Almost every day since mid-June, protesters and bystanders have been killed in firing by government forces on irate groups of stone-throwing people during massive demonstrations for the region's separation from India. The large-scale protests were widespread across the Muslim-majority Kashmir valley. By the end of October, 111 residents, mostly youths, were killed in the intifada-like uprising in which angry protesters fearlessly pitched themselves against armed police and federal paramilitary soldiers. The moral equation changed perceptibly in favour of the agitating people, before the overbearing security establishment cracked down with a stringent shoot-on-sight curfew, and laid siege around populated areas.

This summer's cycle of protests and killings was seen to be triggered by a staged gun battle by Indian Army soldiers in the mountainous Machil area near the Line of Control (LoC), the de facto border dividing Kashmir between India and Pakistan. In May this year a rare police probe found that the army had gunned down three civilians, claiming they were armed militants who had 'crossed over' from Pakistan. This enraged the Kashmiri people, but the reasons behind the civil unrest had been accumulating since much earlier.

Since the Partition of India in 1947, Kashmir has been a site of simmering tensions, alternating with outbreaks of violence. But for the last two decades now India has maintained the presence of an estimated 7,00,000 troops in Kashmir, the disputed Himalayan region with a population of about ten million bordering India, Pakistan and China. Hundreds of armed forces' camps dot the region, keeping a close watch on its residents. Most of these troops were brought in to fight a Pakistan-backed armed rebellion by Kashmiri Muslims in 1990. Citizens deeply resent the overwhelming presence of soldiers amongst them, and their camps in the neighbourhoods. They feel violated by the impunity soldiers enjoy under the Armed Forces Special Powers Act (AFSPA). This law allows the soldiers to search houses without warrants, to detain residents at will, and to destroy buildings, including houses suspected of harbouring rebels. Under the AFSPA, soldiers accused of crimes like rape and the killing of civilians in their custody cannot be prosecuted in civil courts unless the federal government in New Delhi specifically permits it.

Militarization of the region was politically cemented in 1994 with a unanimous resolution by the Indian parliament declaring

Kashmir an 'integral part' of the country. Kashmir's special status within the union, which had been guaranteed in the Indian Constitution, had been slowly eroding for decades. Kashmir enjoyed a significant degree of self-rule until the early 1950s, when only foreign affairs, defence and communications were subject to Indian domain control. The Indian military campaign against a few thousand insurgents has since left about 70,000 people, mostly civilians, dead.

By the year 2002 the popular armed rebellion was largely crushed, but public support for Kashmir's independence from India appears to have deepened over the years. The government claims 500 to 700 armed rebels remain in the fighting, confined to the forested areas of the region, but the concentration of the troops across the region remains unchanged for the most part. However, it is not these armed militants who are leading the most recent protests against the Indian government.

The largely defeated armed insurgency and the sustained crackdown by the Indian counter-insurgency campaign have gradually produced a transition to a less violent mode of mass rebellion in the last few years. It fed on the two-decade-long local memory of arbitrary detention of residents by troops, and widespread torture and harassment. Hundreds of graveyards for the victims of conflict across the territory became shrines to the loss and the 'Kashmir cause'. The pent-up bitterness and a sense of being completely dominated were waiting to explode.

In mid-2008, protests erupted over a government decision to grant 100 acres of land to the Hindu shrine of Shri Amarnath in the Kashmir Himalayas. Many Muslim Kashmiris perceived the land deal as an attempt to effect a demographic change in the Muslim-majority region. Thousands of people took to the streets of the provincial capital Srinagar as well as other towns, in protests spearheaded by separatist leaders, demanding that New Delhi negotiate a settlement of the six-decade-old dispute with Pakistan and them on board.

Defying a curfew, hundreds of thousands of protesters marched towards the heavily militarized frontier west of Srinagar in an attempt to cross over to Pakistan-controlled Kashmir. Government forces eventually fired at the procession before it could reach the border, killing several people, including senior resistance leader Sheikh Abdul Aziz, a former militant commander and a key leader of the hardline All Parties Hurriyat Conference (APHC), the main separatist alliance in the disputed state. By the time that summer uprising was defused, and a siege laid around Srinagar and other towns of Kashmir, a total of around sixty protesters had been killed. Significantly, the armed rebels remained tactically silent during the period.

New Delhi's earlier claims of 'normalcy' returning to Kashmir went up in thin air in the face of the massive demonstrations for Azadi. The situation called for a non-military response. The Indian government's response to the unrest was a plan to stage a fresh round of elections. Many senior activist leaders, including the hardliner Syed Ali Shah Geelani, moderate Mirwaiz Umar Farooq and former armed rebel commander Yasin Malik of the Jammu Kashmir Liberation Front (JKLF), were arrested as the polls for the region's new government were announced in October 2008.

Buoyed by renewed mass support for their campaign against Indian rule, the resistance camp had appealed for a total boycott of the elections, called by New Delhi against the advice of pro-India Kashmiri political parties, which feared very low participation. To facilitate campaigning for votes and ensure security during polling, several thousand more paramilitary troops were brought in. During their lacklustre election campaign, the politicians sought votes for day-to-day governance. They repeatedly told people in small gatherings, and through the media, that the election had nothing to do with the dispute over Kashmir or the territory's future that has been at the centre of animosity between nuclear arch-rivals India and Pakistan.

Meanwhile, hundreds of resistance activists and prominent protesters were meticulously identified by field intelligence operatives from video footage and photographs of demonstrations. They were arrested under the Public Safety Act (PSA) that allows the authorities to detain anyone presumed to be acting against the interests of the state for up to two years without legal recourse. The field was cleared for the pro-India politicians and groups.

The vast and robust Indian intelligence apparatus in Kashmir worked overtime to ensure a good voter turnout where little was expected. Besides nominees from the pro-India Kashmiri political parties, more than a thousand candidates suddenly jumped into the fray for eighty-seven seats. They were fielded by regional parties from mainland India who had no cadres to talk of in Kashmir. Many were also independents, some of whom later revealed that they were backed by government agencies and promised money for bringing out friends and relatives to vote.

In winter, and under highly militarized conditions, polling was held in seven phases over six weeks for what turned out to be a 'watershed election' that registered a turnout of 60 per cent. A huge number were first-time voters, educated young men and women who, while acutely aware of post-9/11 realities and clearly uneasy with the violence around them, had perhaps hoped that a new emerging India would deliver justice this time round. But politicians in New Delhi and the Indian mainstream media described the turnout as a 'victory for Indian democracy' in Kashmir and a 'defeat of separatism'.

The resistance leaders were 'humbled' while people in general felt angered and foxed at their vote being interpreted—once again—as a referendum endorsing Indian rule. Many Kashmiri voters sulked under the media euphoria, and many first-time voters tasted their first 'betrayal'. In January 2009, the elections brought the UK-born Omar Abdullah to centre stage, at thirty-nine the region's youngest-ever chief minister. Lauded by the Indian media, he promised an era of reconciliation, gradual demilitarization and repeal of the contentious AFSPA, as well as restrictions on the use of the widely resented PSA.

Although the results of the elections sidelined the discourse of separatism for several months, trouble returned in May 2009 after two young women were found dead in disputed circumstances in Shopian, a district with a heavy military presence to the south of Srinagar. The victims' families alleged that the women had been abducted, raped and murdered by men in uniform.

Several botched investigations into the incident triggered unrest once again. The state's intelligence chief was changed for 'misleading' the government, and four police officers were arrested and charged with dereliction of duty and destruction of evidence in the case. Shopian remained under a forty-seven-day protest shutdown. An autopsy report confirmed that the women had been raped, and a government-appointed, one-man inquiry commission alleged that four police officers were involved in destroying evidence.

Privately, officials told *Jane's Intelligence Review* that in this process newly elected chief minister Abdullah lost some support, particularly from within the frontline counter-insurgency paramilitary units who were engaged in the fight against armed militants. But the separatist resistance campaign found new energy, with the protests being joined by youths who have grown amid the two-decade-long conflict. The resistance leaders were establishing connections with this new generation of Kashmiris.

Alarmed, the government called in India's premier investigating agency, the Central Bureau of Investigation (CBI), for a fresh probe into the Shopian deaths. The new investigation, conducted on the bodies exhumed four months after the death of the victims, concluded that they had died due to drowning in a local stream. Not many in Kashmir believed the findings, but the CBI filed cases against the doctors who had conducted the previous probes into the deaths, as well as the lawyers who were fighting the original case in the court. They were charged with inciting violence in the aftermath of the Shopian deaths.

While Kashmiris were debating the 'institutional denial' of justice in the Shopian incident, in January 2010 Border Security Force (BSF) soldiers killed a schoolboy in Srinagar, and sparked off yet more protests. Witnesses said the soldiers opened fire on a group of boys without provocation, making it the sixth death of a civilian within a month that local residents blamed on government forces. Abdullah ordered a probe into the death, saying, 'Incidents of unprovoked and innocent killings will not be tolerated.' However, protests meant that a curfew was extended in Srinagar for several days and dozens of activists were arrested, setting the tone for the coming summer.

In April, major protests erupted again, this time in response to the killing of three men by the Indian Army in Machil, near the militarized LoC. The army said it had killed three rebels trying to cross into Indian-controlled Kashmir from the Pakistani side of the border. However, local residents demanded an inquiry into the claims, saying three local men had disappeared from the village of Nadihal three days before the supposed firefight.

Police exhumed the bodies and confirmed that the men had been local civilians. Farooq Ahmed, a senior police officer, said: 'They were innocent citizens killed in a fake gun battle.' The incident sparked protests involving thousands of local residents. Two army officers were removed from duty pending an inquiry into the killings, amid accusations from local residents that the men had been killed so that the troops could win rewards and promotions awarded for neutralizing militants.

Fuelled by existing anger over the January killing, protests over these deaths spread across parts of the Kashmir valley, eventually reaching Srinagar. A tear-gas shell fired by police officers killed a student who local residents said had not been part of the protests. The death sent much of the Kashmir valley into a renewed cycle of intense protests—and more deaths—that continued throughout the summer.

Omar Abdullah later blamed the fresh violence on the deaths in Machil and called for restraint in the use of the AFSPA, saying the army was acting as 'judge, jury and hangman'. 'There is absence of transparency, as a result of which people have lost faith in the system,' he said. Each killing triggered more protests, often coordinated through text messages and over the internet, and led by youths throwing stones at everything that symbolized state authority, most visibly, men in uniform and their armoured vehicles.

Many separatist resistance leaders and activists were soon jailed. However, one man who had just emerged after twenty-two months in jail in June 2010 went underground on his release. Masarat Alam Bhat, a thirty-nine-year-old resistance activist educated in a Christian missionary school and member of the separatist All Parties Hurriyat Conference, started channelling the anti-India groundswell by issuing weekly protest calendars. He urged people to join the 'freedom rallies' that protests in Kashmir most often morph into. An activist for the right of self-determination since his student days, Bhat had been jailed many times.

The fiery young man deployed an idiom of political resistance that immediately connected him with the protesting youths, electrifying the street. Bhat's rotating protest calendars copied the First Intifada of Palestinians, dedicating each day of protests and shutdowns to specific demands, with different forms of protest against 'Indian military occupation' of Kashmir. Encouraged by the ascendant public response, the emerging separatist leader triggered a 'Quit Kashmir Campaign' calling for demilitarization and an end to Indian rule of the disputed region. A charismatic orator, Bhat also appealed to the 'conscience' of the Indian troops deployed in the region and asked people to reproduce his memorandum and deliver copies to military commanders in the hundreds of camps dotting the entire region. A video recording of the appeal and its text was sent to media outlets in Srinagar. An executive order from the authorities barred the press from reporting the contents of Bhat's powerful appeal. However, he kept the pressure up from the underground and started issuing statements calling for social boycott of Kashmiri police officers and bureaucrats for being 'collaborators' of the 'Indian occupation'.

Bhat's clear appeals resonated among the people, particularly youths and students. Local leaders and activists that no one knew about began emerging from neighbourhoods in cities, towns and villages all across Kashmir and kept organizing demonstrations in strict adherence to the 'protest calendars'. The authorities responded with stringent curfews and, occasionally, lethal force. As the toll of civilian casualities mounted, so did the general anger. Protesters, sometimes in their tens of thousands, defied curfew and in a number of instances targeted government buildings, including railway stations. The houses of a few local police officials were also set on fire. The situation stretched the massive security grid to its maximum. At the peak of the unrest, the government brought in several hundred members of the federal Rapid Action Force (RAF), specially trained in riot control, to augment efforts directed at calming the situation.

On 7 July, New Delhi tried to address the situation by allowing the army to be deployed for crowd control in Srinagar and across much of rural Kashmir. This decision, taken for the first time in nineteen years, received heavy criticism from much of Indian civil society, and sections of the political establishment expressed disappointment at the government's failure to respond politically. Indian Army chief General V.K. Singh had already warned of the need to 'handle things politically'. He emphasized that militarily the security situation was already under firm control and told the *Times of India* in July: 'I feel there is a great requirement for political initiatives.'

The sudden and significantly changed ground scenario choked space for field intelligence operatives who had worked for the police, the military and the paramilitary forces in the region, each operating their own separate intelligence-gathering networks. The unrest turned into a frontline contest between the protesting masses and the police aided by federal paramilitaries. Since a majority in the police force is composed of local Kashmiris, the clearly drawn lines made the mobility of its field intelligence staff very risky.

Over two decades, the Criminal Investigation Department (CID) of the police had focused on countering armed militants, like the federal and military intelligence agencies, and developed a frontline cutting-edge capability for anti-militancy operations. This massive intelligence-gathering network had penetrated so deep into the social structure that it was easily possible to get information about the activities of armed militants. The premium had been on the actionable and quick intelligence on armed rebels and their networks. The department's Special Branch and Counter-Intelligence wings, specially designed to monitor separatist politicians and continually interrogate their plans, failed to anticipate and assess the unfolding summer unrest.

'Often, the intelligence we get is not worth the paper it is printed on, and that's a charitable way of putting it,' Abdullah told *India Today* magazine in an interview published on 8 October. 'Most of the reports are simply accounts of what has happened and there are no assessments of what is likely to happen. The presumption that Kashmir is simply crawling with intelligence operatives is ridiculous. You cannot create a network of credible information and analysis overnight. In the last twenty-odd years of militancy, our intelligence system has deteriorated. I am making a huge effort to overhaul the CID structure.'

As anti-India protests spiralled across the region, police and CID operatives became their first targets. Protesters began attacking paramilitary camps with stones and other missiles, as well as police stations that also housed intelligence units. The onslaught demoralized the field operatives and all but restricted them to their fortified offices. A field officer told *Jane's Intelligence Review*: 'It became impossible for us to be seen on the ground. We risked being lynched by the mobs. We started talking to media outlets even for basic information about the scale and spread of protests.' Another intelligence official told *Jane's Intelligence Review* that the state's intelligence grid had collapsed in the face of spreading unrest. Field operatives, both officials and civilian recruits who had over the years become known to the residents as part of various intelligence networks, became virtually useless.

Officials also admitted that over the years a certain amount of complacency had set in with the arrival of sophisticated electronic surveillance equipment. The easy availability of information from tapped mobile telephone conversations 'dampened the cultivation of human intelligence'. They said this outcome had resulted in a lot of civilian sources being abandoned.

Another intelligence official speaking to *Jane's Intelligence Review* on condition of anonymity said: 'Some of these sources were seen participating in and leading protests at many places to save themselves from public wrath.'

The intelligence apparatus, with its access to human intelligence now restricted, was also faced with activists using social media such as Facebook and YouTube to mobilize within Kashmir, and to communicate with the outside world. The CID has started a crackdown on such activity, with one student detained by police officers after they found out he had posted a list of police officials on his Facebook page, calling them 'traitors'. As of mid-October, in Shopian alone three people, including a bank executive, had been arrested in connection with their Facebook activity.

Over the past twenty years, the intelligence apparatus had configured itself to deal with the traditional media and with well-known separatist leaders such as Syed Ali Shah Geelani, Yasin Malik and Mirwaiz Umar Farooq. Now it is pitched against a diffuse leadership, many of whom are well-travelled and university-educated, and able to bypass these traditional focuses for dispersing information. These numerous neighbourhood leaders often have no past police record and no history of political mobilization. The government has found it hard to crackdown on these activists in the absence of a substantial political response from New Delhi.

By late September, New Delhi sent a thirty-nine-member delegation of parliamentarians on a two-day visit to Kashmir to help draft a political response. Most of the senior separatist leaders, who were under strict curfew, declined formal invitations to meet the group, but several members of the delegation visited the separatist leaders' residences, appealing to them to help restore calm in the region. During one such encounter on 20 September, Syed Ali Shah Geelani, who had been placed under house arrest, presented five preconditions for official dialogue, including the demand that government forces stop firing on anti-government protesters. Other demands included a formal acknowledgement by the government that Kashmir was under international dispute, the release of all political prisoners, the announcement of a demilitarization schedule and an investigation into all civilian killings by government forces since 1989. The Mirwaiz further demanded that India and Pakistan constitute parliamentary committees for negotiating a final settlement of the 'Kashmir dispute' and include the Kashmiri separatist leadership. Yasin Malik also reiterated his demand that separatists be made a part of the Kashmir-specific element of the more general Indo-Pakistani dialogue process.

One aspect all of them made clear was that they would not be able to influence the agitating population unless significant political concessions were formally offered. Their position signified the single biggest change the summer unrest had wrought: the separatist old guard no longer has absolute control over the Kashmiri civilian population. Much of the unrest had been orchestrated by little-known leaders who may not even fully trust the old resistance leadership any more.

Apparently aware of the new realities, the leaders appear to have refrained from public disagreements, instead urging demonstrators to remain peaceful during protests and giving clear signals that Pakistan was not in control of the Kashmiri resistance. This gave the protesters a new impetus and a sense of ownership that has led to much greater participation in the protests from students and professionals, including lawyers, doctors and teachers. Recent protests in Iran, Thailand, Tibet and Myanmar seem to have given rise to a feeling in Kashmir that public opinion in the West can be influenced by non-violent protests and the intelligent use of new media.

New Delhi has so far only fanned the smoke away but may have left the embers burning. Meanwhile, an eight-point political package presented by the government in New Delhi on 25 September was greeted with disappointment in Kashmir. Among the initiatives announced were the appointment of a group of mediators to hold 'sustained dialogue' with Kashmiris, the release of several hundred people detained for stone-throwing and a reduction in the number of security forces stationed in the valley. The plan also allows for the review of areas designated as 'disturbed', a move which could result in the rescinding of the application of the AFSPA to parts of Kashmir. Grants will also be awarded to the families of those killed during the summer's unrest. Geelani rejected the initiative, terming it 'eyewash', while other separatist leaders responded to parts of the package.

The parliamentary group's effort could therefore be seen as a lost opportunity for New Delhi to engage with the new activism in Kashmir. The armed rebellion of 1990 had similarly resulted in the central government sending a group of prominent lawmakers to Kashmir. The response then was a major military campaign, parts of which are still in place, fighting remnants of that old insurgency. Governing the restive region has since remained a function of security control achieved through militarization. This time around, such a forceful and security-driven option seems counter-productive.

The Kashmir issue has caught the attention of Western capitals once again as hesitation in attempts by India and Pakistan to make progress on Kashmir remains. In 2004, during Pervez Musharraf's regime, Pakistan had come close to sealing a Kashmir deal with India. Statements emanating from Washington have also encouraged the Kashmir street. Ahead of a visit by United States President Barack Obama to India in November, separatists in Kashmir increased the pressure. If the past three years are any indication, this summer's large-scale mobilization could intensify in 2011, as the stand-off continues between protesters in Kashmir and New Delhi.

The new generation of separatist leaders seems to have made a conscious decision not to take up arms again, even as they push for the same objectives as the armed rebels—a move to retain a moral supremacy over 'Indian occupation'. This represents a major shift in tactics, and one to which political leaders both in Kashmir and in New Delhi may struggle to produce an adequate response. The government is unlikely to meet the protesters' demands in full, not least because it may feel that such a move would hand effective power in the region to the APHC. As such, the most likely outcome in the short term, especially given Alam's arrest and the return to a tentative peace, is an intensified attempt at dialogue, in a bid to keep the temperature low and the streets calm in the coming months.

A version of this article appeared in *Jane's Intelligence Review*, December 2010.

Diary of a Summer

Suvir Kaul

I fly into Srinagar to visit my mother, who is spending a long summer in our ancestral home, away from the heat of Delhi. At Delhi airport, I am startled by the number of army men waiting to catch the hopper flight to Srinagar via Jammu: I had not thought that jawans flew on commercial airlines, but there they were, their presence a foretaste of things ahead. My flight is made up of Kashmiri families, many visibly settled abroad, visiting home, and several Amarnath yatris. Three of them, all young men, large tikas on foreheads, are thrilled when they share the bus to the airplane with four European women tourists—they chuckle, nudge each other, and fondle themselves in sheer joy at this early payoff on their pilgrimage.

Srinagar has turned into a city of shutters. The taxi home makes quick progress as there is virtually no civilian traffic on the streets. We pass a four-vehicle army convoy—my taxi driver makes careful eye-contact with the gun-toting jawan at the back of the last jeep in order to get permission to overtake. A nod in reply allows us to zoom ahead, and I make desultory conversation while reading the occasional hand-written wall-slogan that says 'GO INDIA GO' or the harsher 'INDIAN DOGS GO BACK'. That makes me an unwanted visitor, I suppose, but then, not fifteen minutes ago, as I walked to the airport taxi-stand, one driver called out to his

17

compatriot who had taken charge of me: '*Haiyo yi chui local*' ('Hey you, he's a local'). Poised between an Indian citizenship I wear with pride in my professional life abroad, and a 'localness' which has learned to fear the cynical might of the Indian security apparatus in Kashmir (and elsewhere), I wonder what my time in Srinagar will bring.

Watching television in the evening reminds me of the fundamental absence of interest in the Indian media in the situation in Kashmir. Major news channels report on protests here, particularly if protesters are shot or property is damaged, but there is no attempt whatsoever to ask if these protests are a continuation of two decades of political unrest, and not simply random acts of violence instigated (as our Home Minister would have it, by the Lashkar or some such convenient scapegoat). Last year's assembly elections, and the installation of Omar Abdullah's government, were celebrated as a reminder that Kashmiris were not alienated from Indian democracy. Thus no political initiatives were necessary to address their demands, articulated now for five decades and supposedly guaranteed by Article 370, to define for themselves the forms of their autonomy.

But the last few weeks have seen renewed protests in Kashmir, with stone-pelting and demonstrations recurring in Srinagar, Sopore, Anantnag/Islamabad, and elsewhere. The military has been called out once (only, a 'flag march' is the official word), but the Central Reserve Police Force (CRPF) and the Jammu and Kashmir (J&K) police have fired upon and killed protesters already, and are in any case on edge in the streets. The Hurriyat announces a weekly calendar of protests, but there is widespread awareness that they no longer initiate or control these demonstrations, which seem less orchestrated and planned and more the product of rising anger amongst people brutalized by the daily humiliations of living under a security regime.

Television this evening also brings a reminder of the ways in which public debate within Srinagar is censored. Two channels, *Sën Channel* and *Sën Awaaz* ('*sën*' means 'ours' in Kashmiri), are off the air, and the former broadcasts the legend: 'The Transmission of *Sën Channel* has been Banned by Government, under order no: DMS/PS-MISC/10/840-52, Dated: 29-07-2010.' I ask my mother if she knows why these channels have been banned. Her answer is succinct: they discussed local political events, covered street demonstrations and told the truth.

Every evening at 7 p.m. we turn to ETV, an Urdu-language channel, to listen to their half-hour news bulletin on Kashmir. This is the fullest and most accurate account of all that happens here, and their local correspondent, Manoj Kaul, is measured in his reportage without omitting major details. Kashmiri news channels have been coerced into trimming their news bulletins into vapid coverage of government events, and it is ironic—but precisely symptomatic—that the best source of information operates out of Hyderabad.

In the evening, my neighbourhood is preternaturally quiet, and I cannot help thinking of the silence of a mausoleum.

Friday, 30 July 2010

The authorities have banned the weekly *jumma namaz* at the main Jama Masjid, and several other large masjids, for five weeks now, and each Friday brings about a declared or undeclared curfew. Today is no different. My mother tells me that the local paper has not been delivered for several days now—it is being printed, but the delivery man lives in Maisuma and cannot make his rounds. Maisuma is a neighbourhood that has seen sustained public protests and is thus kept under virtual curfew at all times. Only government employees who carry appropriate identification and those who have curfew passes are allowed on the streets, and even those passes are not always respected by the police or CRPF constables who patrol Srinagar's barricaded streets. Government employees have been told that they must report for duty, but the government offices in our neighbourhood are more or less deserted. (Incidentally, a house close by sports a signboard that would be witty if it was not an example of the growth of high-level bureaucratic offices: Office of the Chairman, Committee for Examination of Demands for New Administrative Units).

To my mind, these empty administrative offices represent one of the worst forms of collateral damage suffered by Kashmiris over the last two decades. An astonishing number of Kashmiri men (and some women, of course) are on government payrolls, and here I do not include the many (some estimate up to 100,000) who receive regular stipends from various intelligence agencies and secret services. Civil services and local administration have been systematically hollowed out over the past two decades; there is virtually no accountability at any level, and receiving a government salary is tantamount to being on the dole. If nothing else, the Indian state has revenged itself on Kashmiris by teaching them how not to work while still drawing salaries. This *salariat* functions as a vast buffer between the Indian state and the elected J & K government and the mass of people whose livelihood depends on daily work and trade, and, like government servants everywhere, they constitute a bulwark against political movements that mobilize common people. This is not always the case, and there have been times when some sectors of government employees have taken to the streets to protest against different facets of Indian rule, but they are, for the most part, at peace with their salaries.

By the evening, reports of demonstrations and the shooting of protesters are confirmed: three dead (two in Sopore) and many injured, including a score wounded by bullets. It is now clear that tomorrow, a day on which the Hurriyat calendar encouraged people to resume normal activities and stock up on supplies, is going to be another day of curfews and mounting tension. There seems to be no official response other than the police action on the street; no ministers or any other government officials are on television to explain the day's events and to offer some account of plans to de-escalate violence. In the absence of official explanations, rumours provide information: a substantial number of the dead and injured sustain head and chest wounds, and it seems that the security forces are shooting to kill rather than to injure or maim. Conversations about cynical politics abound: is it possible that these street protests are not being halted because their random, unsupervised quality undercuts the Hurriyat's claim to being the political leadership of the mass of Kashmiris angry with life under military occupation? Some argue that precisely because there are no known leaders of these demonstrations, can they really be said to serve a partisan political purpose? Some weeks ago, a group of young men in Sopore—leaders of street action—ignored Geelani's call to avoid stone-pelting and rejected the appeal made by Syed Salahuddin, the Pakistan-based head of the Hizb-ul-Mujahidin, to not precipitate confrontations and disruptions that will get in the way of a longer, more sustained struggle. But there is also the crucial fact that the largest mass of people respond to the Hurriyat calendar, and Geelani is the man with the greatest public heft here.

I read a local English-language newspaper that, on its front page, prints in Urdu a revolutionary poem by Sahir Ludhianvi under the caption, '*Bol ki labh azad hain tere*' (which, incidentally, is the title of a Faiz Ahmed Faiz poem). The final lines of the Ludhianvi poem are worth transcribing here, for they take on an uncanny urgency in Srinagar—this most progressive Indian poet now speaks for those subject to the unthinking muscularity of the regime:

> *Yeh kis ka lahu hai kaun maraa,*
> *Ham thaan chuke hain ab jii men,*
> *Har zaalim se takraaenge,*
> *Tum samjhaute ki aas rakho,*
> *Ham aage barte jaenge,*
> *Har manzil ae azadi ki kasam,*
> *Har manzil par dohraenge,*
> *Yeh kis ka lahu hai kaun maraa.*

Whose blood is this? Who is dead?
In our hearts we are resolved,
Every tyrant we will smash.

You can hope for compromise,
We'll continue to stride forward.
Each step ahead we swear by freedom,
Each step we'll swear again.
Whose blood is this? Who is dead?

Saturday, 31 July 2010

We have a young neighbour who steps out at 5 a.m. every morning to see if he can buy *lavasas* or *girdas* (local rotis made in a tandoor) and milk, and he does the same for us. Bakeries and other stores shut by 6 a.m. so that people can be home before the curfew is enforced, but today he comes back to say that the bakery has not opened. Given how wedded Kashmiris are to their lavasas, this is as pronounced a symptom of civic disorder as any.

The curfew, we are told, is to be enforced more closely today, but that does not seem to stop people from taking to the streets all over the valley; the list of towns and villages in which people mobilize knits together north and south Kashmir, as well as Srinagar, in a network of protest: Sopore, Pampore, Naidkhai Sumbal, Pattan, Handwara, Kupwara, Kreeri, Varmul, Bijbehara, Kakpora, Ganderbal (the chief minister's constituency). Two (or is it three?) more are shot by the police and CRPF, many more injured, hospitals in Srinagar report a shortage of blood. The pattern of daily protest and firing is now firmly in place: people gather to raise slogans and march towards government buildings, the young throw stones, the CRPF retaliate in kind (including, in a species of collective punishment, by breaking the windows of homes in the urban areas where protesters originate), use tear gas, and then, after they fire warning shots, shoot to kill and maim.

But there are variations in these seemingly established patterns, new participants in these protests. In several instances, women are at the forefront, and we see images of young women throwing stones at the security forces. Today also sees a demonstration at

Uri, which is close to the border and home to a great army presence; but mercifully, they do not intervene as protesters make clear that their protests are directed elsewhere. Today also sees substantial damage to government property: a building at the Amargarh station at Sopore, police vehicles, two Indian Air Force trucks. And where larger crowds gather, as at Kreeri, they burn a camp of the Special Operations Group (the SOG is a police auxiliary recruited locally, including surrendered militants, and is loathed because they are often used by the security services to do their dirty work for them). One story that makes the rounds—no news channel in Kashmir or elsewhere confirms this—is that two army vehicles were burnt when the soldiers in them refused their officer's order to take action against the protesters who had stopped them. We will not fire on the unarmed, they are supposed to have said.

Kashmir has never seen such widespread anger and mobilization, say those who lived through the worst episodes of armed militancy in the 1990s. Then state forces fought those equipped to fight back, and civilian casualties (and there were many) could be blamed on insurgents and counter-insurgency tactics. Now there are no armed militants, only people, their voices, and their bodies on the road, and of course there are stones. Policemen do get hurt, and isolated government officials are thrashed, but the only people who are shot are civilians. A Delhi-based news channel used the word 'miscreants' to describe the protesters who burned a building, and once again I was reminded of the chasm that divides opinion-makers in Delhi and events on the ground here. Would we ever call those who marched for freedom against the British 'miscreants'? Even those who torched the police station at Chauri Chaura? (It is another matter that Gandhi called a halt to the movement in the face of that incident; but this is another time and place, and there is no Gandhi here).

And that is an important part of the problem in Kashmir. If the British had insisted that Gandhi was not to be dealt with as a politician, that he and his politics had no locus standi, a different map of protest would have emerged all over India. Our home minister's line on Kashmir has been clear: emboldened perhaps by the election results in 2009, he had declared the separatists irrelevant. But they have never been that, and in fact are the only set of politicians who have consistently argued the need to re-examine Kashmir's status within the Indian Union. There are those amongst the Hurriyat who are amenable to the development of political systems in J&K that will in fact put into practice the autonomy, the special status, constitutionally available to this state. There are those who are much more *independentist* in their aspirations, and there are a few (and increasingly fewer) who think of a merger with their Islamic neighbour, if only because that was the principle of the merger of majority populations that was supposed to govern the allotment of territories during the Partition process of 1947. Successive regimes in Delhi have sought to delegitimize this entire range of political opinion, and that has been a huge and arrogant miscalculation. Kashmiris have seen too much suffering over the past two decades (and before) not to see themselves as at the receiving end of the policies of an imperial state. The security apparatus is too visible and intrusive on a daily basis to be understood as anything other than a reminder of an occupation force and a subject people. And there has been no justice offered for even the most egregious acts of violence committed by the military, the paramilitary, or the police. There have been spectacular instances of murder, torture and rape, and no immediate moves to bring criminals to justice, and that has been the case all of this year too, from the killings at Macchil to the unprovoked shooting of boys in Srinagar.

Sunday, 1 August 2010

I read about a statement issued by the Central Committee of the Communist Party of India—CPI(M)—offering an 'Inquilabi Salaam' to Kashmiris who, in their pursuit, of self-determination, are being crushed by their common enemy, the Indian state. The enemy is the same, they say, in Dandakaranya as in Kashmir. What they self-servingly omit to mention is that their political and military methods are not those of Kashmiris today. And this is an important distinction, and crucial to understanding why the valence of the state 'crackdown' is not the same in each theatre of conflict. Some Kashmiris have a different comparison for their struggle: their resistance is like the Palestinian Intifada (minus Hamas), and the visual analogy—stone-pelters versus armed state forces—is compelling.

And the situation worsens today: eight more are killed, including a young woman, scores wounded, another SOG camp is burned, as is a tehsildar's office. Villagers who live in areas adjoining the Jammu–Srinagar highway are blockading sections, which invites swift reprisals, since that is the primary road link between India and the Valley. The range of protests widens, and it is clear that no official response, however swift, is working. There are ministerial delegations visiting districts in north and south Kashmir, but members of the government have no credibility at all, and their meetings with local officials seem to be exercises in futility. Mehbooba Mufti of the Opposition People's Democratic Party (PDP) is refreshingly honest when she says that there is no point in mainstream politicians like her attempting to speak to the people now—they will not listen, she says.

The conversation here shifts increasingly to the imposition of governor's rule, and the handing over of roads and major installations to the army. However, a friend points out that Delhi is able to perform this sort of deployment even when there is an elected government in place, so why would they remove the fig leaf that Omar Abdullah provides them? In any case no political activity of any sort is feasible before this cycle of violence—demonstrations and official reprisals—is broken, and no one, least of all the government, seems to know how to enable that. I am reminded of Jayaprakash Narayan's comment on the imposition of the Emergency: '*Vinaash kale vipreet buddhi*'. It is true that in difficult times, when you need them most, the buddhi, the mind and the imagination, work least well. In this case, the political imagination has been caused to atrophy, overtaken entirely by the polarized power of the state and the single-minded separatist slogan of 'Azadi'. I ask a wise friend here what he thinks might happen if tomorrow the Centre says that they would talk to the entire range of Kashmiri political opinion without preconditions, that is, without insisting that Kashmir's future necessarily lies within the parameters of the Indian Constitution. I don't know, he says, and in any case these moments of heightened violence are not a good time to begin to think about such future possibilities. Times of peace, or rather, times when daily violence is absent, those are the right moments to initiate political dialogue and action, but those are precisely the moments when governments, lulled into a false sense of security and complacence, do nothing. In any case such inaction suits the government, whose actors seem to believe that economic development and employment, thin as they are in practice, will be the magic wands that wave away political aspirations.

There is no peace, not today. In fact there has been enough violence for the Prime Minister to call a late-night meeting of the Cabinet Committee on Security. Everyone waits to hear what will emerge, and the results are predictable. Omar Abdullah's government is asked to intervene more personally and capably, punishment is promised to all those who take the law into their own hands (that is, all those on the streets who disobey curfew restrictions, and worse, revenge themselves upon those elements of the administration they have come to hate). Abdullah has also appeared on television to make a tepid appeal for calm, but it is too little, too late. His pained face and tone lack conviction.

We hear the sounds of massed people in the first half of the night, and occasional shots. But our neighborhood, like so many others in Srinagar where the well-off live, is quiet, quiet enough to let the sounds of struggle elsewhere waft indistinctly but ominously into our homes.

Monday, 2 August 2010

The action on the street shows no let up, and Omar Abdullah is in Delhi for a meeting with the Prime Minister and others. He emerges and makes an eloquent appeal for peace (the police have been instructed to be restrained, but violence will have consequences, he says) in his English-language press conference afterwards. He repeats his request in Urdu later in the day for local consumption here. He calls for a calm that will allow the proper education of children and young adults so that they can be competitive in the job market. He also promises the massive recruitment of young people to an unspecified set of jobs—once again, the government offers its payroll as a solution to the problem of political disenchantment. But he does offer a phrase that should be remembered at all times, not just in this moment of crisis: he has told the Centre, he says, that Kashmir needs a 'political', not just an 'economic' package. There are no details offered, but at least there is now a phrase to work with.

Phrases to work with, a new and respectful semantics—a journalist friend tells me that that is what both the government and Kashmiris need. The government plays strategic games in which the vocabulary they use for the political (not the parliamentary) opposition is charged and designed to belittle: they are the instigators of unrest, they are irrelevant, they are obstacles in the path to development. Small wonder then that Kashmiris see the government as colonial, mainstream politicians as stooges, and the military and paramilitaries as an occupation force. In the absence of a new, more innovative, more polite idiom, there is going to be no way of climbing out of the deep rut in which we find ourselves.

Sadly, eight more people are shot dead, and people have lost track of numbers of the wounded. I keep thinking of the multiplier effects of such violence: for each person dead or injured, there are a score personally affected, and each funeral cortège reminds larger groups of past losses. But then these are the most recent, intense episodes in a longer history of violence. If 70,000 Kashmiris have been killed (regardless of by whom) in the last two decades, then there is virtually no family exempt from the eddying effects of such loss. This is the reservoir of grief, anger and frustration that produces the flood of emotion that moves people into risking their lives on the street; and sometimes, as we know, floods overwhelm the thickest embankments we build to contain them.

There is also the highly intrusive security footprint to think about. I had travelled in Punjab in the worst years of the Khalistan movement, and I remember just how humiliating and fear-inducing it was to be stopped and questioned over and over again, to have your car searched, and occasionally to be patted down. This is how Kashmiris have lived for twenty years now. No one goes anywhere, even in times of relative peace, without being aware of surveillance and check-points. An entire generation—the young on the streets now—have grown up with no other sense of the Indian state. India is the jawan who slaps you because it has been a long day and you are less patient in the checking-line than he would like; India is the officer who smiles sardonically as you are pushed to the ground and kicked for good measure; India is the force that tears you and your family from your home to stand around for hours as entire neighbourhoods are cordoned off and searched. And this is low-level business. There have been far harsher crimes committed by state agents, but no one has been punished, and that fact alone rankles and will not die.

I speak on the phone to a relative who was a career bureaucrat: utter lawlessness, he says, it needs to be put down firmly, no one should feel entitled to damage property or attack the police. He wonders why things have been allowed to slide in the past few days. I suggest that we have been on this slope for at least twenty years now, and that we have a political rather than a law-and-order problem, but he wants none of that. Various friends and relatives have been calling to ask after us—we don't leave the house and are fine, we say. No, we aren't planning to leave. This is home, my mother says, and the weather is lovely.

Tuesday, 3 August 2010

A friend with a press pass escorts me past the razor wire that closes off our neighbourhood from Maulana Azad Road. We are asked a few questions by the police, which I let him answer, and then we step into the shuttered world of the market. On our route, we pass by a government office protected by CRPF jawans. They are used to seeing my mother walk by—she is the only woman in a sari for miles—and they ask my journalist friend about the day's events. He tells them, and then I say to one of them (miles away from his home in Tamil Nadu): this is all terrible, is it not? He nods wanly, and says, '*Kya karein, aisa hi ho raha hai*' ('What to do, this is what is going on'). My mother tells me that these jawans wish her and talk to her each time she walks by them, and that their loneliness is palpable. They are young men, far from home, under-paid, under-rested, and occasionally under-fed, deployed in a situation in which they know that they are loathed for their uniforms. No shining nationalist zeal or commitment brings them here; their poverty renders them cogs in the machinery of the state, and they well know that.

There are only police on the streets—there is after all a 'shoot at sight' order in place—and I smile at the young policeman who has been issued a lathi for offensive action and worn out batsman's pads as defensive equipment. What kind of game do the police authorities think they are playing? What manner of crowd control might be enabled by such equipment? We walk across the market and into the Press Enclave. Reporters and photographers have been spending nights in their offices, since they are never sure that they will be able to make it to their homes at night or back to their offices the next day.

Five more are dead today (twenty-seven in the last five days), and, worst of all, an eight-year-old boy has been beaten to death. The police issue a statement saying that he died in a stampede of protesters, but there are eyewitnesses who say that he, cricket bat in hand, was raising slogans for Azadi and was not quick enough to run away when the CRPF charged. Several jawans beat him, dragged him into their vehicle, and then decided to dump him on the side of the road. He died, not long after, in hospital. Clubbing an eight-year-old boy to death? What kind of harm could he have done, mighty with his cricket bat? (Ah yes, perhaps he too picked up and slung stones at the police.)

There seems no escaping the impasse here: more dead protesters, more angry protest, more protesters killed. Upon the chief minister's request, the home ministry has flown in 2,000 paramilitary men, but it is clear to no one what purpose such reinforcements will serve. They are trained no differently from the hundreds of thousands of uniformed men already in service in Kashmir, so how will their presence be a deterrent? They will join the daily rotation, I'm sure, and allow some others overburdened with duties some respite, but it isn't more troops that are needed here, but different forms of policing. Some very senior retired Indian police officers have issued statements saying that police should be instructed never to fire above the waist of protesters, but that advice seems likely to be ignored.

And it isn't only imaginative policing that is missing. People are so stunned by the turn of events here, and the shocking violence, that nothing seems to emanate from the many civil society organizations at work in Kashmir. Many lack local credibility in any case, but the turn of events here has closed off the possibility of any initiatives or efforts at mediation between people and the state. There is a vast population here holding its collective breath, and I am sure many are wondering, as they have in the past, *after such knowledge, what forgiveness*? And that is what it means to be a Kashmiri in Kashmir today.

This article first appeared as 'Days in Srinagar' on the website http://www.outlookindia.com, 6 August 2010.

What Are Kashmir's Stone-pelters Saying to Us?

Sanjay Kak

Like an obstinate nightmare, Kashmir has returned to haunt India's political discourse in this third consecutive summer of massive protests. For almost two months now we are witnessing the brazen courage of Kashmiri youth, armed with stones in their hands, in groups of no more than a few hundred at a time, taking on Kashmir's much vaunted 'security grid'. This carefully welded network deploys at least 6,00,000 soldiers in uniform, and another 1,00,000 'civilian' intelligence and surveillance operatives. But pinned down by this summer's showers of carefully aimed rocks, the grid has begun to appear clumsy and vulnerable.

As the *sang-bazan,* the stone-pelters, insolently stormed into prime time, they brought with them an intensity that made the newspaper pundits, and the usual chorus of television-studio experts, briefly wilt. Images of boys as young as nine and ten being dragged off into police vehicles, or shot dead by the paramilitary forces, have begun to dent conventional truisms about what is happening in Kashmir. Startling photographs of middle-aged (and middle-class) women in the ranks of the stone-pelting protesters have also destabilized those who have allowed a morbid panic of the 'Islamists', or the fear of Pakistan's venality, to obscure their understanding of events in the Valley. Although reluctant to grant this uprising the same political pedigree, at least some Indians seem to be curling their tongues around the word *intifada*. On the whole, the David and Goliath disproportion of the protests, and its sheer effrontery, has begun to capture the imagination of a growing number of people in India.

So beyond their furious defiance, what are Kashmir's stone-pelters saying to us?

As a Kashmiri who has mostly lived outside the Valley, my engagement with its troubles began quite recently, in 2003, when I returned to Srinagar after a gap of fourteen years. These intervening years were witness to the tumultuous history of the present movement—the *tehreek*—and were accompanied by massive militarization. It had ended in a virtual deadlock: a restive population, locked down by a gargantuan military presence, in what Kashmiris call the 'occupation' of the Valley.

The year 2003 turned out to be significant, partly because it gave the first indications that armed militancy might be on its way out. From a peak figure of almost 30,000 militants in the early 1990s, security forces had dropped their estimates to less than 2,000 active fighters. Typically, and well before anyone could understand what lay behind the ratcheting down of the armed struggle, the government claimed credit for 'breaking the back' of the armed struggle, and trumpeted the return of 'normalcy'. Unorthodox parameters were used to buttress the claim to normalcy: tourism department estimates of tourist arrivals, and the headcount of pilgrims headed for the annual *yatra* to the Amarnath shrine. There was no acknowledgement that tourists and pilgrims were moving along sheltered corridors, tightly controlled by the security forces, and that these had little connection with the everyday lives of Kashmiris. The understandable enthusiasm of pony-men on the pilgrimage route, and shikara-walas and houseboat owners on the Dal Lake, were presented as the turning of the tide against the tehreek. And for? Well, if not for India, then it was seen as turning towards something called Peace. This was a 'normalcy' confected for visitors, not for the vast majority of people in Kashmir.

As the state government quixotically launched road shows to bring Bollywood producers back to the sylvan slopes of Gulmarg, Kashmiris seemed preoccupied with picking up on other parts of their lives. For the first time in over fifteen years, they too were coming up with a set of numbers, not so much to plumb the peace, but to help configure their abnormal past, and consign their losses to a respectful memory. A dogged survey by the Jammu Kashmir Coalition of Civil Society was providing early indicators: 60,000 people killed, and almost 7,000 'missing' in fifteen years. No one had gotten down to counting the men and women injured and maimed in the thousands of incidents of firing; nor had reliable estimates been made of those molested or raped. Interrogation and torture—words used interchangeably in Kashmir—had run their brutal, bloodied hands over several hundred thousand people it was said, but these were only whispered estimates.

They make a desolation, and call it peace, Agha Shahid Ali, the Kashmiri poet, has written.

In 2003, I was in the Valley with twin identities, Kashmiri and Indian. As a Kashmiri, in place of the promised 'normalcy' I could only sense a deeply traumatized society, and one fearful of its own recent past. Not defeated perhaps, but in some inchoate way, overwhelmed. As an Indian, I was acutely disturbed by what I saw, and could see something with far-reaching consequences for India brewing in those troubles. Even today, the sharpest memories of that visit are those that bridge my two disparate identities.

The strongest is always the militarization. However prepared you are for the presence of uniforms and guns; actually facing them, and living with them, is much harder, even for the casual visitor. From the aircraft window, you see soldiers with automatic weapons on the tarmac; outside, dozens of vehicle-mounted machine guns wait to 'escort' the convoys of dignitaries. The streets are endlessly lined with heavily armed soldiers, and roundabouts throw up the unsettling sight of traffic policemen who carry AK-47s. And then the bunkers: everywhere, but most galling when they turn up at both ends of the lane in which you live. Even without a secessionist bone in your body, so many guns can never stand for anything but intimidation.

The second is a compelling sense of the breakdown of the institutions of democratic governance. For a people bruised and battered by fifteen years of an armed struggle, every single mechanism by which they could find representation, or hope to be heard, or access minimal justice, had been dismantled and put away. Elections, the judicial process, the rule of law: all had been hollowed out. In their place we had the draconian provisions of the Armed Forces Special Powers Act (AFSPA), and the Public Safety Act (PSA). Despite the fact that an elected legislature was in place, real power was widely regarded as lodged in three specific sites: Badami Bagh, Srinagar's cantonment, where the corps headquarters of the Indian Army are located; Gupkar Road, where a slew of Indian intelligence agencies are based; and Raj Bhawan, formerly the maharaja's palace, now the governor's home. (Kashmiris don't fail to make the obvious connection that all three sites are implicated in a century of highly oppressive rule by the Dogra maharajas.) Outside of Srinagar, for those living in the *qasba* and the small town, the real face of power was clearer, and usually sign-posted in the middle of the main street. 'Town Commander', the modest tin boards said. Lettered in just below, the name and phone number of a major of the Indian Army.

The third revelation centred on the national media. What was reported seemed so far removed from the reality unfolding on the ground here that it was not long before an acute sense of disorientation began to settle in, a feeling of being lied to, and manipulated. Unlike the ongoing conflict in Manipur, or earlier, in Nagaland, which are shrouded in silence, Kashmir was regularly covered by the mainstream Indian press. There was a large contingent of reporters covering Kashmir for the Indian media, and there were a surprising number of local newspapers and magazines. But this media mirror was hugely distorting, sending out twisted images every day, right on to the front pages of newspapers, and on prime time television. The very abundance of such coverage seemed designed to obscure, a dense smokescreen on which many prominent Indian journalists could project a self-image of caring souls whose hearts bled for Kashmir.

The easy comfort with a military solution, and the near abandonment of the rule of law: many will recognize in Kashmir a set of tactics that the Indian state has since begun to deploy with avidity in other troubled parts of the country.

What has changed in the Valley since 2003?

In 2010, despite occasional lip service to the idea of troop reduction, the military presence remains unaltered, and the civilian population continues to suffer the full weight of the security apparatus. Despite the talk of normalcy, there has been only the rare instance when there was 'troop reduction'. (One particular, well-publicized pullout of a battalion of the Indian Army translated into no more than a 1,000 soldiers on the ground. Out of an estimated 6,00,000.) In Srinagar the cosmetic changes have included replacing the Border Security Force (BSF) with an equal, perhaps greater, strength of the Central Reserve Police Force (CRPF). There has been a visible reduction in the ubiquitous squalor of the brick and barbed-wire bunkers that puncture the daily life of its citizens. But in its place the CRPF have shifted to a more centralized 'quick reaction' deployment, with even more lethal consequences. The recent cycle of protests, for instance, saw patients pour into Srinagar's Shri Maharaja Hari Singh Hospital with severe bullet injuries inflicted by security forces, sixty in the first fortnight of August alone. Surgeons at the hospital told the BBC 'most of the bullet injuries are in the abdominal area, chest, eyes and neck. They are single and multiple bullet wounds. They are all young men, in their late teens or early twenties'. This week a new threat was unleashed in the streets of Srinagar: a 'pressure pump' gun. It fires highly damaging pellets which enter the body and destroy vital organs, but leave hardly any external marks. (The summer of 2010 left thirty-five people blinded in firing, and more than 110 have been killed. The security forces have reported no casualties.)

In the countryside, which has always been 'held' by the army, even less ground has been yielded. If anything, the army has visibly dug its heels in, with the defence minister firmly rejecting the possibility of a troop reduction. Earlier this year the army commander, northern command, waded into the debate around the removal of the draconian AFSPA, with a comment that displayed a dreadful lack of cultural sensitivity, describing the Act as a 'holy book' for soldiers deployed in Kashmir. Debate on the possible removal of the notorious Act has always been upstaged by considerations of the 'morale' of the Indian Army. What this word 'morale' effectively silences is the impact that half a million soldiers have on a civilian population. It starts with the colonization of scarce water resources in villages and the catastrophic effect of their presence on the forests. It is reflected in the high incidence of forced labour, *begaar*, around the army camps. And in the largely unspoken incidence of the sexual exploitation of women.

And yet, in discussions on this summer's protests, all attention has been focused on the incompetence of the Omar Abdullah government, encouraging the impression that it lay within his powers to alter any of the key elements in the crisis. The reality is that within this present structure, were the prime minister of India arrange to have Syed Ali Shah Geelani, the separatist patriarch, recast as chief minister of the state, even he would be hard put to prevent further strife. Incidents like the fake 'encounter' in Machil, Kupwara, came and went, but were never allowed to disturb the tone of the official Indian position. But Kashmiris could not have forgotten that the protests this summer were sparked off by the cold-blooded killing of three innocent civilians in a faraway valley by Indian Army soldiers. That the soldiers were under orders from their officers, who tried to pass off the bodies as those of 'militants' killed in an encounter. Eventually when the story broke, and massive protests erupted, a colonel and a major were charged with murder. (Their motivation was not much more than a few hundred thousand rupees of 'reward' money.) The Machil incident was a timely reminder that India's military presence in the Valley is not seen as some well intentioned—if occasionally clumsy—beast sent to protect Kashmiris. It is seen as an occupying force.

To dismiss such incidents as aberrations would be dangerous. The past two years have seen the unearthing of a series of mass graves in Kashmir, which could hold evidence of hundreds of Machil-style executions. There has been no considered official reaction to these revelations. Meanwhile, the government remains doggedly centred on the role played by Pakistan, the involvement of the Lashkar-e-Toiba, and for the good news, the 2008 elections and its voter turnout.

Over two decades of conflict, Kashmiris have lost the right to speech, assembly and travel; they have lost all guarantees of their freedom from violence, harassment and unlawful detention. They have seen every single substantive attribute of democracy give way under the pressure of militarization and the attitudes of those who administer Kashmir. The rule of law, the independence of the judiciary, and the civic responsibilities of elected politicians: as each of these protective pillars has been hollowed out, all that remains of democracy is the thin patina of elections.

And this record is itself such a shabby one, right from the first election of 1951, where the National Conference (NC) under Sheikh Abdullah won every single seat in the seventy-two-member assembly. (Only two seats were actually contested. No one else was allowed to file nominations, most of which were rejected at the outset.) But as long as he could deliver the Kashmiri 'mandate' to New Delhi, Sheikh Abdullah was left undisturbed. His successors, Bakshi Ghulam Mohammed, and G.M. Sadiq, were allowed to do the same, a tradition that has survived all the way into the present. Not surprisingly, elections are seen locally not as a measure of popular support, but the mechanism by which the writ of the Indian government can be stamped on the dispensation of its choice.

(Ironically, the only election that Kashmir will remember as 'free' was in 1977, in the aftermath of the declaration of Emergency by Prime Minister Indira Gandhi, when the fractious coalition of the Janata Party was in power, and the 'centre' at it's weakest. For a people who had not experienced a fair election in twenty-five years of voting, this brief tryst with democracy electrified Kashmir.

But that moment of fairness passed too quickly, and as soon as the Janata Party coalition collapsed, and Indira Gandhi returned to power, things reverted to normal. This brief experience of free and fair elections, it has been suggested, could well have given a spurt to the secessionist movement in the early 1980s.)

Of course none of this sordid reality ever inflects the debate on Kashmir in India. This summer, while there was some grudging space for a 'human-rights' discourse, attempts to read events politically were viewed with distaste. 'You are bringing politics into it!' our TV anchors said in what could only have been feigned outrage. While on the streets of Kashmir, protesters are unambiguous, chanting *'Go India! Go back!'* and *'Hum kya chahte? Azadi!'* Like an article of faith common to the entire political spectrum, references to the voter turnout of the 2008 election recur all too frequently, from left-liberal to right-Hindutva. (With metronomic regularity, Bharatiya Janata Party (BJP) spokesman Ravishankar Prasad offered us the non sequitur, 'Why don't the separatists stand for elections?' He clearly chooses to be oblivious of the fact that during the last elections most separatists were in detention. Before, during, and after the polls.)

The quicksilver memory of our media allows us to forget that the 2008 elections were called at a moment spectacularly unpropitious for the government of India. It was a time not unlike the present. Through the summer, Kashmir had been rocked by protests against the state government's acquisition of land for the pilgrimage to Amarnath. Massive unarmed marches, often with 20,000 people, had snowballed into the most outspoken expression of public sentiment since the troubles began. After years of looking frayed at the edges, the numbers on the street suggested that the sentiment for Azadi was back. The palpable air of defeat one had sensed only a few years ago seemed to be a thing of the past.

Not surprisingly, the two principal 'pro-India' regional parties, the National Conference (NC) and the People's Democratic Party (PDP), were both visibly reluctant to wade into this flood of separatist sentiment and canvass for votes. In the face of a poll boycott called by the separatists, a lacklustre and largely invisible campaign followed. Omar Abdullah and the NC in particular pointedly sheltered under the caveat that the election was narrowly about 'development' and not about the larger issue of Azadi. Informally, police and intelligence officials made the gloomy admission that a turnout of 35 per cent would leave them very satisfied.

Yet, when the results started to come in, and the turnout began to creep past these modest expectations, and eventually rise to 60 per cent, no one admitted to being surprised. (In 2002 the figure was just under 32 per cent) Such was the din of celebration, deftly orchestrated by the mass media, that an election fought on the mundane platform of *bijli, sadak, pani* was suddenly being served up as a referendum. Kashmiris had embraced Indian democracy, they said. Kashmiris had rejected separatism.

There was no mention that to stall anti-election protests, most districts had been under curfew for weeks before polling. Or that almost 700 key activists of the summer's protests spent the months in the run-up to the election in jail, locked up under the PSA. There was silence about the sudden and ominous reappearance of the dreaded *ikhwani* counter-insurgents, their murderous operations now dressed up in the constitutional uniform of Special Police Officers, as part of the Special Operations Group, and even the Territorial Army. (Word of their renewed presence alone was enough to terrorize people in the villages.) No one drew attention to the fact that in addition to the soldiers already in place, nearly 450 additional companies (50,000 paramilitary troopers) had arrived to 'assist' in the elections, allowing the government to flood each constituency with khaki and olive green before the polling, which was held in an unprecedented seven stages.

Of course there were the more familiar reports of straightforward rigging, of bogus voting and booth capturing. But on the whole the strategy seemed designed not to favour one party or the other, but to simply ensure a turnout. The more subtle strategies included the sudden nomination of thousands of candidates, most of them independents, but others from parties that had little or no presence in Kashmir. In the midst of a fierce poll boycott, and a tense campaign, candidates suddenly showed up from the BJP, the Samajwadi Party (SP), Janata Dal (JD [Secular]), Rashtriya Janata Dal (RJD), Janata Party (JP), Lok Janshakti Party (LJP), All India Forward Bloc (AIFB), Forward Bloc (Socialist), Republican Party of India (Athvale), Samata Party, Socialist Democratic Party, National Lok Hind Party . . . An endless list of Indian political formations had lined up at the hustings. They clearly hadn't hoped to win, and almost 1,100 such candidates lost their deposits. But whatever the inducement to stand, these candidates were probably expected to poll only a few hundred votes each, often just from family and neighbours.

In the end it did all add up, they did deliver a few percentage points in the voter turnout. 'We had several different strategies in place,' I heard from a senior police officer, some months after the elections, 'and all of them luckily fell into place.' He could not stop grinning. 'Of course we will never again have this level of force available to us, never,' he added emphatically, 'so it will be difficult to replicate.'

That is what the 2008 elections in Kashmir eventually was: an exercise in pushing up the turnout to a 'respectable' level, to once again demonstrate the validity of Indian democracy in Kashmir. It did not matter what Kashmiris thought of it. So that when the new coalition government between the Congress and the NC, and headed by the telegenic Omar Abdullah, was sworn in early in 2009, all that grey was forgotten. In the noisy triumphalism generated by the Indian media, the spin masters in Srinagar and New Delhi seemed to so enjoy the din that they appear to have begun to believe in the implausible script they had written. These elections had pulled Kashmiris back into the mainstream, they said. Something akin to a 'post-conflict' euphoria permeated the atmosphere, and the air was thick with talk about a 'reconciliation' commission.

It took only a few months for the illusion to fall apart, to understand what Kashmiris thought of all this delusionary behaviour. By May 2009, the rape and murder of two young women in Shopian, in which the security forces were widely believed to have been implicated, led to another massive round of protests. If the protests in the 2008 Amarnath land issue were marked by huge unarmed processions, now the overwhelming feature was civil disobedience. Shopian town remained shut for forty-seven days, this unprecedented *hartal* itself called by a non-political formation of citizens, the Majlis-e-Mashawarat, the consultative committee. It was the Majlis who made sure that daily wagers and petty shopkeepers were given rations to survive the long shutdown.

But wrapped up in its hubris, and swaddled by a pliant media—and an intelligence structure dulled by complacency—New Delhi was unable to grasp what was developing. Opaque to the terrible bottled-up anger of people, Omar Abdullah's government responded with a series of callous statements about the death of the young women, and the Jammu and Kashmir police followed up with a series of bungled investigative procedures. These eventually threw up so many contradictions, and started to look so shabby, that the government of India had to rope in the Central Bureau of Investigation to put a lid on it. (The CBI promptly concluded that it was a case of death by drowning, in a stream with less than a foot of water). Today the case remains stuck in an extraordinary place: charges have been filed against the doctors who performed the post-mortems, against the lawyers who filed cases against the state, against everybody except a possible suspect for the rape and murder, or the many officials who had visibly botched up the investigations. In Shopian, the anger remains in place.

This week I was suddenly reminded of a conversation I had some years ago with a committed separatist, a former militant, and ex-chairman of the United Jehad Council. (He spoke about carrying an AK-47 for seven years, but was oddly proud of himself for never having fired it.) He's now a quiet scholarly presence, retired to a spartan hut in his sister's compound in Srinagar.

'We didn't want an Azadi where all our young men were dead,' he had said, suggesting tactical withdrawal before the might of the Indian Army, not a defeat.

'There were 30,000 armed militants once,' I insisted, 'what happened to their weapons?'

'Well, guns are not like fruit, my friend, they don't come off trees, they don't just rot with age . . .' he had answered thoughtfully. Then added, 'They must be somewhere, mustn't they? There must be many, many weapons buried in the Valley. Plenty of ammunition too . . .'

I regret not having asked him about the fighters, the survivors amongst the 30,000, those who were not killed, or jailed. (Or arrested and broken by torture.) How many of those are there? Where are they? What must they be thinking of what is going on? As the streets are taken over by younger people, the stone-pelting children of the tehreek, what counsel do they have to offer to this new generation of Kashmiris, who grew up in the tumultuous 1990s? What lessons are these veterans in turn drawing from the young?

The last three summers have seen an argument about resistance slowly taking shape in the Kashmir valley. The tenacity of the sang-bazan only caps a political debate that Kashmiris have been engaged in for the last twenty years. (And in some ways, all the way from 1947.) The difference is that this time the stone thrown on the street is being intelligently shadowed by a sharpened understanding of the oppression. It's no more a secret understanding, open only to a few select leaders. It's available on the Internet, on social networking sites. But it still is a debate. And the form of the resistance is fluid, and can easily swing back to the place where it has come from.

What is buried in the Valley, as my friend had hinted, can always be resurrected.

That is a debate that should engage all of us, Kashmiris and Indians.

This article first appeared in the *Economic and Political Weekly*, 11 September 2010.

Kashmir Unrest
A Letter to an Unknown Indian

Basharat Peer

When poems written about totalitarian regimes echo in the hearts of a people purportedly living in a democracy, it is time for that democracy to take a hard look at the mirror. Over the past two months, as the numbers of Kashmiri protesters killed by Indian troops rose, I kept returning to a poem. In December 1970, the troops of the communist government in Poland fired and killed forty-nine protesting workers at a shipyard in the city of Gdansk. Three iron crosses, cast by fellow workers, stand now at the spot where the workers had fallen. On the memorial remain the words from a poem by Czeslaw Milosz:

> *Though everyone bowed*
> *down before you*
> *Saying virtue and wisdom*
> *lit your way*
> *Striking gold medals*
> *in your honour*
> *Glad to have survived another day*
> *Do not feel safe.*
> *The poet remembers.*
> *You can kill one, but*

another is born.
The words are written
down, the deed, the date.

When pain makes it difficult to articulate coherently, quiet remembrance helps. Like many other Kashmiris, I have been in silence, committing to memory, the deed, the date. The faces of the murdered boys, the colour of their shirts, their grieving fathers—these might disappear from the headlines, but they have already found their place in our collective memory. Kashmir remembers what is done in your name, in the name of your democracy, whether its full import ever reaches your drawing rooms and offices or not. Your soldiers of reason carrying their press cards might dissuade you from seeing it, comfort you with their cynical use of academic categories and interpretations of Kashmir, they might rerun the carefully chosen, convenient images on TV, but Kashmir sees the unedited Kashmir.

The tortured man returns home one day to tell the tale. The pallbearer remembers when the slain boy's body fell on the street. The hands of the doctor who struggled to stitch the torn limb bear witness. We have been remembering for a while, and you don't make it easy to forget. Every new atrocity is a reminder of a previous one. I remember getting my first identity card in 1990; I remember that early morning announcement ordering us to the hospital grounds, the first crackdown as soldiers searched every house. I still remember the eyes of the masked informer in the Border Security Force (BSF) Gypsy, pointing out who would be taken into the makeshift torture centre. I still remember the bruised back and burnt hands of one who limped out of the hospital, where soldiers extracted information. I remember raising my hands in the air and walking between check-posts.

Even when we go about our business, getting degrees in far-away universities and working jobs in far-off lands, we remember. Even when we don't know we are remembering, we remember. Like my friend, who confessed one night in a New York room to a recurrent dream: a boy he had known was running in a lane outside his house in a northern corner of Kashmir, but the soldier chasing him had fired and not missed. The boy has been running in my friend's dream for eighteen years now.

They too remember, the boys whose masked faces you see, carrying stones in their hands. One of them remembers a bunker by a bridge in Srinagar and hot iron rods leaving marks on his forearms that he now hides with a full-sleeved shirt. One of them remembers the cold edge of a dagger on his throat and a question shouted at his grandfather, 'Where did they go?'

On 13 August 2008, a twenty-one-year-old house painter from a tiny village near Sopore saw unarmed people being shot in the village of Chahal near the Line of Control. His mother remembers now, looking at a framed picture of him. The house painter's memory brought him to Srinagar on 7 January 2010, carrying a gun, shooting, and eventually being killed after a twenty-seven-hour-long encounter with the troops, that you might remember.

And now there is much more that is becoming hard to forget. Have you seen that picture from Srinagar? On a stretcher in the middle of a street is a slain young man. Behind his fallen corpse, soldiers and policemen assault the pallbearers and mourners with guns and batons. The mourners run for safety, except for a man in his late fifties. The father trying to save his son's corpse from desecration, spreading himself over the boy, his arms stretched in a protective arc. And have you seen the video of a woman in Anantnag, washing the blood of the boys who were killed outside her house?

We also remember your soft-spoken prime minister speaking in Srinagar of 'zero tolerance of human rights abuses'. We remember a committee he had formed to possibly repeal the law that gives license to kill. Do you remember it—the Armed Forces Special Powers Act? A broken man I met by the Dal Lake remembered it. His sixteen-year-old son, who had argued with a BSF officer, had been killed. He remembered his son wearing sneakers and leaving the house that afternoon. He remembered lowering him into a grave, soon after. A tired son I met in a remote village near the border remembered it. His seventy-year-old father, the 'oldest militant', had been killed. They even remembered that rare thing called justice. They know you don't speak much of it any more.

Your government is sending troops with guns, more loops of barbed wire, announcing more curfews. It might even pacify the Valley again. In his essay, 'On Disbelieving Atrocities', Arthur Koestler says that those not directly touched by atrocity were protected by an ability to 'walk past laughing and chatting'. Koestler addressed the untouched, unaffected people, walking past: 'Were it not so, this war would have been avoided; and those murdered within sight of your daydreaming eyes would still be alive.'

Is that how you seek to be remembered?

This article first appeared in the *Economic Times*, 9 August 2010.

How I Became a Stone-thrower for a Day

Hilal Mir

I left Kashmir a year ago to preserve my sanity, frayed during the past two decades by the internalizing of the conflict. Covering it as a reporter for seven years felt like wading—despairingly—through the five rivers of Hades. My emotions stabilized a bit by the speed and normalcy of life in Delhi, I thought I could now maintain a safe distance from the happenings. With this frame of mind, I landed on 4 July at Srinagar airport on a vacation.

Policemen and paramilitary soldiers were everywhere along the way. Driving me home, my friend Showkat, *Outlook* magazine's Kashmir correspondent, prepared me for the situation by narrating the horror he and a bunch of journalists from the *Indian Express*, *Sahara Samay* and *Tehelka* had faced a day before. While covering a procession marching toward the north Kashmir flashpoint of Sopur, they had been fired at by a policeman on the Srinagar highway. Shouting aloud about their press credentials had only invited abuses. They had to take cover in the nearby paddy fields, surprised that the bullet missed them. Showkat's wife had since asked him to quit journalism and raise chickens. It was the only day I saw shops open and traffic plying normally. From the next day, it was a return to the realm of Hades.

In the morning, one and a half kilometres away from my home, I went to the funeral of a seventeen-year-old blue-eyed, fair-skinned student, as handsome as Omar Abdullah, and a thirty-five-year-old father of two. According to the protesters, the boy had been hit in the head and then thrown into a flood channel by the police. The man had been shot dead during the boy's funeral procession. Women wailed, pulled out their hair, beat their chests and faces, and men shouted freedom slogans while the duo were consigned to the graves. I had seen this countless times in the past, but the rage this time was volcanic, fuelled largely by official lies, apathy and the validation of the bullet-for-stone method. People wanted revenge—though, at the same time, they were aware that their acts of revenge, stone throwing at best, would result in more deaths. It seemed a rage directed more towards one's helplessness than towards an armed soldier. Otherwise why would such 'frenzied mobs sponsored by Lashkar-e-Toiba' not kill a soldier they had cornered on a road, but instead just beat him up, strip him and let him go?

This strange mix of rage and helplessness was to strike me and several journalists I was moving around with in the curfewed, restricted and deserted city. A Central Reserve Police Force (CRPF) soldier stopped us in the old city. A young reporter of a local English daily showed him a curfew pass issued by the government. The soldier tore it up and asked, 'Where is your bloody curfew pass now?' I had had no time to get a curfew pass. I just showed my *Hindustan Times* ID card. I presume the word 'Hindustan' did the trick.

The next few days were spent in exhausting discussions on politics, in parks and the Mughal Gardens, leaving us with an aftertaste of impotent rage. The calm instilled by Delhi was wearing thin. I had always loathed the term 'objectivity' when it really meant balancing truth with a healthy dose of falsehood—or, even worse, 'national interest'. Much of the media were doing that. The state and central governments were in a state of denial, effectively blaming the people for the mess. For the first time I felt like an ordinary Kashmiri and wanted to react like them. I was with other journalists when we went to Kawdara in the old city, where separatist leader Mirwaiz Umar Farooq was leading a demonstration that soon morphed into a clash between youth and CRPF soldiers (camping in a bunker as old the insurgency itself).

I picked up a stone from the debris of the housing cluster burnt by CRPF soldiers in 1990 and threw it at the soldiers, a few of whom were filming the stone-throwers with mini-cams. Caught, I could have been booked under the Public Safety Act and jailed for two years without a trial. I would also have been jobless because no news organization would have a felon on its desk. But I threw more stones. I later realized it was an atavistic reaction, as if it was the only legitimate thing to do in that cursed place. I had thrown stones twenty-three years ago when three people were killed for demonstrating against a hike in power tariff, an event that would catalyse the uprising of 1989. My journalist friends restrained me. Disoriented, I walked to my birthplace, Nawab Bazaar, in the old city, a kilometre from Kawdara.

Nawab Bazaar was as furious as it was twenty years ago. Angry youths whom I had seen growing up were pelting the CRPF bunker there with stones. Back then, militants had attacked it with AK-47 rifles. For me, the bunker represents an occupation of memories. It was built on the spot where a man sold *phirni* and children would line up for the sighting of the crescent, a harbinger of Eid. A short distance away, the Dogra maharaja's soldiers had shot dead my great-grandfather in 1931. Twenty years ago, when the bunker was being constructed, my father's bosom friend, a fanatical Congress supporter, prophesied that 'your eyelashes will turn grey, but the bunker will still be there'. He died last year. His eyebrows had started to grey and all his hair was silver.

Old demons were stirring up inside me. During nights I would look out of the window of my room, holding a digital recorder in any hand to catch freedom songs blaring from mosque loudspeakers and wafting through the quiet air. Twenty years ago I had heard and sung the same songs. The bunker in Nawab Bazaar has grown bigger and uglier, with all those barbed-wire loops, fences, gaudy paint and slits, demonstrating that the state does not tire. But neither do the people.

A shorter version of this first appeared in the *Hindustan Times*, New Delhi, 7 August 2010.

Curfewed in Kashmir
Voices from the Valley

Aaliya Anjum and Saiba Varma

*S*ince 1989, civilian life in Indian-administered Kashmir has been governed through the presence of more than half a million troops, making the region the most heavily militarized zone in the world. This, despite the fact that last year, official government figures put the number of militants operating in the Valley at less than 500.

Since 2008, Kashmiris, especially young Kashmiris, have been waging a new form of rebellion against the Indian state known as the 'second revolution'. Expressing their demands through public protests often punctuated with stone-pelting rather than guns, Kashmiris have launched this 'second revolution' through a massive, sustained and predominantly non-violent, civil disobedience movement in the streets. These protests are expressions of widespread dissatisfaction with what Kashmiris view as a defunct justice delivery system and gross violations of human rights that have occurred under Indian rule in the larger context of their persistent demands for the right to self-determination. In the past nine weeks, such protests have been met with disproportionate force from the Indian paramilitary, leading to the deaths of at least fifty-six civilians and the arrests of hundreds more, heralding what Kashmiris are calling, 'The Year of Killing Youth'.

This piece is part of a collaborative writing project called 'Voices from the Valley', composed of youth voices from Kashmir. We asked *poets, lawyers, writers, activists and doctors to submit their interpretations of the current crisis. Rather than have others speak for them, we wanted to create a forum where Kashmiris could speak for themselves.*

⁓

Writing this, we await the stomach-churning news of more deaths. The cursor blinks at 62—tenuously, tentatively. Any moment now, we think. Friends are phoned anxiously, 'facts' are double and triple checked, even though we know that in the inevitable act of putting type to paper, things will be lost. This piece too, will become history.

In the eerie quiet, mobile phones have become umbilical cords, Facebook pages, arteries. Information—found in the liminal space between fact and rumour—spreads like wildfire: the Internet is going to be banned, warns Mehran Khan, one of our contributors, so finish your piece quickly.

Journalists scramble to guarantee accuracy, as numbers are what matter now. And what numbers? Only the dead can be affirmed. We mark these on neat and orderly spreadsheets— who, how old, when, where, how. Dilnaz Boga, a journalist friend, sends us the Excel spreadsheet that she updates daily, which she has named 'Body Count'. We are grateful for the orderliness of it—the way she has bolded the names of those deceased, assembled a narrative that grows and grows, but for the moment stops at '75 civilians so far'. This 'Body Count' sheet starts in January, when the first teenage civilian death of the year—sixteen-year-old Inayat Khan— was reported on 8 January. Although there have been regular strikes and protests in Kashmir since Inayat's death, the confrontation between Indian security forces and Kashmiri civilian protesters became particularly intensive in the first week of June, prompting frequent comparisons to the Palestinian Intifada.

On a recent Facebook status update, Sajid Iqbal, a lawyer, writes of the scarce heed paid by the international media to the persistent civilian killings in Kashmir in these past weeks: 'After over forty deaths, the BBC finally does a full length story on us, in one of their main evening programmes, *The Hub with Nik Gowing*. Congratulations everyone, our body count is finally respectable. . .' Besides gaining Kashmir a small amount of international media attention—a piece in the *Guardian*, the *LA Times*, the *New York Times*, *Christian Science Monitor*, the *Huffington Post*, occasional coverage on the BBC and Al Jazeera websites on exceptionally violent days—the casualty figure is the only thing we have left to hold on to. It is the lone fishing vessel in a sea of rumours, proxies and hurdles.

> *Along that solitary gravelled path*
> *Into a crimson evening,*
> *My eyes chase you and chase you*
> *Until you ask them:*
> *'Where do these boys go after they kill them?'*
> *'What happens to their hearts, the love-lakes, now mad with*
>   *the tempests of freedom?'*
>
> *In Kashmir, in my village, Bumthan,*
> *A cold summer morning*
> *Whispers into the leaves of an elm,*
> *Why the dearest ones have to leave us before autumn?*
> *Ah! You have taken away the summer rain,*
> *And the news of our own death smashes us*
>   *under the glaring sun.*

(From 'The Shining Stars of my Sky' by Feroz Rather)

This excerpt captures how Kashmiris will remember the summer of 2010 as a season of loss and longing.

'It's almost two months now,' says Ahmad Umar, 'during which Indian paramilitary forces killed over fifty young people, including nine-year-old children, as well as women, besides leaving hundreds of others injured or crippled.' As the Indian media establishment prepares itself for yet another round of brouhaha, it is sometimes easy to forget how all of this began. That there was something *before* and something other than images of burning police stations and masked teenage boys hurling stones.

Body counts

> *Into the sunset, a scream rises from*
> *the stones rebelling in the streets of the Old City,*
> *Our hearts turn crimson,*
> *The blood seeps into the lake,*
> *And in our eyes Tufail floats like a new leaf*
> *Amid the wreaths of lotuses . . .*

(From: 'The Shining Stars of My Sky' by Feroz Rather)

The most recent wave of state violence began on 11 June with the death of seventeen-year-old Tufail Ahmad Matoo. Tufail, a bright student who had just passed his examinations with distinction, was playing in a park in Srinagar when local police shot him in the head with a teargas launcher. As crowds poured into the streets to protest his death, Indian paramilitary forces responded with a 'bullet for a stone' policy amidst an atmosphere increasingly charged with restrictive curfews, arbitrary arrests, stone-pelting, and consequently, increasingly violent protests. Incidentally, the J&K police registered a First Information Report (FIR) on Tufail's death a total of thirty-six days later, on 18 July.

As the number of civilian casualties mounted, India called in its army to Srinagar on 7 July to enforce 'law and order' for the first time in twenty years, making it clear that such a move was intended to deter the protests. While the army-imposed curfew succeeded in stopping the haemorrhaging for a total of ten days— the return of Jammu and Kashmir Chief Minister Omar Abdullah's civil administration heralded yet another round of killings in the month of July. By the end of July, the civilian death toll in the months of June and July had reached twenty-two.

Meanwhile, the Indian establishment began carrying stories

about how the agitations were being sponsored by 'anti-social elements'—coded language that the protests were being backed by Pakistan. Officials, including the home minister, declared that armed militants had infiltrated the protesting crowd, but the fact that there hasn't been a single paramilitary casualty does not support that theory. The home minister's stance was also echoed by Omar Abdullah, as recently as 1 August. Since 2 August, however, the narrative has shifted once again, with Omar Abdullah declaring the crowds as 'leaderless'. Omar, who until very recently was being touted as a poster boy of everything from secularism to technical savvy, even dazzling the Indian Prime Minister Manmohan Singh with a PowerPoint presentation reviewing ongoing developmental works in the Valley, has now become a punching bag, with the Indian government and media blaming the current crisis on his misgovernance.

The chief minister, meanwhile, has shied away from expressing his thoughts on the ongoing chaos as frequently as he is expected to. Of late though, in desperation, he has appealed to the people to help him restore calm amid dashing off to Delhi for meetings, asking for troop reinforcements and promising 50,000 government jobs to the youth, whose single most pressing concern, according to his analysis, is unemployment. How his token concern for Kashmiris was perceived by those injured was demonstrated by the anger and resentment he faced on his first visit to a Srinagar hospital on 6 August. Apparently, he had to leave hurriedly as attendants shouted slogans against him, and some reports say more serious humiliation was meted out to the young chief minister. One of those injured was quoted as saying, 'Who is Omar Abdullah and who gives a damn?' More recently, on 15 August, during Indian Independence Day celebrations, a defiant J&K policeman hurled his shoe at Omar while chanting pro-freedom slogans. Although the cop was arrested after the incident, he was widely celebrated on the streets of Kashmir for capturing the sentiments of the people; thousands of people visited his home in Bandipora and decorated it as a wedding house. Meanwhile, the chief minister—perhaps missing the cultural significance of a thrown shoe—retorted: 'It is better to throw shoes than to throw stones.'

The soft knife of everyday violence

> *I am incarcerated, in these dark walls*
> *I see nothing, coerced to smell*
> *Filthy, dirty, plagued floors*
> *You caught me by my collar*
> *Dragged me to these walls*
> *Which I won't call a 'place'*
> *Some days ago*
> *Just the sore words I whispered*
> *'We Want Freedom!'*

(From 'As I Die' by Jasim Malik, 19 January 2010)

The death toll is, of course, the most spectacular example of ongoing sufferings. But there are other sufferings, which have not gained as much media or public attention, partly because these 'facts' are more difficult to verify. The daily *Greater Kashmir*, quoting the Hurriyat Conference (G), reported that as of 28 July, approximately 1,400 people, mostly teenage boys, have been detained and charged with crimes ranging from rioting to attempted murder. According to this report, approximately seventy youth have been booked under the Public Safety Act of 1978 (PSA), a preventive detention law that has been criticized by Amnesty International, as well as by both Indian and Kashmiri civil society groups and political parties. In contrast, the National Crime Bureau puts the total number of those booked under the PSA in J&K at *two*. The truth lies perhaps somewhere in between. Under the PSA, a person can be jailed without trial for two years to 'maintain public order', without speedy and fair trial guarantees. The PSA has also been used to detain prominent legal activists, including the president of the Jammu and Kashmir High Court

Bar Association, Advocate Mian Qayoom, who has also been charged with sedition.

The current climate of uncertainty, has been exacerbated by intensive restrictions on media and communication in the Kashmir Valley, including blocks on SMS services since 30 June, complete jams of cellular services in more sensitive pockets, and limits on local print and televised news reports, as ordered by the J&K government. Further, while the curfew passes of local journalists have been dishonoured, and they also have been assaulted and arrested under special security legislations, journalists from outside Kashmir have been given unobtrusive access to volatile areas. To protest what they describe as 'discrimination', on 8 July, the Press Guild of Kashmir unanimously decided to suspend local news publications.

Yet, it is not only journalists who find their curfew passes dishonoured. In a similar vein, Dr Junaid Nabi describes how the government invalidated curfew passes for medical practitioners as well: 'Being a doctor I had a horrible time not being able to make it to the hospital. I just want to know what happens if a person falls ill or something untoward happens. How would I help them? No one has any answers.' As doctors like Junaid struggle to deliver their duties, those who do manage to reach hospitals have to go through the trauma of a sea of injured protesters pouring in daily. Further, local doctors report that a significant number of those injured have been shot at from point-blank range, and almost all have been shot in the upper body. Many of them have been left maimed for life. The hardships, and in some cases, life-challenging perils, caused to the sick due to non-availability or lack of access to medicine and medical supplies, including blood, were also causes for serious concern until very recently. These medical crises were not mitigated by governmental efforts, but rather by those outside of the state fold: the International Committee of the Red Cross donated medical aid worth Rs 40 lakhs to the Government Medical College in Srinagar, and volunteers, who donated 180 pints of blood in a single day on hearing news of blood shortages.

Apart from the number of civilian casualties, gross restrictions on movement and the sudden structural transformation of local neighbourhoods have also been deeply disturbing. Indian armed forces have severely restricted civilian mobility by blockading roads, neighbourhoods and entire towns with barricades, check-points and spirals of concertina wire. Police and paramilitary units guard the streets and often intimidate local residents by shattering the windows of their homes, chasing them off the streets and at times beating them without provocation. Past experiences of life under curfew have led some neighbourhoods to set up their own rock and cement pipe barriers to deter police vehicles from patrolling their streets and causing further damage. In such circumstances, neighbourhoods resemble not so much war zones, but rather prisons or ghettos of collective punishment. Umar Ahmed, an activist, describes this atmosphere as one 'between a wall of physical oppression and a hard place of psychological suppression', where Kashmiris are left with 'no option as an option and no choice as a choice'.

As with other communities who have experienced this scale and duration of violence, Kashmiris have revived declining cultural practices to try to adapt to such conditions of uncertainty. For example, because the landlocked Valley used to be cut off from the rest of the world, particularly in winter, Kashmiris developed techniques of efficiently storing food, such as by drying (*hokhea syun*) or pickling vegetables. Although these practices had to some extent dwindled as Kashmir moved away from a self-sufficient agrarian economy, there was a resurgence of many of these practices—such as the tendency to 'hoard' non-perishable items—during militancy, when there would be curfews in place for months at a stretch. A professor of linguistics at Kashmir University, Aadil Kak commented that, 'while people in Delhi buy one or two kilos of rice at a time, we keep two to three months' supply of rice at all times. *Yeh humari purani aadat hai* (This is our old habit).' In other words, while the armed struggle may have waned, many of the (war-time) habits of Kashmiris—what the French sociologist

Pierre Bourdieu has termed *habitus*—continue to be part of the contemporary Kashmiri cultural toolkit.

Yet despite these commendable efforts to use resources available to them, almost every household in Kashmir currently faces an extreme shortage of supplies. For many Kashmiris, then, such periods of unrest bring together feelings of victimhood and agency, the familiar and unfamiliar, the everyday and existential.

Stonewalled: representations

For the last two months, in India, newspapers and television channels have been dominated by images of Kashmiris enacting violence against the state: a gang of youth setting fire to a government vehicle; boys cornering a policeman and beating him to the ground; stone-pelters breaking the windows of a police vehicle disabled in the midst of a street clash. During the first few days of protest, the establishment, including the ruling Indian Congress Party, asked the Central Reserve Police Force (CRPF) and other security personnel to 'exercise maximum restraint' against protesters.

However, as the 'anti-social' argument gained momentum within the Indian establishment—buttressed by images of anti-state violence, such as the ones above—the burden of acting responsibly was shifted to the protesters. The only admission of responsibility came in the suggestion that these troops—who have mostly been trained in counter-insurgency operations—needed to be better trained for 'riot' control.

One of the less visible and longer term effects of blaming the protesters is that it obscures the Indian state's failure to find a long-lasting political solution to the Kashmir dispute. It also obscures the non-accountability for (at least) recent human rights abuses—particularly the Machil fake encounter—that kick-started the ongoing cycle of killings–protests–more killings–more protests—and the pressing need for revocation of the Armed Forces Special Powers Act (AFSPA), which gives unbridled powers to the Indian armed forces. Ironically, in the months before June, civil society groups from Kashmir and beyond had finally made inroads in their longstanding demands for the repeal of AFSPA, gaining support even from the upper echelons of the Congress party, much to the chagrin of the army chief and the Bharatiya Janata Party (BJP). While Prime Minister Manmohan Singh reiterated in his 15 August address that AFSPA will be reviewed and made more humane, in the days that followed his speech, both the Indian home minister and Chief Minister Omar Abdullah ruled out the possibility of its repeal.

In contrast to the Indian narrative, Kashmiri media outlets have been circulating a proliferation of images of state brutality and people's anguished responses to it: a father kneeling in the street and mourning over his dead son's body; crowds carrying corpses through the narrow lanes of the old city in massive funeral processions; a mother wailing on hearing that her son has been killed by the forces; a lone agitated woman hurling a brick at a group of a dozen police personnel in full riot gear. Pertinently, the only local cable TV channel that Kashmiris would turn to for garnering an 'actual' understanding of the situation on the ground—as it carried exclusive coverage of the ongoing protests—has been banned by the state.

The juxtaposition of these images in national and local circulation gives rise to two mutually exclusive ideological narratives—one backed by the coercive authority of the Indian state, and the other backed by the popular authority of the Kashmiri people. In particular, it seems that the mainstream Indian media has been unwilling to make sense of the spontaneous uprisings after Tufail's death within the context of a broad-based, Kashmiri movement for self-determination. 'By trying to discredit all stone-pelters as "hired agents",' says Sajid Iqbal, 'the armed forces, the home ministry, and the powerful Indian media houses are in effect implying that Kashmiris are perfectly fine dying without protest at the hands of the armed forces, since all "mobs" are sponsored. They are trying to pass us off as an insensitive people, who experience no pain, have no heart, no feelings and no emotions.'

The end result is that the rhetoric and representations in the mainstream Indian media continue to de-legitimize the genuine disillusionment faced by Kashmiris resulting from non-accountability for years of human rights abuse in the larger context of their persistent demands for their right to self-determination. On such representations in the Indian media, Mehran Khan says, 'They can't feel or represent our sentiments. They blame us for protesting against India's brutal and inhuman acts, rather than blaming them for killing our youth and opening fire at their funerals.'

Frustrated with these representations—as *either* victim *or* perpetrator—Kashmiri youth have taken responsibilities of representation into their own hands. Youth from all across the political spectrum have turned to YouTube and Facebook in a major way to express their thoughts on the current situation. On the walls of Facebook groups that have mushroomed in the last two months, stories proliferate describing the human consequences of curfew: pregnant women unable to reach the maternity hospital in time for their deliveries, families unable to access local graveyards to bury their dead and ambulances turned back at check-points, leaving patients with no access to clinical care.

This turn to Facebook as a contingency news network in recent months is reminiscent of its use by youth in political crises in other parts of the world, notably during the Iran election crisis. (In the case of Iran, of course, Facebook was used to organize people before the election, but it was also blocked after the vote. This prompted Iranians to turn to the microblogging site, Twitter). As then in Iran and now in Kashmir, the turn to social networking and new media represents a fundamental shift in the way politics is, and will be, done here—including the manner these sites are monitored. Although not to the same extent as in Iran, the online activities of Kashmiris on Facebook are also being closely followed by the Indian state and media. An NDTV reporter recently made an analogy between a stone and a computer's mouse, implying that both are equally dangerous weapons in the hands of Kashmiri youth. This representation, of course, mirrors the Indian state's decision to survey Kashmiri Facebook users, even making arrests on the claims that users are 'provoking people' to 'anti-state activities'.

Is anybody listening?

While Kashmiri youth are dying in the streets, the international community has all but ignored the ongoing human rights and humanitarian crisis in South Asia's most volatile region. This is nothing new. Historically, the only moment in recent years when Kashmir made international headlines was in the year 2000, when former US President Bill Clinton described it as a 'nuclear flash point' and termed South Asia as 'the most dangerous place on earth'.

On 10 July, US State Department spokesman Mark Toner explained the administration's reluctance to intervene, stating that the US 'regretted the loss of life', but regarded the current climate of repression as 'an internal Indian matter'. Most recently, a controversy was adrift around whether the UN secretary general, Ban Ki Moon, made any statements expressing 'concern' over the prevailing security situation in Kashmir on 29 July. The Indian ministry of home affairs and the mainstream Indian media proclaimed in unison that Ban's spokesperson of Pakistani origin, Farhan Haq, had concocted the secretary general's remarks. Ban's chief spokesperson Martin Nasirky, expressed his displeasure with the Indian media's suggestion that Farhan's ethnicity might have inspired his alleged 'concoction' and sternly told the journalists at the UN briefing that he 'won't tolerate insults being directed' at his colleagues. No statements from the Indian government or media followed this incident.

On the part of the Indian state, after over seventy days of deaths, scores of injuries and tough talk, the Indian home minister finally expressed his 'regret' for the killings and condoled with the affected families. However, such empathetic statements were watered down by Mr Chidambaram's continued defence of the Indian armed forces and his reiteration that the responsibility to end the violence lay solely in the hands of protesters. Clearly, the number and manner of civilian deaths and injuries do not support his contention. In addition, such statements also do not acknowledge the forms of everyday violence that Kashmiris suffer, and indeed, have grown accustomed to suffering, in times of strikes and curfews. They also do not take into account the alienation experienced by armed forces personnel in Kashmir (and elsewhere). On this point, we have limited information; what we do know is that on 18 August, the Defence Minister A.K. Antony told the Rajya Sabha that 170 armed force personnel had committed suicide in the last nineteen months.

After weeks of denial that the civilian deaths were nothing but the consequence of unruly teenagers run amok—or alternately, the handiwork of Pakistan—on 17 August, Mr Chidambaram finally admitted that (at least) twelve of the civilian deaths were 'unprovoked' and would be investigated. Does this pithy acknowledgement by the home minister, that at least *some* of these deaths were improper, signal the beginning of the end of the vicious cycle of killings–protests–more killings–more protests, violence and death? Probably not. But it might indicate that there is a space now opening up for a grounded understanding of Kashmiri sufferings. In the words of the singer-poet Leonard Cohen, 'There is a crack in everything/That's how the light gets in.'

There are at least two sparks of hope. A viewer poll conducted by CNN/IBN on 5 August showed that 82 per cent of its viewers thought that the Indian state needed to completely overturn its Kashmir strategy. This suggests that there is an appetite amongst at least some sections of the Indian public for a new way forward. The last ten days or so have also seen a spate of writing in the Indian mainstream media by Indian public intellectuals which contradicts the state narrative, from Suvir Kaul's eyewitness account of life in Srinagar, to Karan Thapar's appeal to the PM to apologize for civilian deaths.

These lone, but powerful, voices find resonance with the voices of young Kashmiris who also continue to speak out—online, through poetry, photography, art, and most of all, street protests. Such public demonstrations provide tools for preserving their memories of the past, negotiating the uncertainties of the present and carving out a collective future.

Meanwhile, the counting continues . . . In a poem dedicated to Tufail and to many others who have gone unnoticed, Jasim Malik carries forward the memory of loss through the voice of a Kashmiri youth who speaks from beyond the grave:

> *This silence has lots of stories to tell*
> *Each word in these Chronicles pierces my page*
> *Stories which no pen dares to jot down*
> *Accounts which no ink can 'give tongue to'*
> *Blood ruptures by my eyes, I feel lazed*
> *I can't even say, 'till we meet again'*
> *For I am not sure about the future*
> *At last I must confess, as I leave you forever,*
> *I stole a jam bottle from the kitchen last week*
> *And I love you the most.*

This article first appeared in the *Economic and Political Weekly*, 28 August 2010.

I See Kashmir from New Delhi

Suvaid Yaseen

Gaemit dam phuit che saeri, bey-qaraari chakh dilan andar,
dapaan wanehav paenin ahwaal,
Aesi ma laaey azaedi?

None dares to speak out, there is restlessness in their
    hearts,
Wish we could speak of our condition,
Might freedom not turn hostile?

—Mahjoor, Kashmiri poet, 1885–1952

Living in Delhi for the last few years, Kashmir has never been very far away. It's as close as it could ever be, even if the physical body remained a thousand miles away. Thoughts and memories transcend distance. They live in a dimension of their own, across space and, often, time.

So it is. Back in Kashmir a happening would normally be talked about over a cup of tea, or dinner, as it would be with anyone. These discussions are usual. Counting deaths, however, is different. Discussing death, the metaphysics of it, might be a good thing to argue over, or contemplate. But when you are discussing people who existed, who walked the same streets you have grown up walking upon, and then ceased to exist—through murder, through torture, through the manifestation of the oppressive predatory mechanism which the occupation sets in motion—it becomes very intense, very painful.

From recent memory you can hear the thundering of bullets being showered on the protesters. You remember the bullet-torn bodies of youngsters, red with their blood, in ambulances en route to the hospital. You hear the sirens. You feel the tear gas. You feel the tears filling the lashes to the brim, seeking an escape—freedom. You hear the abuses on your identity, your family, your nation. You remember that you have witnessed the mockery of civilized values when, back home, an alienated soldier, a dispensable pawn in the ego game of his masters, goes on a killing spree. You remember, even though you are alive, that you are a *shaheed*, a martyr, a witness to the brutality which has led to innumerable other martyrs—those who ceased to live but were never forgotten, and are now alive in your memories.

Counting the years one has lived, already more than that teenaged boy shot dead in a lane you know so well, makes you angry, helpless, even guilty at being relatively safe, away and distant from the firing line. For you too suffer the same suffocation that makes the boy step out on the street and protest.

You want to shout. You want to scream. You want to let the people know about the massacre of a generation as they go on with their lives, praising the shooters who won gold medals in the Commonwealth Games. You want to alert them to the story of other perfect shots which their country's forces are firing—in their name—in an occupied territory.

Feelings, however intense, must be brought in front of the world in a language that adheres to convention. A protest. You assemble at the place, holding placards, sit and address the gathering, trying to inform people who take an interest.

On 7 August 2010, Kashmiris assembled at Delhi's Jantar Mantar for a night-long sit-in. Emotions were moulded into convention. In those weeks, Kashmir's days were curfewed, so in the night people poured into the streets. Songs of freedom blared from the mosques' loudspeakers. When they took away the day, people reclaimed the night. The night-long sit-in was in solidarity with those people awake back home, telling them that Kashmiris elsewhere were also awake with them.

In India, a Kashmiri is always suspect. And he is aware of that. He tries to focus on his work—education, business, profession—refraining from making his political views public. He keeps his tales, his perceptions, his subjectivity deep inside his bosom, revealing them only to close, trustworthy fellows. However, that day was different. He had ceased to be a student avoiding suspension from the university, a businessman not wanting to offend his customers, or a professional avoiding 'irrelevant' talk. Inhibitions were discarded. Words usually uttered in hushed tones or pondered over in silence by Kashmiris far from their homeland were now loudly vocalized in public, just as in Kashmir. For one evening, Jantar Mantar was Kashmir's Lal Chowk.

For the first time in sixty years, the slogan '*Hum kya chahtey? Azadi!*' came to this city, even though at a place officially designated for protest. In the history of protests at Jantar Mantar, this one must have been one of the more unique ones. The perpetual question—'What do Kashmiris want?'—was answered right in the vicinity of the Indian Parliament, if anybody was willing to listen. Azadi resonated the loudest, as one commentator said, 'sometimes spoken with joy, sometimes with anger, sometimes as a lament, sometimes with hope—with the vowels elongated to mean a myriad complexities that are rendered unspoken by the simplifying violence of the occupation.'

This was significant, for Kashmiris in India live their lives under constant scrutiny from the state, and sometimes from self-imposed caution. The latter is reinforced by the consequences of the former, which also prejudices the views of common people about them.

But that day in Jantar Mantar, the Kashmiri in India had turned as political as any of his fellows in Kashmir. And he was as open about it, as he would be on a Kashmiri street.

The gathering at Jantar Mantar was made up mostly, though not entirely, of Kashmiris. Not only had Kashmiris living in Delhi assembled, but also those from Aligarh and adjoining satellite cities of Delhi. All kinds of people were present—students, professionals, businessmen, families, activists, those related with struggles in Punjab, Andhra Pradesh, Tamil Nadu, Manipur, Nagaland, central India. A solidarity based on the demand, identification and struggle for justice seemed to have come about. It was a substantial gathering that asserted their rights, articulating a longing for greater freedom—Azadi.

Varavara Rao, noted revolutionary poet and Maoist ideologue, spoke of the solidarity and support to the people's struggle for self-determination in Kashmir. He read out a poem he had written about Kashmir—*Apna naam kal Vietnam, aaj Kashmir* (Yesterday our name was Vietnam, today it's Kashmir)—which spoke of how the children of Kashmir had answered the bullets with stones, how the women had answered the curfews with open defiance and mass gatherings, and how suppression was answered with the call to Azadi. There were others who spoke and expressed solidarity and support for the demand for justice and self-determination. The discourse wasn't just limited to the symptom of human rights violations but creatively extended to the redressal of the disease of occupation.

People spoke of their experiences. Of their anger. Of their pain. Intermittently they spoke with slogans, the language of convention back home in Kashmir.

Aaj teri mout paey ro raha hai aasmaan, ro rahi hai ye zamin ro raha hai aasmaan, cried the people—the skies and the land of Kashmir echoing their pain—as they lamented the numerous deaths their homeland had witnessed.

As-salaam, as-salaam, aey shaheedo as-salaam, they chanted, greeting their martyrs.

Shaheed ki jo maut hai, wo quom ki hayaat hai, they intoned, honouring the spirit of martyrdom that has sustained the movement in the face of the persecution.

Qatl-e-aam band karo, Kashmir ka masla hal karo, qaatiloun ko saza do, Kashmir ka masla hal karo, they recited, seeking justice for the murdered people, and the occupied nation.

Then came the battle-cry: *Awaaz do, hum ek hain!* (Call out, for we are one!)

They also shouted *Naara-e-Takbeer, Allah-u-Akbar*, invoking the divine for help, since the mortal calls seemed to have lost their appeal in face of the latest cycle of tyranny that had besieged their nation.

Poetry adorned the posters of protest.

One verse by Kashmiri poet Zarif Ahmad Zarif said:

> My gaze has been silenced! What frenzy is this?
> I lost the city of love I had found! What frenzy is this?

A research student at Delhi University recited Faiz:

> *Ab tout girein gi zanjeerein, ab zindanoun ki khair nahi,*
> *jo darya jhoom ke uthey hain, tinkoun sey na taalein*
> *jaayeingey!*
>
> Now the chains will fall away, prisons will no longer be
> safe;
> These rivers arisen in a wave, what trifles will overcome
> them!

A young woman read out Ahmad Faraz:

> *Khwaab martey nahin: Khwaab to roshni hai, nava hai,*
> *hawa hai,*
> *jo kaaley pahadoun sey ruktey nahi, zulm ke darakhtoun sey*
> *phuktey nahi.*
>
> Dreams don't die: dreams are light, music, air;
> mountains of darkness don't stop them, heights of
> oppression do not snuff them.

A poem dedicated to Agha Shahid Ali, by an Indian friend, Manas Bhattacharya, was read out. It recounted the irony of *The Country*

Without a Post Office: 'It is time your country tells less politely, what Gandhi told the British about India: Leave India to anarchy, or if that is too much, leave it to God!'

Everything that evening at Jantar Mantar seemed to speak of protest, even the two-minute silence in the memory of the martyrs. Even the orange–red flames of the candles flickering in the evening zephyr. The energy was high, and passions soared. But despite this the overall discipline of the gathering remained immaculate, graceful.

When a handful of familiar faces from Roots in Kashmir (an organization which claims to represent the Kashmiri Pandits) appeared to protest against the protest—as they do in almost every Kashmir-related event in the capital that talks of Azadi—it initially created a stir, and led to sloganeering. But the shallow intent of these provocateurs soon became visible to the others who sat down and carried on listening to the speakers. The provocateurs were invited to sit down and join in the protest. They didn't. While they shouted slogans aimed at disrupting the proceedings, people shouted back slogans of unity among the people of different religions in Kashmir. Eventually, as the protest carried on, they left silently.

This was a time when people in Kashmir were being killed almost on a daily basis. Close to fifty people had been killed in less than two months. Amongst the civilians killed at least thirty-eight were aged under twenty-five. The count of the injured had already been lost, scores maimed and blinded for life.

At Jantar Mantar that day people listened to others' stories and related their own. They questioned, they hoped.

A businessman who spoke in Kashmiri-accented Urdu shouted 'Shame! Shame!' at the irony of stone-throwing youth greeted with bullets, despair and anger writ large on his forehead.

A young man, whose father was suffering from cancer, tried to explain the reason for the call to the divine, answering the question raised by a request to refrain from 'communal slogans'.

A doctor, having come to the protest straight from duty, spoke of having learned resistance from his parents, then lifted his months-old baby in his arms and declared that his child would learn resistance from him.

An old man sitting on the perimeter of the crowd, dressed in a white 'khan-dress' with a skullcap on his head, suddenly got up and shouted '*Hum kya chahtey?*' He was greeted with a loud roar— 'Azadi!'

A young girl spoke of the lost dreams of her childhood, and the pain she felt at each death in Kashmir, as if one of her own kin was lost.

A young boy spoke of the irony of protesting Kashmiris being called anti-nationals when they in fact refused to be part of the Indian nation.

There was a line painted in red on a placard: 'They silenced the street. And assassinated ALL questions, and all the questions!'

Someone from the crowd shouted:

Ye Khoon Rang Laayega, Inquilab Aayega!
This bloodshed will bring life, there will be Revolution!

Kashmir's Abu Ghraib?

Shuddhabrata Sengupta

Facebook, YouTube, Kashmir

Two days ago, on the night of the 8/9 September, 2010, I noticed a video posted by somebody on my Facebook page. It was yet another video from Kashmir. It was tagged 'brothers please watch, sisters please do not watch'. In later incarnations of the video, posted repeatedly on Facebook sites, YouTube channels and on blogs, it was tagged 'Kashmir—India's Abu Gharib (sic)'. Notwithstanding the misspelling of Abu Ghraib in these tags, there was something compellingly accurate in the designation. What I saw, and what I have seen unfold subsequently as a response by the Indian state to the circulation of this video, makes Abu Ghraib look like child's play. Welcome to the virtual, viral, televisual reality of the nightmare of Kashmir.

For the past several weeks, I have been watching, and forwarding, several videos uploaded on to YouTube and Facebook from Kashmir. Every video that I have seen contains evidence of the brutality of the Indian state's footprint on the Kashmir valley, and of the steadfast, resilient courage of its people, and of the innovative use they have been making of the internet to bear witness to their oppression.

I have seen paramilitary and police personnel open fire on unarmed or stone-pelting crowds, mercilessly beat up young people and children, attack doctors, patients and nurses in hospitals, smash windows of homes, steal chickens and livestock and hurl the most vulgar invectives at ordinary people. I have watched the armed might of the Indian state retreat in the face of the moral courage of the opposition it encounters on the streets of Kashmir.[1]

The first video

But nothing prepared me for what I saw when I clicked on the video that said 'brothers watch, sisters don't watch'. I am a person who works with moving images. I think about moving images, about video. I watch all kinds of things. Not all of which are pretty, or edifying. But the sheer extent of humiliation that was visible in this video was not something that I was prepared to see, not even from Kashmir.[2]

The video, not more than three minutes long, is a piece of uncut, unedited footage, in all probability (judging from the quality and resolution of the image) taken from a cellphone. It

---

[1] A good example of a video showing banal street brutality by security forces in Kashmir can be seen on this YouTube web-page: http://www.youtube.com/watch?v=AA5s3tqG8CM.

For details of some more of these videos, and links to web pages that carry them, see 'Indian Police Brutality in Kashmir Caught on Cameras' by Afroze Ahmed Shah, *Eurasia Review*, 8 September 2010 [http://www.eurasiareview.com/201009087884/indian-police-brutality-in-kashmir-caught-on-cameras.html].

[2] The second video is currently accessible online on the *Aalaw-Kashmir Calls* website at http://aalaw-kashmircalls.org/wp-content/uploads/2010/09/Facebook-3-Messages-spread-it-on-other-pages-n-fake-profiles-not-on-alaw-directly_-let-is-spread-first-dwnload-kar-k-rak_-sk_messagestid_1470911928816.mp4. The contents of this video, as indicated, are very disturbing, and viewer discretion is advised.

shows four young Kashmiri men walking across what appears to be freshly harvested fields (so it could be October–November, or, March–April), egged along by what appear to be paramilitary personnel and some policemen. Some of the security personnel wear khaki, others wear olive green fatigues. One wears the black bandanna of a commando. Others wear helmets and caps. Some have bullet-proof vests. The four young men they are 'escorting' are naked. They hold their clothes in their hands. From what one can make out in the video, their faces reveal their acute shame, distress and embarrassment.

This video needs to be seen as part of a global trend of the usage of ubiquitous recording devices such as mobile phones in the production of atrocity images by state and non-state combatants.[3] These recordings can range from images of harassment such as a video of an Israeli soldier 'dancing' provocatively in relation to a captive Palestinian woman clinging to a wall, to humiliation, such as the now well-known Abu Ghraib pictures, which also constituted a step-by-step guide to the (mis)treatment of prisoners, to the truly horrific, such as the decapitation videos circulated by some Islamist groups in Chechnya as well as recordings of summary executions, carried out by soldiers, which have emerged recently from Swat in Pakistan and the Jaffna peninsula in northern Sri Lanka.

---

[3]For the *Daily Telegraph* story on 'Dancing Israeli Soldier Video', see: http://www.telegraph.co.uk/news/worldnews/middleeast/israel/8043714/Footage-aired-of-Israeli-soldier-dancing-round-blindfolded-Palestinian-woman.html.

For the Channel 4 Story on execution videos from Sri Lanka, see: http://www.channel4.com/news/sri-lanka-execution-video-evidence-of-war-crimes.

For the *Guardian* story on execution videos from Swat, Pakistan, see: http://www.guardian.co.uk/world/2010/oct/08/pakistan-investigate-execution-video.

For the CNN story on 'Alleged Extra-judicial Execution of Pashtuns in Swat', see: http://www.youtube.com/watch?v=bB-zlxik9ac.

(The Swat recording, which shows Pakistani armed forces personnel lining up and then killing several captives, resurfaced briefly on Kashmiri Facebook groups as the false trace of an atrocity carried out by Indian soldiers in Kashmir. The irony of a Pakistani atrocity being briefly misattributed as an Indian one only underscores the fact that when it comes to the everyday operationalization of state-terror, the security apparatuses of India and Pakistan aspire to the same low standards, which make it quite possible for those seeking to score a few cheap propaganda points on either side to—deliberately or otherwise—confuse one perpetrator for another.)

In what rapidly became known as the 'Kashmir Naked Parade Video' the paramilitaries and policemen can be seen taunting the four naked men as they walk. The main voice is that of a person who seems to be holding the device that is capturing the image. We hear him speak in perfectly legible colloquial Hindi:

'Move, Move, Move, Keep moving, sisterfuckers.'

'Raise your hands, I'll hit you otherwise.'

'Your shoes are very good. Sisterfucker.'

We hear another, more muffled voice say what seems to be:

'Why are your shoes so dirty?'

And then, so that the genitals are not covered:

'Fold your clothes, collect them, hold up the clothes.'

'The sisterfuckers have been making us run after them since the morning.'

'The police station is where we need to take them.'

The video does not appear to have been taken in the recent weeks. The fields have been harvested. It has to be either autumn or spring. But it has not been taken that long ago either. It has to be from after cellphones were allowed to be used in Kashmir, and after cellphones capable of shooting video became cheap, and popular, which places the incident, and its recording, roughly within the last two to three years. In some of the official and media responses that are beginning to trickle in, this business of 'the video is not recent' is getting some mileage. As if somehow the reality that the video portrays needs to be distanced from the current meltdown in Kashmir. Assuming that is the case, the implications of what the video shows become even more disturbing. It proves that a systematic humiliation of the Kashmiri population is part of the standard operating procedure of the security establishment of the Indian state in Kashmir. This is neither anything new, nor associated with the current wave of unrest. It has been in operation for several years now.

The banal violence of the scene is in some ways far more distressing than the images of gun battles and blood on the streets that we have become accustomed to harvesting from the past few months in Kashmir. At least in the pitched street battles, we see adversaries, albeit unequal adversaries, policemen, paramilitaries, soldiers one side, and the angry tide of stone-pelters on the other. Here, there are no adversaries. Prisoners are not in a position to be adversarial when surrounded by heavily armed men in uniform. What we see instead are unarmed captives, people who are in no position to threaten or endanger the security forces. That such people should be made to undergo a humiliation such as this is proof of the extent to which the forces of the Indian state in Kashmir have become brutalized by the experience of serving in Kashmir.

The men in uniform do not need to strip people naked and make them walk in public. There is something utterly, lethally, gratuitous in their action. There is nothing that says that arrested or detained citizens should be marched to police stations without their clothes on, in public view. No imperative of self-defence, defence of the realm, public safety and security, or the Indian Constitution requires them to visit this indignity on the four young people in their charge. Nowhere is it indicated that one can behave like this even with convicted criminals, captured terrorists or under-trials. That they choose to act as they do only indicates that the laughing, taunting men in uniform see the four young men, and by extension, any Kashmiri that they can lay their hands on, as sub-human beings, as animals. By doing this, they only expose the extent to which they have allowed the state to turn them (the men in uniform) into racist, colonizing brutes.

The primary voice on the video betrays a calculated, cold, cynical disregard for human dignity. You can recognize that mocking tone, even if you do not understand the language, the moment you hear it. The paramilitaries are walking casually, some carry sticks, others carry guns. They walk at leisure, without any urgency, as if parading captives naked through open fields was a perfectly normal, routine thing to be doing in Kashmir. (And suggests, horrifyingly, that it is indeed a perfectly normal, routine thing to be doing.)

While the making of atrocity images such as these have for long been a part of the apparatus of violence, the ubiquity of mobile phones as recording devices, and of internet-based social networking sites as vectors of circulation has taken the phenomenon to a new level. We have no clear understanding of what motivates the making of these images. Are they meant as evidence of a 'job well done'—to be shown to superiors who actually sanction torture and humiliation but have no way of assessing their effectiveness or actual operation because of the legal difficulty involved in maintaining official records of 'unofficial' secrets? Or, are they simply testosterone-fuelled perversities, operating in the same sphere as MMS messages of pornographic sadism?

There is need for further research on questions such as whether or not the makers of these atrocity images are also consciously seeking each other out, both as audiences and as competitors, in a new economy of prestige linked to the capacity to represent and circulate one's own cruelty. In other words, are the makers of the videos in Kashmir, or in the Jaffna peninsula, aware of, and in some senses seeking to out-do the actions of their peers and predecessors in Abu Ghraib? Also, is there an informal network of know-how, pertaining to techniques for torture and humiliation that lubricates the virtual matrix inhabited by the protagonists of the so-called 'global war on terror', that operates in much the same way as the networks that bring together paedophiles and sex offenders on online platforms in the darker parts of the internet? Finally, how and why do these videos leak out of these networks into the wider public domain? Are there weak, conscience-stricken, anonymous whistle-blowing links at the fringes of even the darkest recesses of power (as is evident from the centre of the WikiLeaks storm) that cannot bear the burden of carrying power's dirtiest secrets?

The second video

Some days later a second video, far more disturbing than the first, also surfaced. This too seemed to be recorded with a mobile phone camera. The video features several armed and uniformed men, bearing the insignias of security forces deployed in Jammu and Kashmir. The men are seen walking through a wooded area. One of them, wearing a bullet-proof jacket, is seen carrying a wounded, possibly tortured man, who is clearly unable to walk. The banter between the uniformed men insists that the man being dragged through the ground is feigning injury. He is repeatedly insulted, and threats to sodomize him are uttered several times. Some of the uniformed men feign as if to sodomize the man with their bamboo sticks. I made no attempt to share this video, as I felt its public circulation would add nothing to our understanding of torture in Kashmir, but could in fact add to the humiliation of the tortured person, as his face (unlike in the first video) was clearly visible and recognizable. The brutality of the men in this video had a sickening edge which also made it difficult to consider circulating.

We have all heard (from ex-prisoners, human rights activists and lawyers) that sexual humiliation of young men is a routine practice during interrogations in Kashmir. That men are asked to simulate sodomy on each other, and that they are photographed in the course of doing so, and that these images are held out as means of blackmail and intimidation. On seeing the first clip, Khurram Parvez, a human rights activist with the Jammu and Kashmir Coalition for Civil Society said: 'There is nothing new in the video clip. Stripping off the detainees, parading them naked and inserting wire in their private parts was a normal practice in jails and interrogation centres. The video has created a furor because it has been released in public domain (sic).'[4]

Contemporary definitions of torture have expanded to include non-invasive and psychological terror methods, foremost amongst which is sexual humiliation.[5] The sobriety of rural Kashmiri society is not geared to deal with the humiliating spectacle of naked young men being made to march out in the open. Such an act is bound to leave deep scars on the consciousness of whomsoever it has been perpetrated on and whosoever was unfortunate enough to have observed it. It is designed to do so.

---

[4]Parvez is cited in a report titled 'Video Showing Kashmiri Boys Paraded Naked Sparks Outrage' by Izhar Ali, dated 8 September 2010, that was published in the *Kashmir Observer*, and several other websites. The report as it appeared in the *Kashmir Observer* can be accessed at: http://www.kashmirobserver.net/index.php?option=com_content&view=article&id=5529:video-showing-kashmiri-boys-paraded-naked-sparks-outrage&catid=15:top-news&Itemid=2.

The report goes on to state that on occasion captives in Kashmir have been made to simulate acts of sodomy with each other while they are filmed by their captors.

[5]The seriousness of the situation was underscored by the recent WikiLeaks disclosure on torture by Indian forces in Kashmir by ICRC (Red Cross) personnel to US Embassy officials in New Delhi in 2005. The ICRC statements refer to widespread use of several torture methods, including sexual abuse, carried out by Indian forces in prisons and detention centres in Kashmir.

See 'WikiLeaks: India "tortured" Kashmir prisoners', BBC News South Asia, 17 December 2010 [http://www.bbc.co.uk/news/world-south-asia-12014734].

See also 'ICRC Defends WikiLeaks expose on Kashmir Torture', *Greater Kashmir*, 23 December 2010 [http://www.greaterkashmir.com/news/2010/Dec/24/icrc-defends-wikileaks-expos-on-kashmir-torture-17.asp].

Nakedness and humiliation

Why do coerced nakedness and humiliation make such a perfectly repulsive pair? Perhaps because we think of being naked only with ourselves, or with someone whom we can be intimate with, or who is able to care for us. Children can be naked to their parents, lovers can be naked to each other. A patient can be naked to his or her doctor. Or, one can choose, lucidly, joyously, to be naked, (the insane do not 'choose' to be naked, they simply 'are' naked) even in public, in moments of total abandon, when all inhibitions can be thrown away in a free act of the will. In the woods, in a river, by the sea, on stage. In any instance, being naked somehow suggests a condition of freedom, or care, or intimacy. Something we freely enter into and govern for ourselves. It is this condition of intimacy and care that is twisted and turned inside out when nakedness is coerced. Coerced nakedness takes place in contexts that are the very opposite of intimacy and care. It invariably takes place in contexts that are cold, violent, brutally impersonal but horrifyingly intimate. This is a kind of nakedness that lays bare the darkest secrets of power. That it really doesn't care about the humanity of the person in its clutches. In its transparency, what it makes most naked, is power itself. It is no wonder, therefore, that this video will now stand alongside the images of naked Jewish prisoners being made to line up in Nazi concentration camps, and the disturbing legacy of the, now all too familiar, images from Abu Ghraib.

That the uniformed representatives of the Indian state should choose to wear the nakedness of their violence with such pride and aplomb says something shocking and profound about the sheer immorality of India's ongoing military occupation of the Kashmir valley. After this, it is not necessary to give even a shred of consideration to the frayed patchwork of arguments that constitutes the Indian state's line on Kashmir. And no, this is not an exception. The uniformed men in the video do not behave as if they were performing under 'exceptional circumstances'. It looks like a jolly outing. A stroll with a few trophies.

At the tail-end of the three-minute video we hear high-pitched keening voices, and then mocking echoes, and laughter. The keening voice can be heard lamenting, in Kashmiri, '*Hata Khodayo*' (something like 'Oh God') several times. It is not possible to determine whether these voices are of onlookers (perhaps of women and/or older men), or of the paramilitaries themselves. What is impossible to dispute is that the lamentations/mock lamentations are in Kashmiri, proving conclusively that the incident occurred in the Kashmir valley. All attempts at suggesting that the video is 'not from Kashmir' fly against the face of this fact.

In any case, we soon hear, in counterpoint to these 'laments', such as they are, a set of mocking, echoing responses that mirror the music and cadence of the lamentations exactly as a chorus would echo a soloist. The chorus is interrupted by cackling laughter. It is as if·the men in the uniform of Indian security forces were not content with the mere humiliation of bodies. That in fact, they needed to pervert and mock the ways in which a people mourn their indignities in order to extract the pleasure that they felt entitled to in the course of this grotesque incident. When even the lamentations of the Kashmiri people are not safe because of the predatory presence of the occupying force, then it is time for the world to sit up and say that we have had enough of the Indian state's mayhem in Kashmir.

The strange case of the disappearing links

Characteristically, the video was pulled down, on both Facebook and YouTube, repeatedly, in the course of last evening, last night and today. There was some discussion on different Facebook pages about whether this occurred due to the 'nudity' in the video. I too was persuaded for a while that this might be the case. But a quick search for nude content on YouTube showed up a whole range of things—from naturist videos to medical material—that featured nudity. In fact there is a whole discussion on 'Non-sexual Nudity' on YouTube that indicates that it is not YouTube policy to remove content merely because it may contain nudity.[6]

Notwithstanding all this, the video repeatedly disappeared shortly after being posted on YouTube. And even posts of links to it, or discussions of it, began disappearing from Facebook pages. This suggested something more than the automatic application of 'no nudity' rules. It suggested what has been suspected for some time, that the Indian state—or some of its 'organs'—'lean' on platforms like Facebook and YouTube to ensure that content that is problematic for its image simply gets erased. Through much of last night (8/9 September, 2010), a concerted online effort across two Facebook pages (*'Aalaw'* and *'I Protest the Indian Occupation of Kashmir'*) by a constellation of people who did not know each other prior to this incident made sure that the video was momentarily up on YouTube. Notices went out across Facebook walls to download the video from the concerned YouTube site so that the video could have a distributed, viral presence across several hundreds, if not thousands of computers. By the morning of 9 September, the effort to 'erase' the video from public consciousness had failed. News of the video made it to newspapers like *Greater Kashmir*. The Kashmir-based newspapers carried extensive reports, quoting the shocked responses of the people who had seen the videos. These included some responses from several people who are non-Kashmiri Indian citizens.[7]

Responding to the after-image of an absent video

By the afternoon of 9 September 2010, the response of the state had changed. From attempts at erasure, the state moved into a

---

[6]To view a discussion on the question of Non-sexual Nudity on YouTube, see: http://www.google.com/support/youtube/bin/answer.py?hl=en&answer=117432.

[7]'Facebook Clip Triggers Rage' by Gowhar Bhat, *Greater Kashmir*, 8 September 2010 [http://greaterkashmir.com/news/2010/Sep/9/video-shows-cops-parading-youth-naked-29.asp].

state of denial, and characteristic intimidation. The *Indian Express* reported that the Union Home Minister P. Chidambaram had questioned the authenticity of the video on the grounds that the *'people seen in it have not spoken up'*.[8] Were a mass grave of anonymous dead people to be discovered in Kashmir (as happens from time to time), Mr Chidambaram would probably question the authenticity of the report on the grounds that the cadavers had not identified themselves or spoken of the circumstances of their deaths and burial.

On the other hand, a Central Reserve Police Force (CRPF) spokesman denied that such an incident could have taken place, because in his opinion 'it is difficult to keep even rapes secret in Kashmir'. (Which involves the interesting tacit assumption that attempts are made, from time to time, to keep rapes secret).[9] A spokesperson of the Jammu and Kashmir (J&K) police, however, said that charges would be filed against Facebook, YouTube and all those who have uploaded and distributed the videos on the grounds of 'maligning the forces' by distributing such objectionable material.[10] In the J&K police's version, neither the authenticity nor

---

[8]'Naked Parade: Centre to look into Video Clip on Kashmir', *Indian Express*, 9 September 2010 [http://www.indianexpress.com/news/kashmir-police/679592/].

[9]'Such a thing is not possible in Kashmir,' CRPF spokesman Prabhakar Tripathi was quoted as saying. 'The video seems manipulated to tarnish the image of the force and police.' Tripathi said it was hard to imagine how such an incident, if it had happened, could remain under wraps so long. 'In this place, even rape doesn't remain a secret,' he said. 'This video can never be proved to be genuine.'
See 'J&K Cops to Sue Facebook, YouTube', *Outlook* website, 9 September 2010 [http://news.outlookindia.com/item.aspx?692932].

[10]See 'Naked Parade of Boys: Police to Register Case against YouTube, Facebook', *Rising Kashmir*, 9 September 2010 [http://www.risingkashmir.com/news/%E2%80%98naked-parade-of-boys%E2%80%99-police-to-register-case-against-you-tube-face-book-1298.aspx].

(Contd.)

the veracity of the video is an issue; what is offensive is the effort to circulate the material in question, because the contents of the video can 'malign' the forces. The varied wings of the Indian state have displayed the full spectrum of ostrich-like obduracy, from attempts at erasure, to incredulity, to denial, to attempts at intimidation, but none of these efforts seem to be of any avail. It needs to be noted that, so far, the Indian state's response to this scandal has been far short of the expectations set by international precedents.

The US army may not have come off with a shining reputation from Abu Ghraib, but the US government realized the gravity of the situation and took action to punish at least the primary perpetrators of the outrage (even if those who dictated the policies that made the outrages occur went scot-free).[11] The recent incident of a former Israeli conscript, a woman named Eden Aberjil who posted photographs of herself posing with blindfolded Palestinian

---

(Contd.)

Also see 'Police Crackdown on Netizens for Naked Parade Video in Kashmir', *Rising Kashmir*, 9 September 2010 [http://www.risingkashmir.com/news/police-crack-down-on-netizens-for-naked-parade-video-in-kashmir-1329.aspx].

[11]The Abu Ghraib incidents have been very well researched, documented and commented upon. Amongst the most comprehensive accounts are:

- 'Abu Ghraib: The Hidden Story' by Mark Danner, *New York Review of Books*, 7 October 2004 [http://www.nybooks.com/articles/archives/2004/oct/07/abu-ghraib-the-hidden-story/]
- *The Schlesinger Report : An Investigation of Abu Ghraib* by James R. Schlesinger, Harold Brown, Tillie K. Fowler, and General Charles A. Horner (United States Department of Defense, 2004; Cosimo Reports, 2005)
- For a discussion of the imagery of the Abu Ghraib pictures, see 'Cloning Terror: The War of Images 2001–04' by W.J.T. Mitchell in *The Life and Death of Images: Ethics and Aesthetics*, edited by Diarmuid Costello and Dominic Willsdon (Tate Publishing, 2008)

prisoners[12] attracted severe criticism worldwide, including within Israel. Several serving Israeli women conscripts condemned Aberjil's conduct in public and even the Israeli army (not an organization known for its sensitivity in human rights matters), took a stern view of the matter. The *Huffington Post* (August 2010) report on the issue says: '"These are disgraceful photos," said Capt. Barak Raz, an Israeli military spokesman. "Aside from matters of information security, we are talking about a serious violation of our morals and our ethical code and should this soldier be serving in active duty today, I would imagine that no doubt she would be court-martialed immediately," he told *Associated Press Television News*.'

Contrast these responses with the conduct of responsible officers of the government of India, from the Union Home Minister downwards. If ever there were to be an 'object lesson' in how not to handle a situation like this—we will only have to turn to the conduct of Chidambaram and his minions.

As of now, the video is up, on distributed servers, in several locations and circulating, through emails, MMS messages, Bluetooth transfers, blog posts and Facebook notices (not of the videos themselves any longer, but of descriptions and commentary). There is no way that the Indian state can any longer evade responsibility for the venality of its actions, especially as they are visible on this video. Even if the state can set its house in order, speak in one voice, persuade the lunatics who run the army in Kashmir to see the pointlessness of making a fetish of the Armed Forces Special Powers Act (AFSPA) and announce some kind of tepid 'package' by way of an insult to the people of Kashmir on the occasion of Eid, then too, it will not succeed in fooling either the people of Kashmir, or the world.

This one video, with the perfect timing of its appearance, has succeeded in pulling the fig leaf off the true character of the Indian state's rule in Kashmir as nothing else has. It has exposed how the

---

[12]'Eden Aberjil Facebook Photos Controversy' on the *Huffington Post* website: http://www.huffingtonpost.com/2010/08/17/eden-aberjil-facebook-pho_n_684611.html.

state acts, it has shown us that the state is 'leaking' information about its own misdeeds, and it has proven that the resistance in Kashmir and about Kashmir is getting increasingly sophisticated. If the state wants to prevail, it can do so only by recourse to massive armed force, or fraud and dissimulation at a hitherto unimaginable scale.

As of tonight, the mainstream Indian media has not covered this incident with the seriousness it deserves.[13] Neither television nor print media have tried to look beyond the state of denial that the home minister is in, vis-à-vis this scandal. If this were any other civilized country, there would be immediate demands for his resignation. If such demands do not gather force, we will demonstrate how far we are, as a nation, from being civilized. The conduct of the Indian security forces in Kashmir threatens to make barbarians of all Indians in the eyes of the world.

I do hope that even all those who consider themselves to be genuinely patriotic Indians will be disgusted by what the video reveals about Indian might in Kashmir. If they hold their patriotism in the slightest regard, then they should realize that the continuing occupation of Kashmir, which breeds perversities such as this, is only a blot of shame on what they hold dear as the fair name of their country and on their patriotism. I hope that they will find it in themselves to act with the honour that they take pride in, and refuse any longer to be complicit, willingly or unwillingly, in the nightmare that haunts the waking and sleeping hours of the people of Kashmir today.

---

[13] The *Indian Express* did, however, find it possible to highlight the news of the footage of alleged atrocities committed by the Sri Lankan army, including summary executions of naked prisoners on its front page. See 'TV Anchor among Naked Men, Women "Killed" by Lanka Soldiers on Video', *Indian Express,* 3 December 2010 [http://www.indianexpress.com/news/tv-anchor-among-naked-men-women-killed-by-sri-lanka-soldiers-on-video/719807/].

A version of this article first appeared on the website Kafila.org, 10 September 2010.

'The People Are With Us'
An Interview with Masarat Alam Bhat

Dilnaz Boga

Booked under the draconian Public Safety Act seven times since the 2008 Amarnath land row in Kashmir, Masarat Alam Bhat was released from jail in June this year. A science graduate who speaks fluent English, Bhat is now leading the Quit Kashmir campaign against India, giving the Union and state governments sleepless nights. The Muslim League leader, who is currently underground, began the campaign by issuing weekly 'Protest Calendars' and calling for an overall strike in the Valley since the latest round of demonstrations began after the killing of a teenager on 11 June 2010 by security forces. In an exclusive interview, Dilnaz Boga catches up with Kashmir's most wanted man.

Tell us about the current phase in Kashmir's struggle. And is it different from the past?

It is not that different. The only difference is that this time the people of Kashmir have succeeded in giving a clear message to the world community as well as to the Indians—that the people of Jammu and Kashmir (J&K) want total liberation from India. They want total independence; they want the Indian forces to quit Jammu and Kashmir. This nation has been striving for a just cause for the last sixty-three years but this is a decisive phase.

What makes you think this is a decisive phase?

Now people are fed-up with this long chapter of tyranny, deception and occupation. This time around, they have seen with their own eyes that children as young as eight have been beaten to death. Unarmed young boys have been needlessly shot in the streets. So the feeling is that we should do it once and for all. Let them kill every Kashmiri if they have to. The Indian armed forces have to leave.

This has been tried before. How are you going to make this work?

We are discussing how to strategize and how to channelize this movement. Fortunately, the sentiment for freedom is alive this time in every corner of this state and everybody is involved in it. This movement has gone outside our offices, outside the organizational set-up. Everybody is involved; you just give a call asking people to write, 'Go, India, go back' on the walls and the roads, or get on Facebook and campaign for the same and the next day you see graffiti on every road, and on the Internet there is [a] flood of these messages. People are following the movement with utmost faith. We will pressurize the state and force them to give due attention to this issue and fulfil the promises they had made about giving the people of Kashmir the chance to go in for a plebiscite. Then the people will decide their future—whether they want to remain with India or they want to accede to Pakistan or they want to be independent.

But independence is not a choice in the plebiscite promised by India.

India is an oppressor and has occupied this land since 1947. So, first India should go from here. After that, the people of Jammu and Kashmir are mature enough to decide their future as a nation as they have seen so many things . . . the situation has educated them. But the first phase, and the most important one, is that India should quit J&K.

What have you learnt from the past? And what do you see in the future?

We have learnt many things from the past—the need to involve people in the movement, not just [Syed Ali Shah] Geelani or Masarat. You have to put your case in clear terms to the world. Let there be no ambiguity. It is up to us whether we make this a long-term programme or a short-term one. People have to be ready for this. People have already suffered a lot for their freedom. By 2011, our luck will be much better. This year is very important for us. We should resist the state in a continuous way. Our social network is also strong, thanks to the people spread across many places. This is for the first time that we are spending time with the people and not remaining confined to our offices. We will chalk out our future strategy keeping their views in mind. Views of other leaders, including mine, don't matter at this point; it is clearly a peoples' movement. Sixty-three people have been killed since June. Facebook has played its role, non-resident Kashmiris have played their role along with people in India. The outcome is that the world community has listened to us.

What about the role of stone-throwers?

Stone throwing is not new in Kashmir. In the 1980s, this used to happen, but it wasn't so broad-based at the time. I am a stone-thrower since my childhood. In those days, the only source of resistance was [throwing] stones. In winters, we used to throw kangris[1]. In 1989–90, the gun came, followed by torture and subjugation by the state. There have been so many deaths because the demonstrators were unarmed. You don't allow them to express their anger or their feelings, but attack them, and then you expect them not to retaliate by throwing stones. People throw shoes, coke tins and trash in the US. Gujjars in Rajasthan threw stones when their demands were not met.

---

[1]Earthen pots with hot coals carried in a wicker case to keep warm.

But why are they targeting the common man?

We have told them not to indulge in this. Some are miscreants and we will check them within a few days. We have set a principle that no oppressed person will bother another. We regret if it has happened, and we apologize. We have information that *ikhwanis*[2] are now being used to harass people and break the strike.

And there are people from within you who collaborate. How do you plan to tackle them?

We have appealed to them and their kith and kin to resist—because nations don't forgive traitors or collaborators. Don't be at war with your own people. Not all the police personnel are against us. The bureaucrats are also collaborators, but they don't pose any major threat to us. Renegades like Moma Kanna and these [Kuka] Parrays have publicly announced that they are not going to do anything against the movement and will not turn against their own people. For those who fail to comply, people will punish them eventually. They won't leave them. People won't leave us either if they feel we have wronged them. The question of forgiving the killers doesn't arise. They will get a place in Delhi . . . six feet under. Collaborators should see how renegade Kuka Parray is buried in his house, despite having so much backing and might. He wasn't even allowed in his village. The collaborators have to decide [what they should do], along with their families. Can't they smell the blood of the children in the food, the big houses and the cars they have? They have to decide. Our fight is with the army not the local police.

How did you conceive the Quit Kashmir campaign?

The idea was that our movement was mismanaged and we were not able to give a message to the world community in clear terms—somebody was talking about self-determination, others

---

[2]Ex-militants or renegades.

wanted tripartite talks, somebody else was talking about bilateral talks, others wanted autonomy. So we gave a slogan that India should quit J&K. Now, for the first time in sixty-three years, in the Indian Parliament the home minister recognizes this voice of freedom. For the first time, the largest opposition party, which is the Bharatiya Janata Party (BJP), had their senior leader Murli Manohar Joshi clearly stating in Parliament that the people of J&K are not striving for employment or roads but they want Azadi. This was our achievement. The second thing is that we have been able to mobilize everyone in the state, whether they are students, shopkeepers, employees, doctors or lawyers. About the next phase of our strategy, Hurriyat (G) chairman Mr Syed Ali Shah Geelani has given five points to India that can be looked at as confidence-building measures. First, India should comply with demilitarization, release all political prisoners, etc., and then we will talk and halt this phase of agitation. But if India fails to fulfil these five points, we will intensify the movement. Strikes and curfews won't last forever. We will make it more intense. If India is sincere about peace, here's the chance to do it. They should start demilitarization now.

What is India saying at this point? Any message from back-door channels?

Why should we go on Track II? We should not deceive people; we should be honest and clear and do everything openly.

But there are some people who don't want to support your calls for strike. Your party workers often try to stifle this voice of dissent. Why?

We respect dissent. But if you are going to stage something else, then there's a problem. We are addressing the genuine troubles that people have. We are taking people's suggestions into account. And though we have to suffer, we are trying our best to minimize the sufferings. Whoever has achieved freedom, they all had to suffer. If people think they will get freedom without being affected, then they are living in a fool's paradise. People should set up committees at local levels for food distribution and education. People have been helping poor people. People should teach locally. Until India agrees to our demands, we will have to pull along. Things are going to get more intense after the festival of Eid.

What has the role of the media been?

There's a complaint against the media. We request the media: please speak the truth. Don't write to [sell] the newspaper. People are monitoring which newspaper has picked up which issue. So please behave. Today we have warned the police; tomorrow we might have to warn the local media. We want to ask the Indian media why they are biased about Kashmir. Are we not human beings? They should listen to us, tell our stories. We have behaved as a nation; for this they should admire Kashmiris. Our community is tolerant. Still they try to divide us. Why did they try to divide the Sikhs and now us? We have information that they are trying to incite violence between the Shias and Sunnis. Now we are mature enough; we will not fight. We are brothers.

Do you have a message for the people of the state?

Everyone is facing bad times. I haven't been home in three months. Even our families have suffered a lot. But we have sacrificed for our community. So the community should also be ready to sacrifice. This is not public posturing. I can truthfully say—and I have met thousands of people here—that I have never seen a crestfallen or a tired Kashmiri. People are with us. Why don't we deal with this once and for all to save our future? This is not a directionless movement. We will wait for an opportunity to intensify public demonstrations, which will be harder to handle. It is this sentiment which rules the nation this time around.

This article first appeared in the *Times of India, Crest* edition, 18 September 2010.

Masarat CD Creates Ripples

Greater Kashmir

In a jittery move aimed at preventing the dissemination of the contents of a compact disc of Tehreek-e-Hurriyat leader, Masarat Alam Bhat urging the armed forces to join the ongoing 'Quit Kashmir Campaign', the government Tuesday 'by default' facilitated wide circulation of the CD's transcript 'with a warning against publishing the same'.

The district magistrate, Srinagar, Meraj Ahmad Kakroo, vide his letter no: DMS/PS-Misc/10/827-31, addressed to director, Information Department and also circulated to the press, said: 'This office is in receipt of a communication which reveals that Masarat Alam Bhat of Tehreek-e-Hurriyat has circulated a video CD in which he is not only trying to spread dissatisfaction among the security forces working in J&K but is also asking the security personnel to Quit Jammu and Kashmir. The transcript of the CD is enclosed.'

Curiously, district magistrate, Srinagar while asking the director, Information to 'issue instructions to the print and electronic media to desist from printing/publishing the CD', puts no such bar on the CD's transcript circulated by his office.

The transcript of the Masarat Alam Bhat's CD (circulated by the district magistrate, Srinagar), titled 'Quit Jammu Kashmir' addressed to the 'armed forces' reads: 'We appeal you to lend solidarity with the people of Jammu and Kashmir for the state's rightful self-determination, and the right of the people of Jammu and Kashmir to be free. We call on your conscience to end the long chapter of deception, tyranny and death. Your actions have killed 1,00,000, disappeared 10,000 and orphaned 60,000.'

Interestingly, the one-page transcript has been forwarded to the principal secretary, to Chief Minister Omar Abdullah, additional director general of police, CID, J&K, Srinagar, divisional commissioner, Kashmir, and senior superintendent of police, Srinagar.

'You thought your violence would kill our dreams for freedom. They have not. You thought our spirit would break; we would turn against each other. We will not. You have succeeded in murder, but not in the death of our dreams. Before more violence, before more sorrow, before more graves, we ask you to stop,' the transcript read.

'Ours is a rich and resilient culture. We are proud people whose hospitality has defined our history. We welcome guests, invited or uninvited, not invaders. We understand your deception, your psychological warfare. You will be tired of killing us; some day you might be horrified at what you have done to humanity. We will never tire of struggling for our history, for our future, our freedom. We will not forgive.'

Masarat said, 'We are against terror and in solidarity with all who oppose violence and repression. We seek truth, justice and freedom.' Masarat, through the CD, called for civil disobedience against the government.

This article first appeared in *Greater Kashmir*, Srinagar, 27 July 2010.

'Respected Shobha Rani'

Aijaz Hussain

In the heart of Srinagar, in the winding streets of its downtown, the protesting stone-pelters—mostly school and college students—had organized themselves into small, compact units. When not busy clashing with the police and the paramilitary forces, they engaged in endless discussions. These were wide-ranging, from narratives of love affairs to the unravelling of the Kashmir problem and the search for a solution, as well as the comparing of notes on the various instruments and techniques of stone-pelting. As the curfew became stricter, the debates also bloomed.

On one of those curfew days, a new officer arrived to take charge of one of the countless paramilitary camps downtown. Shobha Rani was soon briefed about the geography and sociology of her operational area. This included acquainting her with the area's prominent personalities—its main stone-pelters.

The arrival of this young and beautiful woman officer swelled the blood of the young stone-pelters, producing many conflicting emotions. She soon became the hot topic of their discussions. A few revolutionaries held the opinion that taking on a woman was below their dignity. Some saw a deep conspiracy in the deployment of a lady officer. Still others were of the view that once they don a uniform, men—or women—are all the same. Yet another school of thought pitied India for sending women to fight its wars.

In the midst of these relentless debates, a very active stone-pelting unit, made up of five close friends, became victims of a strange dilemma.

One of the friends disclosed that he had been arrested by a weakness for Shobha Rani. Thereafter, one by one, the others too divulged that they had been afflicted by similar, unrequited love.

Events soon began to freeze up this group of five stone-pelting friends. In place of the sounds of bullets and the clatter of the tear-gas shells they now started to seek refuge in the melancholic songs of Mohammad Rafi. This change in their outlook could not go unnoticed. For this was a place where just the depth of a furrowed brow could let people distinguish between someone coming back from a meeting with a lover, or returning from a rendezvous with a spook. Now doubtful of their commitment, the shadows of the grapevine were briefly aflutter with whispers.

But nationalistic fervour and revolutionary zeal soon jolted the five friends out of their dormancy. Steeling their resolve, they once again became active participants in the street protests, gaining greater prominence than ever before.

However, as they threw stone after heavy stone, they were still weighed down by an overwhelming longing for the object of their love. It was as if the very image of her tresses had made a Medusa of her. They managed to encircle Shobha Rani more than once, but their limbs grew heavy, and simply refused to hurl stones at her.

Ultimately, they tried to end the dilemma of this extreme test of conflicting emotions.

They sent her a joint letter.

Respected Shobha Rani jee, it said.

We Gudde, Rajje, Mithe, Gugge and Saebe do all love you.

We promise, that if you choose any one of us as your life-partner, we will give up stone-pelting.

But we have a condition too.

We will continue demanding Azadi.

Translated from the Urdu by Aijaz Hussain and Arif Ayaz Parrey.

Captive City

The routine: waking up, morning chores, breakfast,
out on the streets to hurl stones and abuse at the visible
symbols of occupation, no lunch, more stones, more abuses,
getting chased, hurt, tear-gassed, shot . . .
The next morning, the same routine.

Yirvun Kreel

Captive City

Wasim Bhat

> This city is built of bones,
> Plastered with blood and flesh,
> And filled with
> Ageing, death, conceit, and hypocrisy.
>
> —*Dhammapada*, 150

Srinagar appears through a haze from the ancient heights of the Shankaracharya temple, hewn in massive rock, an enduring invocation to Shiva by a devout king.[1] An expanse of earth, water and mountain so intermingled, so intricate, so engaged, each with the other, a tapestry unique.

The vantage of the temple atop the Takht-i-Sulaiman hillock offers an enchanting view of the old town. Across the expanse of the Dal waters, the Hari Parbat hill, with the Afghan fort sitting on top, looks like a restive lion keeping a vigil over the old quarter of the city. Shifting one's gaze sideways one can just make out the

---

[1]The temple is originally said to have been built by Jalauka, in 200 BC, who controlled Kashmir just after the death of Emperor Ashoka. Jalauka was probably a native of Kashmir and an ardent Shaivaite. Dedicated to Shiva and believed to have been later rebuilt by Raja Gopaditya between the third and fourth centuries.

structure of Jamia Masjid, the Grand Mosque, in the heart of the old town. Just beyond it the wooden spires of the Khanqah-i-Muala, or the Grand Hospice, fade in the dust and light.[2]

This is where Islam leaves its first mark in Kashmir in around the early fourteenth century. Syed Sharfudin, a Sufi divine of the Suhrawardi order, popularly known as Bulbul Shah, lies buried here in Bulbul Lanker. His shrine is a place of deep veneration for Kashmiris. It was at his hands that the Ladakhi Buddhist chieftain Rinchen Shah became Sultan Sadrudin, the first Muslim ruler of Kashmir. The depth of Rinchen's spiritual engagement with Bulbul Shah is suggested by the fact that he, a king of Kashmir, was buried in the precincts of the same hospice that he had built for his spiritual preceptor.

Nearby is the Mazaar-i-Salateen, the Royal Cemetery. Zainul Abidin, the most notable of the Shahmiri sultans, built it for his mother, and is also buried there.[3] The Mazaar is built on the remnants of an edifice of the Hindu period. A millennia and more of history just there, at the very doorway of the Mazaar. It is around here that Pravarsena II had laid the foundations of his capital in the sixth century AD. Remnants of his exertions still remain in the weathered engravings carved on massive slabs of stone in the Mazaar, and in the neighbourhood of Kalashpora, which used to be Kali Shri Pora, where Pravarsena had raised a magnificent edifice to the goddess.

This is around where the Khanqah-i-Muala was raised in honour of Syed Mir Ali Hamdani, popularly called Shah Hamdan, leader of a group of Sufi missionaries who first visited Kashmir in

---

[2]In late fourteenth century, a Shahmiri king, Sultan Sikander (1389–1413) built a seminary in honour of Syed Ali Hamdani, and that came to be called the Khanqah-i-Muala. The seminary is built along the banks of the Jhelum in the centre of what is the old quarter of Srinagar.

[3]The Shahmiris were the most notable dynasty that ruled Kashmir for around two hundred years from the middle of the fourteenth century to the mid-sixteenth century.

the latter part of the fourteenth century, and is credited with spreading the message of Islam in the Kashmir valley and some of its outlying regions.

And all along flows the Jhelum, the Hydaspes, the Vyeth, the Vitasta. Through its many names never missing a spire, not a shrine or temple ghat.[4] It touches everything and blesses everything. It connects everything, in space, in history and in spirit.

And now the Jhelum is red. Its waters are swollen with the blood of its children. It is nauseous and it wants to vomit. This is where in 1992 Abdul Hamid Sheikh, a rebel leader of the Jammu Kashmir Liberation Front (JKLF), was killed while crossing the river in a boat. Much closer in time, in July this year, Faizan Ahmad, a thirteen-year-old, was allegedly drowned by policemen of the Special Operations Group, as they were chasing protesters near the Azadgunj bridge, way downstream in Baramulla town.[5]

The old quarter of Srinagar was once at the crossroads of the Silk Route traffic, feted for the skill of its famed pashmina, papiermâché and shawl artisans. A vortex of spirituality, the blessings of Qadiri, Kubrawi, Suhrawardi, Naqshbandi divines and many other saints and mystics jostle and huddle with each other, suffuse the air and make it dense. This multiform density of history, space and spirit has always nurtured a free and eclectic temperament. It has grown and matured between the interstices of history, watered by the flow of the Jhelum, as it wets the ghats of the Khanqah as well of the much older Ganpatyar temple upstream.

In the evenings, the river front seems to float on equal measures of light and water.

It has the sombreness of a profound thought awaiting discovery.

The very quintessence of this mosaic is now in a quivering ferment, transforming the streets and lanes of the city into a

---

[4]The Greeks called the Jhelum Hydaspes, its Sanskrit name is the Vitasta and in Kashmiri it is the Vyeth.

[5]*Greater Kashmir*, 19 July. Faizan left for school never to return.

gridlock of rebellion. Tangled masses of much used razor wire, spiked barricades and battered grey armoured vehicles grapple to keep this rebellion at bay. Grim and tense, hundreds of paramilitary soldiers are fielded in their latest riot gear, Darth Vader in cheap black plastic, worn over standard ill-fitting khakis. Their AK's slung carelessly around their shoulders while they provide cover to armoured vehicles that move surreptitiously past in convoys across the curfewed streets.

The narrow streets are a maze of barricades, check-points and bunkers, snarling and gnawing unending coils of concertina. Draped in camouflage nets, squat brick bunkers gaze at the people through narrow slats. Memorizing faces and calculating their defences against the multitude. From one bunker to the next and the next, the city is in omnipresent crosshairs.

The tumult of this summer saw a curfew that was brutal and unrelenting for days and weeks on end, a collective punishment for an ever-restive population.

Democracy has its limits and one can only ask for so much. Freedom is not on the list.

On 11 June this year, I was on my way home when I got a call saying that protests had broken out after a seventeen-year-old boy had been killed in downtown Srinagar. He was hit by a tear-gas shell which split his skull. It was only later that I got to know that the boy named Tufail Ahmad Matoo lived just across the road from my house. It's an old neighbourhood that sits between the crumbling outer fortifications of the Afghan fort, and the waterways of the Dal. A narrow lane leads to a modest rust-coloured house that was Tufail's home. I knew the family well. Tufail's death was a trigger that ignited a gargantuan explosion of resentment unlike anything Kashmir had ever seen, though the mixture had been brewing from many summers past.

The extreme militarization of all spaces in Kashmir, the sheer embeddedness of the military machine, it's all-pervasive influence and control over aspects of civilian lives for several decades, provide an immediacy of context to the long festering political questions of the region. This is why when a young boy like Tufail is killed in police action in Kashmir, the demand is not of justice from the state but Azadi, or freedom. And it is in this context that the extreme and disproportionate reaction of the state to the people's agitation in Kashmir can be understood.

There is a certain familiarity about this in Kashmir, where seemingly diverse and disconnected events and demands lead to just one clarion call in the end. A cyclical historicity.

When on 27 December 1963, the sacred reliquary containing the hair of the Prophet Muhammad was stolen from the Hazratbal shrine, the news of the theft of the Muy-i-Muqaddas threw Kashmir into an unprecedented crisis. Tens of thousands gathered in Lal Chowk and Budshah Chowk, the main commercial centres of Srinagar city, and a cry grew into a crescendo. So serious was the situation that Jawaharlal Nehru, then prime minister, felt that it might 'seriously jeopardize India's position in the Valley'.

The intensity of this agitation stemmed from the deep mystical and sacred significance the holy relic has for the Kashmiri Muslim. Its arrival and presence transformed Kashmir, in the words of the poet Qalandar Beg, into Medina, *Kashmir Madina Shud az Muy i Nabi*.[6] What is noteworthy here is that the underlying cause of the agitation was purely religious, and it had started off by simply demanding the restoration of the holy relic. Very soon, however, the movement transformed and took on political connotations, and with the formation of the Awami Action Committee that spearheaded the agitation, the settlement of the Kashmir dispute became a central demand of the movement.

This September, on Eid day, Syed Ali Shah Geelani, a leading separatist leader, announced his plans to offer prayers at Hazratbal,

---

[6]Khwaja Nurudin Ishbari, a rich Kashmiri merchant is reported to have acquired the relic from Syed Abdullah of Bijapur in 1699. Ishbari did not make it home and died on the way but the relic was brought to Srinagar along with his dead body to a state of a rapturous and reverential welcome.

and address people there. The act has a special significance: it was Sheikh Abdullah who in 1943 first brought Hazratbal under the control of the Auqaf[7], deploying it as an effective political platform. Particularly after his expulsion on the orders of Nehru in 1953, the massive gatherings at Hazratbal on the birth (Milad) of the Prophet, and on his ascent to heaven (Miraj) were celebrated as de rigueur occasions for the National Conference leadership to launch into fiery speeches, to reaffirm Kashmir's destiny as inextricably linked to their own. So this year, Geelani's announcement was predictably met with house arrest. After Eid prayers, protests broke around Hazratbal. Amid cries of 'We want freedom', the dull bangs of tear shells exploding, and frantic policemen firing in the air, a police post was burnt down.

The supremely spiritual is still the pre-eminently political in Kashmir.

On 12 June while Tufail's family was still in shock, and yet to receive his body, hundreds of young men swarmed his house and claimed him for themselves, a martyr for the cause, a *shaheed*. They shouldered his coffin through the tense streets, fought pitched battles with the police and paramilitaries deployed in strength. Through the stench of tear-gas smoke and the deafening noise of shells exploding and gunshots singeing the air, Tufail was taken to the martyrs' graveyard at Eidgah, around six kilometres away, and laid to rest. In the aftermath, a hundred and more coffins would be shouldered this summer, the smallest that of an eight-year-old.

Sameer Ahmad Rah, the eight-year-old, died on 2 August. He lived in Batamaloo, an old quarter of Srinagar that sits huddled around the shrine of Baba Daud. The locality takes its name from this revered Rishi sage of the valley, popularly known as Bataa Moul, the Nourisher. Like other Sufis of the Rishi order of Kashmir he was a vegetarian and it's in deference to this practice that people of Batamaloo do not cook meat for seven days around

---

[7]Wakf or auqaf is an Islamic endowment for the upkeep of religious institutions.

the time of the annual Urs of the sage. And it is somewhere here in a dark lane that Sameer was bludgeoned to death. His parents said that he just went out to an uncle's house nearby and was caught by patrolling paramilitaries. 'They killed a seven-year-old boy, the light of my home. He was holding a pear, not a gun, not even a stone,' is the poignant and muted cry of his hapless father.[8]

The upheaval of this summer was tragic in the loss of young lives, heroic in its fearlessness, and proletarian in its character. A perusal of the names of those who died and those who were injured reveals that it was a protest of the working class, of the lower middle class in cities and towns, and the peasantry in the villages. The urban educated middle class were fence-sitters, and largely lent their support in drawing room discussions and on Facebook by saying 'I Protest', never leaving their living rooms. Some made it to television talk shows and talked of Azadi.

Azadi is what the peasantry wants; and it's the cry of the city worker too. The peasantry and the working class in urban areas are the ones who have the smallest stake in the status quo. For a corrupt, semi-feudal, elitist system benefits them the least. At the same time it's they who have been at the receiving end of the counter-insurgency grid for over two decades, and this is what makes them most receptive to exploring possibilities of change.

The middle and upper middle class, and the landed elite in the rural areas, on the other hand, have had their hands full for decades, milking—to borrow that delightful phrase—'the mammaries of the welfare state' in myriad and endless manners. They live in 'posh' colonies of Srinagar, in pockets of the Civil Lines area, while the powerful lord it at their Gupkar Road addresses, manned by stark men in grey safari suits, Uzis snuggling under their armpits. Tinted SUVs parked, revved and ready to go at all times. Lavish golf courses and, of course, one of the best views in the city, are all the accoutrements of this privilege.

---

[8] *The Hindu*, Wednesday, 24 November 2010, 'Feel our pain say Kashmiris', Nirupama Subramanian.

Any radical change would be cataclysmic for them. Unless of course it was presented as a fait accompli. Or a better deal than the one they enjoy at present. This explains their drawing room support to the people's movement. Just enough of a foot in the door, enough to keep open the possibility of new alignments, and secure their position as significant players in altered dispensations.

The complexity of this fragmented political articulation in Kashmir has to be understood in the context of a particular history. In its facilitation (and legitimization) of patently bourgeoisie, elitist and undemocratic processes in Kashmir over the past six decades, the Indian state has meticulously cultivated a diverse and pliant native elite. The challenge before the state has always been to support and legitimize the prominence of this elite in the region, while at the same time attempting to expand and diversify this 'client family' base. Over the decades, the compliance and complicity of this elite has achieved compromises around not just the political and legal status, but also around the ecological and environmental condition of the state of Jammu and Kashmir. In return for what amounts to an economic dole, the largesse and patronage caters to sections that live in the unquestioned abundance of this status quo.

The native elites legislate and govern, while the Indian state rules.

The current ecological decline in the many water bodies, waterways and wetlands in and around Srinagar is a result of decades of compromised, undemocratic and incompetent policy-making. The tons of sewage flowing into the Dal and its back waters, transforming once vibrant waterways into cesspools, and the flouting of environmental, forest and land laws for commercial purposes are burdens that these once pristine waters are no longer able to bear. The opening of the Boulevard Avenue for construction of hotels and the filling up of the Nallah Mar canal that once passed through the old quarter of the city, were catastrophic urban planning decisions, the latter effectively decimating the city's natural drainage.

The Mar Canal, the Nallah Mar, used to be a waterway that coursed through the heart of Srinagar city. The surplus waters of the Jhelum flowed into this canal and Sultan Zainul Abidin had it extended up to Shadipur on the outskirts of Srinagar where it emptied itself at the confluence of the Sind and the Jhelum. Spanned by seven masonry bridges, the canal was an important source of traffic, both of goods and leisure. Bohri Kadal, now a busy intersection in the old town, used to be the busiest vegetable ghat along the Nallah Mar. Children would learn to swim at the ghats, business would be transacted and leisure would be enjoyed. In place of that ghat, a traffic beat box stands in the middle of a crowded chowk. It is here that police and paramilitaries get pelted by stones as processions are taken out.

The Nallah Mar was filled up and converted into an arterial road that would bisect the old town of Srinagar. This was done ostensibly so that modern vehicular traffic could be moved easily into the old town, and because maintaining the pristine nature of the waters of the canal had become a rather complicated task. Filling it up solved both, and when Ghulam Mohammed Sadiq was chief minister in 1970, the decision to bury this unparalleled piece of heritage was taken.

Only a few decades ago, a shikara ride through the maze of interlocking waterways of Srinagar, shrouded by dense drooping willows, was still a serene experience. The backwaters of Rainawari with its beautiful waterfront mansions, temple spires, ghats, quaint bridges were the enchanted backyard of my childhood. The backwater is still there, it's just that it's not so pretty any more, and it smells.

Srinagar is a city that still lives on water, though no longer with it.

It is this backwater route that many used when the downtown was placed under a severe lockdown this summer. A forty-five-minute ride through the backwaters and one would land at the Boulevard Road, the busiest tourist hangout in Srinagar. The fact that Srinagar sits on so much water also makes it unmanageable, for there is so much then that cannot be monitored and put under surveillance. Even though there are patrol boats and sentries overlooking bridges who try to enforce the curfew on the waters as well. In the initial tumult of the militancy of the 1990s, the Dal backwaters were a bastion for the militants who would just melt away after making a strike, or lie low if there were search operations on the mainland.

The city in its density—in the medieval huddle of the old quarter, the intricate loop of its waters—offered its denizens spaces, interstices, gaps, gasps of breath without which they would not have survived the harshness of this summer. Or that of summers past.

Without which they would not have survived the harshness and vagaries of centuries past.

This city is their refuge and their fortress. Through most of the summer this year, the 'Go India, Go Back' graffiti was omnipresent, painted in black or white on walls, shutters and streets across the city. The local cable news that most people used to watch was banned; newspapers were not delivered for weeks on end. In the web edition of the *Greater Kashmir* newspaper every day, the section called 'Latest News' carried news of some more young men getting shot at in protests. The Darth Vaders stood impassively just outside our gates, from morning through the blazing summer noon, till dusk, fiddling with their AKs. Indian talk show hosts tried their vacuous best, 24x7, to unravel what it meant when Kashmiris cried 'Azadi'.

The milkman used to make the delivery at 12 at night:

'The city from where no news can come is now so visible in its curfewed night.'[9]

How many gun barrels stare at us? Enough to keep us anxious and edgy, always looking over our shoulders. We are the children of a war that has no scruples. The war that moves in the billion

---

[9]'I See Kashmir from New Delhi at Midnight', Aga Shahid Ali, *The Veiled Suite: The Collected Poems*, p. 178.

synapses of our brain, releasing chemicals that make us anxious and wary, tiring us and making us old. Catching us unaware, it has captured the rhythms of our being.

The winter is about to ride its crest. The birds I saw in my childhood are no more. Songs are forbidden in this forgotten city. The snow has not yet covered the mountain gorges, the crevasses are a frenzy of rock and gravel. The dogs bark incessantly throughout the night, lost in the streets and dark alleys. The cars are a blur and the pedestrians wary. Olive green and irritated, the trucks snarl and rumble through narrow potholed roads, blaring horns and flashing headlights.

They are the overlords of this earth, the plumed birds have fled. The constant din keeps the city awake, in enduring captivity.

This article first appeared in the *Honour* magazine, Srinagar, December 2010.

'I Protest'

MC Kash

They Say When You Run From Darkness All You Seek
 Is Light . . .
But When The Blood Spills Over, You'll Stand An' Fight!!
Threads Of Deceit Woven Around A Word Of Plebiscite,
By Treacherous Puppet Politicians Who Have No Soul
 Inside
My Paradise Is Burnin' With Troops Left Loose With
 Ammo,
Who Murder An' Rape Then Hide Behind A Political
 Shadow . . .
Like A Casino, Human Life Is Thrown Like A Dice . . .
I'll Summarize Atrocities Till The Resurrection Of Christ!!
Can You Hear The Screams, Now See The Revolution!!
The Bullets, Our Stones, Don't Talk Restitution . . .
'Cuz The Only Solution Is The Resolution Of Freedom,
Even Khusro Will Go Back An' Doubt his Untimely
 Wisdom!!
These Killings Ain't Random It's An Organized
 Genocide . . .
Sponsored Media Who Hide This Homicide.
No More Injustice We Won't Go Down When We Bleed,
Alive In The Struggle Even The Graves Will Speak!

Chorus:

> I Protest, Against The Things You Done!
> I Protest, Fo' A Mother Who Lost Her Son!
> I Protest, I Will Throw Stones An' Neva Run!
> I Protest, Until My Freedom Has Come!
> I Protest, Fo' My Brother Who's Dead!
> I Protest, Against The Bullet In his Head!
> I Protest, I Will Throw Stones An' Neva Run!
> I Protest, Until My Freedom Has Come!

> Democratically Held Elections—Now That's Completely Absurd,
> I'll Tell You Some Stuff That You Obviously Neva Heard!!
> A Ten-Year-Old Kid Voted With All his Fingers . . .
> A Whole Village Gang-raped, A Cry Still Lingers . . .
> These Are The Tales From The Dark Side Of A Murderous Regime,
> An Endless Occupation Of Our Land An' Our Dreams.
> Democratic Politics Will Cut Our Throats Befo' We Speak,
> How They Talk Abo' Peace When Thea's Blood In Our Streets? (huh?)
> When Freedom Of Speech Is Subjected To Strangulation!!
> Flames Of Revolution Engulfs The Population.
> They Rise Through Suppression An' March To Be Free,
> Face Covered In A Rag, Labelled A Revolutionary.
> Through This Fight Fo' Survival I Want The World To See,
> A Murderous Oppression Written Down In Police Brutality.
> Stones In My Hand—It's Time You Pay The Price,
> Fo' Plunderin' An' Rapin' A Beautiful Paradise!!

Chorus:

> I Protest, Against The Things You Done!
> I Protest, Fo' A Mother Who Lost Her Son!

I Protest, I Will Throw Stones An' Neva Run!
I Protest, Until My Freedom Has Come!
I Protest, Fo' My Brother Who's Dead!
I Protest, Against The Bullet In his Head!
I Protest, I Will Throw Stones An' Neva Run!
I Protest, Until My Freedom Has Come!

Let's Remember All Those Who Were Martyred This Year:

Inayat Khan, Wamiq Farooq, Zahid Farooq, Zubair Ahmed Bhat, Tufail Ahmad Matoo, Rafiq Ahmed Bangroo, Javaid Ahmed Malla, Shakeel Ganai, Firdous Khan, Bilal Ahmed Wani, Tajamul Bashir, Tauqeer Rather, Ishtiyaq Ahmed, Imtiyaz Ahmed Itoo, Shujaat-ul-Islaam, Muzaffar Ahmed, Fayaz Ahmed Wani, Yasmeen Jan, Abrar Ahmed Khan, Faizan Rafeeq, Fayaz Ahmed Khanday, Farooq Ahmed, Tariq Ahmed Dar, Mohammed Ahsan, Showkat Ahmed, Mohammed Rafiq, Nazir Ahmed, Javed Ahmed Teli, Mudassir Lone, Nayeem Shah, Rayees Wani, Afrooza Teli, Basharat Reshi, Irshad Bhat, Ashiq Hussain, Rameez Ahmed, Hafiz Yaqoob, Tariq Dar, Khursheed Ahmed, Bashir Ahmed Reshi, Arshid Ahmad, Sameer Rah, Mehraj-ud-din Lone, Anis Ganai, Suhail Ahmed Dar, Jehangir Bhat, Riyaz Ahmed, Mohammad Yaqoob Bhat, Iqbal Khan, Shabir Malik, Ghulam Nabi Badyari, Rameez Reshi, Fida Nabi Lone, Farrukh Bukhari, Mudassir Zargar, Ali Mohammad Khanday, Asif Mir, Sameer Lone, Umar Ahmed Dar, Irshad Ahmed, Mohammad Abbas, Milad Ahmed Dar, Nazir Wani, Mudasir Nazir, Bilal Ahmed Sheikh, Umar Qayoom, Irshad Ahmad . . .

And you will fight to the death of it . . .
And you will fight to the death of it . . .
And you will fight to the death of it . . .

This song first appeared on the online music site Reverbnation [http://www.reverbnation.com/mckashkashmir].

Kashmir Rapper Uses Rhymes to Protest Indian Rule

Aijaz Hussain

If you ask MC Kash, he's just speaking the truth. But Kashmir's breakout rapper's songs court rebellion and could land him in jail. Kash calls himself a rebel who uses sharp rhymes and beats instead of stones or guns to protest India's rule over the mostly Muslim region in the Himalayas. Kash, twenty, whose real name is Roushan Illahi, has won a fan base among Kashmir's youth, whose summer uprising against Indian rule inspired his local hit 'I protest'. The lyrics—'Tales from the dark side of a murderous regime, an endless occupation of our land an' our dreams'—tread dangerously close to sedition in India, where questioning the country's claim to the disputed region of Kashmir is illegal.

'Rap is about straight talk and telling truth in the face, however uncomfortable it may be,' the rapper said on a gloomy autumn day in the region's capital, Srinagar. 'Rap is rebellion. Kashmir is rebellion. MC Kash is rebellion against injustice, oppression and falsehood.' Kash admitted he was scared last month after remarks by Booker Prize-winning author Arundhati Roy questioning India's claim to Kashmir generated angry demands for her arrest. 'Then I thought, revolutionaries don't fear persecution or execution,' Kash said. 'If they throw me in the prison . . . I'll write on the [prison] walls.' Authorities deny going after those who are using the

Internet or music as an outlet for their protests, saying their focus instead is on street protesters who hurl stones at law enforcement officers. 'Youth by nature are rebellious. But if it's going out of control, we would like to check it,' said Shiv Murari Sahai, a top police officer.

Both India and Pakistan claimed sovereignty over Kashmir when they were divided at the end of British rule in 1947. Since then, India has governed most of the territory and Pakistan holds much of the rest. Stuck in the middle of the dispute are Kashmir's ten million people, and for many, anti-India sentiment runs deep after decades of violent turmoil. Separatist insurgencies and crackdowns by the hundreds of thousands of Indian troops deployed in the Indian-administered portion have killed more than 68,000, most of them civilians. Since June, tens of thousands of Kashmiris have risen up against Indian rule again. At least 111—mostly teenage boys and young men—have been killed in the five months of clashes with government forces, and hundreds more have been arrested.

Kash grew up with his physician father and schoolteacher mother in Srinagar at a time when India's army was hammering the region to crush a rebellion that erupted in 1989. Government forces were engaging in regular gun battles with the rebels, raiding homes in search of suspects and arresting people off the streets. Neighbourhoods were cordoned off and security check-points set up across the region. 'People like Illahi are a new generation of Kashmiri artists who have experienced enough fear not to be intimidated any more,' local sociologist Wasim Bhat said. There is a long tradition in Kashmir of writing protest songs, but they are usually in the local Urdu and Kashmiri languages so do not have much impact outside the region. There is even a popular, rap-like genre of traditional Kashmiri folk music called *ladi shah*, in which artists go from village to village to sing about contemporary issues.

But Kash said he chose to rap in English because 'I wanted the world to know what's happening in Kashmir.' He started writing poetry when he was ten, and now studies business administration in a college in Srinagar. Using his own money, he went to a local studio last year and with a computer recorded his first rap song,

'Moment of Truth,' after watching a film on the 2008–09 Israeli-Palestinian war in Gaza. 'I cried and cried because the same thing was happening here in my land,' Kash said. Since June, authorities in Kashmir have continued to impose rigid curfews as separatist leaders call for more strikes and protests. Kash made his third song, 'I protest,' in September. 'I thought about these young martyrs and their mothers, and then I thought to put this pain of Kashmir in music,' he said. The result was a highly political and emotional song naming the sixty-five people killed up to September, and saying 'these killings ain't random, it's an organized genocide.' Kash released the song on the online music site Reverbnation, where his profile photo shows a crew-cut youth wearing a red-hooded sweat shirt and a tough expression. The song rails against 'A Murderous Oppression Written Down In Police Brutality' and vows, 'I'll Throw Stones An' Neva Run. I Protest, Until My Freedom Has Come!'

It was an instant hit with Kashmiri students, some of whom combined the song with videos and photos on YouTube and Facebook. Kash was not arrested, but police raided the recording studio and questioned the staff about his whereabouts, according to one worker who refused to be named for fear of police reprisal. 'Police were particularly asking if any separatist leader was behind the rapper,' the studio worker said. The studio will not let Kash record his new song, also about Kashmir. Kash said he was looking for other outlets, including possibly a local concert with Indian rappers. But already within Kashmir, Kash has inspired a handful of other youths to start rapping, recording hip-hop compositions on home computers and connecting with artists outside Kashmir. One sixteen-year-old boy who calls himself Renegade recently uploaded two songs on Reverbnation, but removed them after a few days, fearing reprisals. A nineteen-year-old, Saqib Mohammed, is soon releasing 'The Revolution', his first rap song. 'MC Kash is showing us a way to express our desire through art,' he said.

This article was first published by the Associated Press, 26 November 2010.

The Islamism Bogey in Kashmir

Najeeb Mubarki

It was Bertolt Brecht who once suggested, in his sharp, almost genial way, while talking of a different uprising, in 1953 in East Germany, that the state could, as a solution, dissolve the people and elect another. That, perhaps, would for many be a consummation devoutly wished for when it comes to Kashmir. For, faced with the kind of uprising, the narrative as exists in Kashmir these days, it seems the counter-narrative can only attempt to subvert or subsume the facts. And if one were to employ a bit of hyperbole, beyond the propaganda seems to lie a desire to somehow do away with the present lot of Kashmiris, and elect, or invent, another. Paradoxically, this consists of either seeking to invent a people more to one's liking or, inversely, creating an image of a people so prone to extremism that empathy with them is simply impossible.

There are broadly two main strands to the discourse on Kashmir that attempt that act of dissolving the reality. One would be the staid, stale assertion that the protests in the Valley, if not instigated from across the border, are managed by a mischief-prone minority, and are not really representative of the people's feelings. In the third month of protests, and after sixty-three killings (thus far) by the state police and the Central Reserve Police Force (CRPF), that 'assertion' seems to have died a natural death. Thus, the supposed silent majority, the potentially 'likeable' lot, the people who would have been hijacked by the minute number of protesters, can't really be brought to life.

It is the second strand, which invokes charges of Islamic extremism, that the counter-campaign in the Indian media now seems to have settled on. On the surface, this campaign is conducted purely at the level of deploying images: by playing up the pictures and statements of an Islamist or two (preferably a female for better effect) and attempting to conjure a link to wider Kashmiri society. It is a classic case of a biased media seeking—and using—the few scattered instances which can reinforce that pre-existing bias. Quite like highlighting those 'letters', pasted on a few walls, addressed to a minority community, to whip up visions of some imminent pogrom.

At a wider, deeper and much more serious level, it is insinuated that some larger Islamist game plan is at work in Kashmir. It doesn't take a politically incisive mind to realize that, at a global level, it is far easier these days to label a movement, a group or just a section of people as Islamists than it is to deal with the political aspects of what those movements or sections might be trying to articulate: that they may well be aspiring to something that is far from, or actually negates, religious extremism. In India, that fact is aided by a wider failure to understand Kashmiris, or just a plain lack of awareness about their history and culture.

Of course, the majority of people in Kashmir are Muslims. And of course, elements among those who raise the Islamist bogey in Kashmir are, inversely, people who simply dislike that fact of Kashmiris-as-Muslims. We could call it a border-world application of a certain brand of mainland communalism. And that attempt at displacing one's own communalism on to Kashmiris neatly dovetails with the wider phenomenon of how Muslims are, post 9/11, subjects of suspicion in the West.

Is there actually any truth to the charge? You don't need to be a sociologist or an ethnographer to learn that forms of faith, of religiosity, inflect many aspects of life within a community, particularly in a community in crisis, under siege, facing a situation where it feels its very existence and identity to be under threat. Thus, for example, while the larger meaning of the slogan of 'Azadi' might be some form of secular Kashmiri nationalism, the slogan of 'Allah o Akbar' (God is Great) also attends it. While it is, in essence, a slogan of defiance, it is also a culturally determined one. Of course there are other slogans too—or have been—which would suggest a decidedly Islamist vision of what Kashmiri society should look like. Beyond the empirically evident gap between slogans and immediately achievable political reality, such slogans were quite often echoed without any real political subscription.

For beyond the level of sloganeering in the streets, there is the fact of centuries of Kashmiri cultural history. One that is unique in the subcontinent. A history and lived life that tempers and inflects even those who would ordinarily be labelled hardliners. With crisis and violence, however, there is a certain hardening, perhaps even some acceptance, of the logic of religious difference, identity and politics. (And the issue of the Kashmiri Pandits, while linked to this, is a topic that needs separate, detailed attention.)

Take, for instance, the rise of Hamas in Palestine. It hasn't meant that Palestinian nationalism, avowedly secular, has turned Islamic, but that responding to the failure—internal, and also enforced by the total unacceptance of any real demands by the opposing side—of that secular leadership, the people voted a hardline faction into power, without necessarily sharing its religiously driven objectives. Similarly, the fact of a Geelani becoming the de facto acknowledged leader of the 'movement' (as it is called) in Kashmir is also due to the perception that he remained steadfast and incorruptible. His viewpoint may not be shared by all in some aspects, but he represents leadership for many.

The dominant form of Islam in Kashmir is Sufism—in its peculiar Kashmiri variety, the religiosity of the Muslims reflected in equal, if not more, measure in the countless Sufi shrines as in mosques. Real, hardcore, Taliban-style extremism is simply alien to, and untransplantable on, the Kashmiri DNA, as it were. A section among Muslims does exist which disapproves of some rituals in Sufi shrines. But that, in Kashmir, doesn't translate into a rejection of the Sufis themselves. Indeed, even the disapprovers hold the Sufis themselves in respect. In effect, then, the thought of the vast majority of Kashmiris 'changing over' to extremism is akin to asking someone to actually convert. An Islamic view of things exists in Kashmir, but it is just one of the viewpoints.

The drive to seek, invoke, an Islamization of Kashmir is insidiously linked to regurgitating, within Indian public opinion, the subcontinental history of Partition and the creation of Pakistan. It is also an act of dissolving the Kashmiris and electing the 'Muslim anti-national'. That done, Kashmir can be presented as once again reflecting the danger of that partition—which then becomes a major roadblock in even attempting to articulate to the wider Indian public what Kashmir is really about, leave alone seeking a solution to the problem.

This article first appeared in the *Economic Times*, 26 August 2010.

Spring seems to have ceased to be the season of life in Kashmir. The battles would intensify as the snows melt.

This spring of 2010 was stained by deaths of Kashmir's youngest generation.

Feb 2010. Wamiq Farooq killed in Srinagar by a police fear gas. Age 13

March 2010. Zahid Farooq killed in Srinagar when Border Security Force shot him after an argument. Age 16

A few months later in June, news came of three other murders.

Three young men disappeared in Kupwara district near the disputed border with Pakistan. A rare police investigation led to the arrest of a policeman, Bashir, who worked as an informer for the Indian army.

Bashir had lured the three young men on the pretext of getting them a labourer's job with the army.

He took them to meet an Army officer in a border village, Machil.

Bashir was asked to return with the three men, a few days later.

The army spokesperson announced their deaths as the "foreign terrorists killed in a gunbattle" on the border.

And then a Major, whose tour of Kashmir was ending and who seemed desperate to show some 'kills' which are needed for promotions, took them to the Line of Control and shot them there.

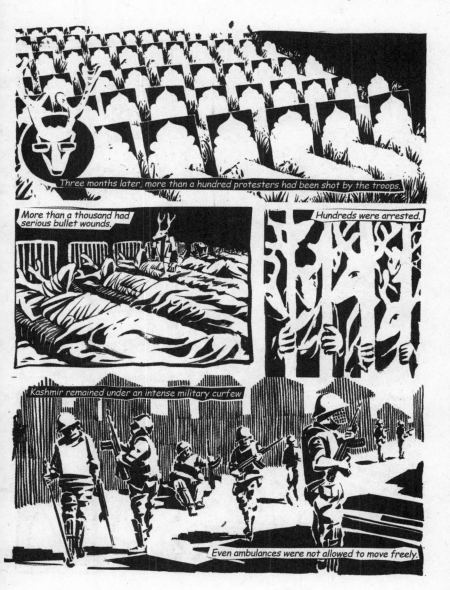

Three months later, more than a hundred protesters had been shot by the troops.

More than a thousand had serious bullet wounds.

Hundreds were arrested.

Kashmir remained under an intense military curfew

Even ambulances were not allowed to move freely.

The protesters flee

I joined the boys in the house a few streets away.

I am curious about their lives, their motivations, and their fear.

We talk. They speak in generalities about the abuses of civilians by Indian troops, about idea of justice, about excessive militarization, and about Kashmir desire for independence.

A little later, as the rants stop, a sense of melancholy pervades the room. They speak of what they have lived through. Young lives filled with grief, loss and violence.

Kashmir
A Time for Freedom

Angana Chatterji

'Freedom' represents many things across rural and urban spaces in India-ruled Kashmir. These divergent meanings are steadfastly united in that freedom *always* signifies an end to India's authoritarian governance.

In the administration of brutality, India, the post-colony, has proven itself equal to its former colonial masters. Kashmir is not about 'Kashmir'. Governing Kashmir is about India's coming of age as a power, its ability to disburse violence, to manipulate and dominate. Kashmir is about nostalgia, about resources, and buffer zones. The possession of Kashmir by India renders an imaginary past real, emblematic of India's triumphant unification as a nation-state. Controlling Kashmir requires that Kashmiri demands for justice be depicted as threatening to India's integrity. India's contrived enemy in Kashmir is a plausible one—the Muslim 'Other', India's historically manufactured nemesis.

What is at stake?

Between 11 June and 22 September 2010, Kashmir witnessed the execution of 109 youth, men and women by India's police, paramilitary and military. Indian forces opened fire on crowds, tortured children, detained elders without explanation, and coerced false confessions. Since 7 June, there have been seventy-three days of curfew and seventy-five days of strikes and agitation. On 11 September, the day of Eid-ul-Fitr, the violence continued. The paramilitary and police verbally abused and physically attacked civil society dissenters. Summer 2010 was not unprecedented. Kashmir has been subjected to much, much worse.

The use of public and summary execution for civic torture has been held necessary to Kashmir's subjugation by the Indian state. Militarization has asserted vigilante jurisdiction over space and politics. The violence is staged, ritualistic, and performative, used to re-assert India's power over Kashmir's body. The fabrications of the military—fake encounters, escalating perceptions of cross-border threat—function as the truth-making apparatus of the nation. We are witness to the paradox of history, as calibrated punishment—the lynching of the Muslim body, the object of criminality—enforces submission of a stateless nation (Kashmir) to the once-subaltern post-colony (India).

Kashmir is about the spectacle. The Indian state's violence functions as an intervention, to discipline and punish, to provoke and dominate. The summer of 2010 evidenced India's manoeuvring against Kashmir's determination to decide its future. The use of violence by the Indian forces was deliberate, their tactics cruel and precise, amidst the groundswell of public dissent. This was the third summer, since 2008, of indefatigable civil society uprisings for 'Azadi' (freedom).

What is the Indian state hoping to achieve? One, that Kashmiris would submit to India's domination, forsaking their claim to separation from India (to be an independent state or, for some, to be assimilated with Pakistan), or their demand for full autonomy. Or, that provoked, grief-stricken, and weary, Kashmiris would take up arms once again, giving India the opportunity to fortify its propaganda that Kashmiri civil society dissent against Indian rule is nurtured and endorsed today by external forces and groups in Pakistan and Afghanistan. If the latter transpires, India will manipulate this to neutralize Kashmiri demands for de-militarization and conflict resolution, to extend its annexation of Kashmir, and further normalize civic and legal states of exception.

If India succeeds in both provoking local armed struggle and linking Kashmiri resistance to foreign terror, it will acquire international sanction to continue its government of Kashmir on grounds of 'national security', and will 'have proof' that Kashmiris are not organically debating India's government of them, but are pressurized into it by external forces. India can then reinforce its armed forces in Kashmir, presently 671,000 strong, to prolong the killing spree.

Such provocation as policy is a mistake. Such legitimation of military rule will produce intractable conflict and violence. All indications are that Kashmiri civil society dissent will not abate. It is not externally motivated, but historically compelled.

Dominant nation-states overlook that freedom struggles are not adherent to the moralities of violence versus non-violence, but reflect a desire to be free.

Dominant nation-states forget that the greater the oppression, the more fervent the resistance. The greater the violence, the more likely the provocation to counter-violence.

Whether dissent in Kashmir turns into organized armed struggle—or continues as mass-based peaceful resistance—is dependent upon India's political decisions. If India's subjugation persists, it is conceivable that the movement for non-violent dissent, mobilized since 2004, will erode. Signs indicate that it is already slightly threadbare. It is conceivable that India's brutality will induce Kashmiri youth to close the distance between stones and petrol bombs, or more. If India fails to act, if Pakistan acts only in its self-interest, and if the international community does not insist on an equitable resolution to the Kashmir dispute, it is conceivable that, forsaken by the world, Kashmiris will be compelled to take up arms again.

Misogynist groups such as the Lashkar-e-Toiba, Al-Qaeda, or the Taliban are mercenaries looking for takers in Kashmir. By the Indian state's record, there are between 500–700 militants in the

Kashmir Valley today. These groups have not been successful because Kashmiris have been disinterested in alliances with them, and not because the Indian Army is successful in controlling them. This time, an armed mobilization by Kashmiris would include an even stronger mass movement than that which occurred between 1990 and 2004–07, led by youth whose lives have been shaped by the two-decade-long violence of militarization.

Who wants that? Can the South Asian subcontinent, already nuclearized, survive that? India is accountable to keep this from happening. Not through the use of unmitigated force, but through listening to the demands for change made by Kashmiris.

Will to power

This summer, India's violence on Kashmir was threaded through with strategic calculation. The police, military, and paramilitary have, without provocation, brutalized widespread peaceable protests across Kashmir that were dissenting against the suppression of civil society by Indian forces. Hostile Indian forces acted with the knowledge and sanction of the government of India and the government of Jammu and Kashmir. The repeated repression by state forces provoked civilians, whose political means of expression and demands have been systematically denied, to engage in stone pelting. The conditions of militarization prompted them to be in non-compliance with declared, undeclared and unremitting curfews. In instances, civilians engaged in acts of violence, including arson.

Each instance of civilian violence was provoked by the unmitigated and first use of force on civilians and/or extra-judicial killings on the part of Indian forces. Peaceable civilian protests by women and men opposed the actions of the Indian forces. Individuals, caught in the midst of the unrest, or mourning the death of a civilian, were fired upon by the Indian forces, leading to further killings by the Indian forces, more civilian protests, greater use of force by the police and paramilitary, torture, and more state repression.

In the summer of 2010, dominant discourse focused on the use of stone-pelting and on the instances of violence by the youth in Kashmir as the reason for armed action on the part of the state. Indian Prime Minister Manmohan Singh focused on the need for efficient tactics in 'crowd control'. India's elite intelligentsia, inculcated into 'rational' conduct, and no longer outraged by suffering, assessed the costs and benefits of militaristic violence.

Civil society demonstrations in Kashmir are not a law and order problem, as they have been reported. Stone-pelting, and incidents of arson and violence, are not causal to the violence that is routine in Kashmir today. Stone-pelting does not seek to kill, and has not resulted in death. Pro-freedom leaders (termed 'separatists' by the Indian state) have emphasized non-violent civil disobedience, and have appealed to civil society to not engage in violent protests in reaction to the violence and killings by the Indian forces.

Indian potentates disregard the fact that suppression acts to catalyse the resistance movement in Kashmir. The government of India continues to monitor the resistance movement, shifting the boundaries of acceptable practice of civil liberties. Kashmiris are allowed to protest in New Delhi, while in Kashmir sloganeering ('Go India, Go Back', 'Indian Dogs Go Home', 'Quit Kashmir') is met with force. When Masarat Alam Bhat, a rising pro-freedom leader, issued an appeal to Indian soldiers in July to 'Quit Kashmir', Indian authorities banned its circulation.

Acts of violence by protesting civilians increased as military violence continued. On 13 September, crowds in Kashmir torched a Christian missionary school and some government offices while protesting the call to desecrate the Qur'an by Florida Pastor Terry Jones. On 13 September, eighteen civilians were killed by the Indian forces in Kashmir (a police officer also died). Provocation is easy in a context of sustained brutality. Provoking Kashmiri dissenters to violence serves to confirm the dominant story of Muslims as 'violent'. Even as several pro-freedom leaders condemned the attack on the Christian school and renewed their call for non-violent dissent.

On 13 September, the government of India stated its willingness to engage with Kashmiri groups that reject violence. New Delhi did not apply the same precondition to itself. Nor did it acknowledge that pro-freedom groups have repeatedly opposed the use of violence in recent years.

The Kashmiri Muslim is caricatured as violent by India's dominant political and media apparatus. There is a refusal to recognize the inequitable historical-political power relations at play between Muslim-prevalent Kashmir's governance by Hindu-dominant India. The depiction of the Muslim, as 'Other' and barbaric, reveals the xenophobia of the Indian state. Distinctions in method and power, between stone-pelter and armed soldier, between 'terrorist' and 'freedom fighter', are inconvenient.

The Indian state's discourse is animated by the prejudice that Kashmiri inclinations to violence are subsidized by Pakistan. Such misconceptions ignore that while Kashmiris did travel to Pakistan to seek arms training, such activity was largely confined to the early days of the armed militancy, around the late 1980s through the mid-1990s. Pathologies of 'violent Muslims' legitimize the discursive and physical violence of the Indian 'security' forces, which is presented as necessary protection for the maintenance of the Hindu majoritarian Indian nation.

I have spent considerable time between July 2006 and July 2010 learning about Kashmir, working in Kashmir. In undertaking the work of the International People's Tribunal on Human Rights and Justice in Indian-administered Kashmir, I have travelled across Kashmir's cities and countryside, from Srinagar to Kupwara, through Shopian and Islamabad (Anantnag), with Parvez Imroz, Zahir-Ud-Din, and Khurram Parvez. I have witnessed the violence that is perpetrated on Kashmiris by India's military, paramilitary, and police. I have walked through the graveyards that hold Kashmir's dead, and have met with grieving families. I have sat with witnesses, young men, who described how Indian forces chased down and executed their friends for participating in civil disobedience. I have met women whose sons had 'disappeared'. I have met with 'half-widows'. I have spoken with youth, women and men, who are enraged. I have also spoken with persons who were violated by militants in the 1990s. Peoples' experiences with the reprehensible atrocities of militancy do not imply the abdication of their desires for self-determination. The Indian state deliberately conflates militancy with the people's mass movement for liberation.

I have met with torture survivors, non-militants and former militants, who testified to the sadism of the forces. Men who had petrol injected through the anus. Water-boarding, mutilation, being paraded naked, rape of women, children and men, starvation, humiliation, and psychological torture. An eagle tattoo on the arm of a man was reportedly identified by an army officer as a symbol of Pakistan-held Azad Kashmir, even as the man clarified that the tattoo was from his childhood. The skin bearing it was burned. The officer said, the man recalled, 'When you look at this, think of Azadi'. A mother, reportedly compelled to watch her daughter's rape by army personnel, pleaded for her release. They refused. She then pleaded that she could not watch, asking to be sent out of the room or be killed. The soldier pointed a gun to her forehead, stating he would grant her wish, and shot her dead before they proceeded to rape the daughter.

Who are the forces? Disenfranchised caste and other groups, Assamese, Nagas, Sikhs, Dalits (the erstwhile 'untouchable' peoples), and Muslims from Kashmir, are being used to combat Kashmiris. Why did thirty-four soldiers commit suicide in Kashmir in 2008, and fifty-two fratricidal killings take place between 21 January 2004 and 14 July 2009? Why did sixteen soldiers commit suicide and two die in fratricidal killings between January and early August 2010?

Laws authorize soldiers to question, raid houses, detain and arrest without charge-sheets, and prolong incarceration without due process. They blur distinctions between military/paramilitary, 'legality'/'illegality'. Citing 'national security', Indian forces in Kashmir shoot and kill on uncorroborated suspicion, with impunity from prosecution. Yet, revoking the Armed Forces Special Powers

Act, for example, will not stop the horror in Kashmir. India's laws are not the primary contention. India's political and military existence in Kashmir is the issue. Legal impunity is the cover for the moral impunity of Indian rule.

Is the military willing to withdraw from Kashmir? Since 2002, the government of India has procured five billion US dollars in weaponry from the Israeli state. Authoritarian alliances between once-subjugated peoples mark another irony of history. Five billion dollars is a colossal sum for India, where 38 per cent of the world's poor reside. Eight of the poorest states in India are more impoverished than the twenty-six poorest countries of the African continent. Five billion dollars, in addition to the other monies and resources invested in the militarization of Kashmir, do not evidence an intent to withdraw.

Human rights violations in Kashmir will not stop without removing the military. The military cannot be removed without surgically rupturing India's will to power over Kashmir.

Inflexible diplomacy

India needs to make the 'Kashmir problem' disappear. India's diplomacy is directed toward assuming a role as a world power, a world market, and a world negotiator in global politics. India is also seeking a seat on the United Nations Security Council.

What constitutes India's dialogue with Kashmiris in conditions of extreme subjugation? The government of India has scheduled a hurried timeframe in propelling Track II diplomacy into success, to secure a proposal for resolution that is acceptable to India and Pakistan, and, ostensibly, to Kashmiris. The terms of reference set by New Delhi exclude discussions of self-determination or heightened autonomy, boundary negotiations, the Siachen glacier and critical water resources, and renegotiations of the Line of Control.

New Delhi and Islamabad appear to be in collusion. If Pakistan overlooks India's annexation of Jammu and Kashmir, India would be willing to forget Pakistan's occupation of another fragment of Kashmir. The Musharraf Formula is no longer acceptable to the government of Pakistan. Afghanistan is the current priority, not Kashmir. Conversations on the phased withdrawal of troops by India and Pakistan at the border, local self-government, and the creation of a joint supervision mechanism in Jammu and Kashmir, involving India, Pakistan and Kashmir, are at an impasse.

The government in New Delhi is looking to neutralize Kashmir's demand for self-determination or unabridged autonomy, pushing forward a diluted 'autonomy', seeking to assimilate Kashmir with finality into the Indian nation-state. New Delhi is seeking a buy-in, which it hopes to push through using the collaborator coterie in Srinagar. Local self-government would be New Delhi's compromise—a weak autonomy—with a joint supervisory apparatus constituted of India, Pakistan and Kashmir.

New Delhi hopes that the Kashmiri leadership, including pro-freedom groups, can be restrained, for a price, and weakened through infighting. Certain segments of the pro-freedom leadership have, through history, lacked vision, honesty and the ability to prioritize collaboration for justice and peace in Kashmir. Certain segments of the religious and political leadership have been unable to collaborate meaningfully with civil society, with devout Muslims and less devout ones, and with non-Muslims. The spiritual commitment to justice in the Islamic tradition has receded as religious determinations embrace instrumental political rationality. The determination of what 'freedom' is has been deferred since 1931; instead there has been a focus on immediate and small political gains.

This has plagued and rendered ineffectual, segments of the complex Hurriyat alliance in the present, which is often unable to capitalize on the exuberant people's movement on the streets and pathways of Kashmir. Segments of the pro-freedom leadership have focused on New Delhi rather than Kashmiri civil society. New Delhi has fixated on enabling this dynamic, using vast resources to create a collaborator class in Srinagar that undermines the will of the Kashmiri people.

While Pakistan's politicians have pointed to India's injustices, they have not reciprocally addressed issues in the management of Pakistan-held Kashmir, including the deflation of movements for the unification of Kashmir. The crisis of state in Pakistan, and the role of its ruling elite in vitiating people's democratic processes, remains a pitfall for regional security.

The logic that Muslim-prevalent Kashmir must stay with secular India or join Muslim-dominated Pakistan is configured by India's and Pakistan's internal ideological needs and identity politics. Neither is inevitable. Neither speak to the foremost aspiration of Kashmiris.

The government of India's 'inclusive dialogue' this summer has systematically disregarded Kashmiri civil society demands, thrusting a violent peace brokered by New Delhi's agents of change. New Delhi has invited various Kashmiri stakeholders from civil society as well. Their articulations, however, have not shifted the agenda, even as bringing people to the table is used to legitimize India's visage of inclusivity.

What do the majority of Kashmiris want? First, to secure a good faith agreement with New Delhi and Islamabad regarding the right of Kashmiris to determine the course of their future, set a timeframe, and define the interim conditions necessary to proceed. Following which, civil society and political leaders would ensure processes to educate, debate and consult civil society, including minority groups, in sketching the terms of reference for a resolution, prior to negotiations with India and Pakistan.

Significantly, pro-freedom leader Syed Ali Shah Geelani's statement of 31 August sought to shift the terms of engagement, not requiring the precondition of self-determination or the engagement of Pakistan. Unless New Delhi responds, the protests in Kashmir will continue. Geelani's statement, supported by the All Parties Hurriyat Conference leader Mirwaiz Umar Farooq, testifies to this. The mood in the streets testifies to this.

New Delhi's current approach repudiates what Kashmiris want. The omissions made by New Delhi are roadblocks to constituting a minimum agenda for justice and an enduring and relevant peace process.

The government of India's 'inclusive dialogue' this summer does *not* recognize Kashmir as an international dispute.

The government of India's 'inclusive dialogue' this summer does *not* include: an immediate halt to, and moratorium on, extrajudicial killings by the Indian military, paramilitary and police; an immediate halt to, and moratorium on, the use of torture, kidnapping, enforced disappearance and gendered violence by the Indian military, paramilitary and police; a plan for the release of political prisoners, the return of those exiled, and contending with the issue of displacement; agreements on an immediate 'soft border' policy between Kashmir, India and Pakistan, to enable the resurgence of Kashmir's political economy; agreements to non-interference in the exercise of civil liberties of Kashmiris, including the right to civil disobedience, and freedom of speech, assembly, religion, movement and travel. New Delhi has refused to acknowledge the extent of human rights violations, and how they are integral to maintaining dominion. New Delhi has not explained why militarization in Kashmir has been disproportionately used to brutalize Kashmiris, when ostensibly the Indian forces are in Kashmir to secure the border zones.

The government of India's 'inclusive dialogue' this summer does *not* include a plan for the proactive demilitarization and the immediate revocation of all authoritarian laws. Nor does it include: a plan for the transparent identification and dismantling of detention and torture centres, including in army camps; a plan for the installation of a Truth and Justice Commission for political and psychosocial reparation, and for reckoning loss; a plan for the international and transparent investigations into unknown and mass graves constitutive of crimes against humanity committed by the Indian military, paramilitary and police. Such omissions are a travesty of any process promising 'resolution'.

Islamophobia and realpolitik

New Delhi has been the self-appointed arbitrator in determining the justifications of Kashmir's claims to freedom. Kashmir's claims are historically unique and bona fide. History—the United Nations Resolutions of 1948, Nehru's promise of plebiscite (to rethink the temporary accession determined by the Hindu-descent maharaja, Hari Singh), Article 370 of the Indian Constitution—is jettisoned by an amnesic India. Official nationalism seeks to rewrite history, affixing Kashmir to India, to overwrite memory. Within the battlefields of knowledge/power, official 'truth' becomes the contagion sustaining cultures of repression and mass atrocity, creating cultures of grief.

The Indian state is apprehensive that any change in the status quo in Kashmir will foster internal crises of gigantic proportions in India. Across the nation there is considerable discontent, as dreams and difference are mortgaged to the idea of India fabricated by the elite. Adivasis, Dalits, disenfranchised caste groups, women, religious, ethnic and gender minorities are fatigued by the nation's deferred promises. Forty-four million Adivasis have been displaced since 1947. Central India is torn asunder, and as Maoists are designated as the latest 'national threat', national memory forgets the systematic brutalization of peoples in the tribal belt that led to a call to arms. Then there is the North-East, Punjab, the massacre of Muslims in Narendra Modi's Gujarat, riots against Christians in Orissa, farmer suicides, the plight of peasants and Adivasis of the Narmada valley where dams are not the 'temples of India', but its burial grounds. Kashmir cannot remain India's excuse to avoid dealing with its own internal matters.

Indian civil society decries that Kashmir is not deserving of autonomy or separation, as it, as an assumed Islamist state, would be a threat to India's democracy. To assume that a Muslim-majority state in Kashmir will be ruled by Islamist extremists in support of global terror reflects majoritarian India's racism. Dominant Indian (left-oriented) civil society must rethink its characterization of Kashmiri civil society as prevalently *'Jamaati'*. *Jamaat* is Arabic for assembly. 'Jamaati' is used by Indian civil society to imply Islamist or fundamentalist. The reference can often be translated as Muslim = Jamaati, and Muslim-devout = fundamentalist.

Indians of Hindu descent largely overlook that India's democracy is infused with Hindu cultural dominance. Indian civil society assumes that Islam and democracy are incompatible, supported by the inflamed Islamophobia in the polities of the West. Importantly, India forgets that in its own history with the British, freedom fighters had noted that the oppressor cannot adjudge when a stateless people are 'deserving' of freedom.

Freedom is fundamentally an experiment with risks that Kashmiris must be willing to take. The global community must support them in making such risks ethical. Jammu and Kashmir is a Muslim-majority space. The population of India-held Kashmir was recorded at approximately 6,900,000 in 2008, of which Muslims are approximately 95 per cent. Kashmir's future as a democratic, inclusive and pro-secular space is linked to what happens within India and Pakistan.

Kashmiris who wish to be separate from India and Pakistan must assess the difficult alliances yet to be built between Kashmir, Jammu and Ladakh, and between Muslims and Hindu Pandits, Dogra Hindus, Buddhists, Sikhs, Christians, indigenous groups and others. Then, there is the question of what lies ahead between Indian-held Kashmir and Pakistan-held Kashmir. Minority groups, such as Kashmiri Pandits, must refuse the Indian state's hyper-nationalist strategy in using the Pandit community to create opposition between Muslims and Hindus in Kashmir, as part of a strategy to bring religion into the issue and govern through communalization.

Where is the international community on the issue of Kashmir? In present history, Palestine, Ireland, Tibet and Kashmir share correspondence. In Tibet, 1.2 million died (1949–79), and 320,000 were made refugees. In Ireland, 3,710 have died (1969–2010). For

Israel, the occupation of Palestine has resulted in 10,148 dead (1987–2010), with 4.7 million refugees registered with the United Nations (1987–2008). In Kashmir, 70,000 are dead, over 8,000 have been disappeared, and 250,000 have been displaced (1989–2010).

During British Prime Minister David Cameron's recent visit to India, he was asked to refrain from bringing up the 'K' word. United States' President Barack Obama's proposed visit to New Delhi in November 2010 is already laden with prohibitions. India's rule in Kashmir and its larger human rights record are among them. Right-wing Hindu advocacy groups have been successful in securing the silence of many on Capitol Hill on the issue of Kashmir. The Kashmiri diaspora has been partly effective in bringing visibility to the issue, even as the community remains ideologically and politically fragmented. International advocates have propagated an 'economic' approach to 'normalcy'. This avoids the fact that militarization impacts every facet of life, making economic development outside of political change impossible.

The United States and United Kingdom have debated the reasons for their involvement in Kashmir. In 2010, as of 23 September, 351 soldiers from the United States have died in Afghanistan, while the United Kingdom sustained ninety-two fatalities. Of paramount concern for both is bringing their forces home without compromising the principles of NATO (North Atlantic Treaty Organization) operations in the region. To accomplish this would require that Pakistan move sizeable forces from the Indo-Kashmir-Pak border to the Af-Pak frontier. This cannot be done without cessation in Indo-Pak hostilities, which cannot be achieved without the resolution of the Kashmir dispute. However, Kashmir's resolution cannot mean a sanction to Pakistan's encroachment on Afghanistan, which, given the political situation in the region, remains a highly likely possibility. For the United States and India, the containment of China is another issue, also linked to Kashmir.

Kashmiris in Kashmir are caught amidst world events and regional machinations, and the unresolved histories of the subcontinent. The Indian state's military governance penetrates every facet of life. The sounds of war haunt *mohallas*. The hyper-presence of the military forms a graphic shroud over Kashmir: detention and interrogation centres, army cantonments, abandoned buildings, bullet-holes, bunkers and watchtowers, detour signs, deserted public squares, armed personnel, counter-insurgents, and vehicular and electronic espionage. Armed control regulates and governs bodies. It has been reported that, since 1990, Kashmir's economy has incurred a reported loss of more than 1,880,000 million Indian rupees (40.4 billion US dollars). The immensity of psychosocial losses is impossible to calculate. The conditions of everyday life are in peril. They elicit suffocating anger and despair, telling a story of the web of violence in which civil society in Kashmir is interned.

For India, constituting a coherent national collective has required multiple wars on difference. National governance determines territory and belonging, disenfranchising subaltern claims. Local struggles for self-determination are brutalized to reproduce obedient national collectives. Systemic acts of oppression chart a history, as relations of power are choreographed by nation-states in the suppression of others. Massacre, 'gendercide', genocide, occupation, all function within a continuum of tactics in negation/annihilation.

India's relation to Kashmir is not about Kashmir. Kashmir's aversion to being subsumed by the Indian state is not reducible to history. If violence breaks lives, Kashmir is quite broken. If oppression produces resistance, Kashmir is profusely resistant. From the writings of Michel Foucault to Achille Mbembe, and so much in-between, we are reminded of the myriad techniques in governance that seek to subjugate, while naming subjugation as subject formation, as protection, 'security', law and order, and progress.

Realpolitik triumphs against a backdrop of persistent refusal. Through summer heat and winter snow, across interminable stretches of concertina wire, broken windowpanes, walls, barricades, and check-points, the dust settles to rise again. The agony of loss. The desecration of life. Kashmir's spiritual fatalities are staggering. The dead are not forgotten. Remembrance and mourning are habitual practices of dissent. 'We are not free. But we know freedom', KP tells me. 'The movement is our freedom. Our dreams are our freedom. The Indian state cannot take that away. Our resistance will live.'

This article first appeared in *Greater Kashmir*, Srinagar, 25 September 2010, and later on the website http://www.countercurrents.org.

Kashmir's Anonymous Graves Summon Darkest Days

Tim Sullivan

He left home on a rainy Wednesday morning, walking through the gate of his solid middle-class house and into the narrow streets of Srinagar, Kashmir's largest city. He needed to pick up some medicine for his elderly father.

It was the summer of 1996. Ali Mohammad Mir was forty years old, a gentle-spoken building contractor and a father of three. In the lush Himalayan valley savaged by cycles of guerrilla attacks and government crackdowns, a place where politics and violence almost always went together, he was utterly apolitical. Desperately non-political.

His family never saw him again.

Here, in this quiet mountain village about sixty miles away, is where Mir may have ended up, in a grave marked only by a mound of dirt, surrounded by the graves of hundreds of other unidentified men. Or perhaps he's in the cluster of unmarked graves in the forests of Parra–Gagarhill, or among the bodies buried in the cow pasture in the village of Kichama. 'He is out there somewhere,' said Mir's son, Zahoor Ahmad Mir. He has spent years researching his father's final hours, and now believes he was killed by some militia tied to the Indian Army. 'They killed him and they threw him aside. Now he is buried somewhere. He must be.'

Dozens of these anonymous burial fields have been identified by human rights workers over the past eighteen months, nameless graveyards where Indian security forces dumped nearly 2,400 nameless corpses.

In a region struggling to emerge from two decades of violence that have left 68,000 people dead, the graveyards have deeply shaken Kashmir, digging up memories of the estimated 8,000 people who disappeared at the height of the militancy. At a time when support for separatist violence has waned, and many Kashmiris have become more focused on jobs than politics, the graveyards brought waves of renewed anger against the government. Days of rioting broke out after rights workers released the first list of burial fields.

The graves have also become constant reminders that while violence is less, it is far from over. Bodies have been buried as recently as the past few months. 'There is no place in Kashmir where innocent blood has not been spilled,' said Zarif Ahmad Zarif, a Kashmiri poet. But who were the dead? Security officials dismiss them as Muslim militants killed in gun battles and some, certainly, were fighters. But rights workers say most were innocent civilians who fell into the maw of the security forces.

They were young men grabbed for their money or killed to settle personal scores. Some were mistaken for militants by terrified Indian soldiers. Indian security forces are largely shielded from prosecutions by a thicket of emergency laws, and while there have been a small handful of investigations, most of the disappearances may never be explained. Two decades after the insurgency broke out, only a tiny fraction have been accounted for.

The bodies themselves give a few clues. According to villagers ordered by police to bury them, they are often of particular sorts: there is blood and shattered bones where they are shot, or they are burned beyond recognition. Many show signs of beatings. At one cemetery, police told villagers they would bring seven bodies for burials. They brought seven heads.

'This is a hidden issue here,' said Pervez Imroz, the Kashmiri lawyer who helped prepare the reports and whose teams are scouring Kashmir for more graveyards. He has repeatedly urged an official probe, but to no avail. 'They can't hold this investigation because it will cause a huge embarrassment to the Indian state.'

Security officials declined to comment on the graveyards. Outside of Kashmir, in the Indian Parliament and media, the graves get barely any attention. Omar Abdullah, the state's top elected official, would only say: 'It's being looked into.' Mir's eldest son doubts that.

Zahoor Ahmad Mir's life has been consumed by his father's disappearance. Over the years he has spoken to witnesses, soldiers and thugs. He has filed dozens of legal requests. Slowly, a story took shape. He says his father was grabbed off the street by a Kashmiri militia often used by the Indian military to target civilians. The son has no idea why it happened—perhaps it was a mistake, perhaps an extortion attempt, but the elder Mir was beaten, driven out of the city and finally hanged from a tree behind an army base.

Officially, though, none of that happened. Instead, one day he simply ceased to exist.

'I don't care much about justice any more,' said the son, his connection to his father reduced to a worn plastic bag stuffed with court documents, fading newspaper clippings and tattered photocopies. 'I don't think justice can happen here. I just want my father's body.'

Kashmir has a long experience with violence. A mountainous region of pine-covered hills, apple orchards and rushing rivers, Kashmir—the only majority Muslim state in a largely Hindu India—is divided between India and Pakistan but claimed by both.

In 1989, its nightmare began after rigged state elections ignited a separatist insurgency which, in turn, provoked brutal military crackdowns. India began accusing Pakistan of supporting the militants with money, training and weaponry, a charge Pakistan denies.

The fighting savaged Kashmir. Tens of thousands of people were killed, many of them civilians. The economy withered. Unemployment soared. But the past few years have seen the beginnings of change. First came 11 September 2001, and pressure on Islamabad to rein in Kashmiri militants on its soil. Then in 2003, India and Pakistan launched a peace effort that, despite many stumbles, helped mend relations to some extent. Finally, politically minded Kashmiris, wearied by the relentless bloodshed, began shifting focus away from militant violence. Over the past two years, massive protests—with violence usually limited to stone-throwing—have filled the streets of the region's cities, a reflection of both enduring anger with India and exhaustion with the insurgency.

The result: deaths connected to the insurgency dropped from 4,507 in 2001 to 541 last year. Today, Kashmir sways regularly between brutal violence and its own strange version of normalcy. Srinagar now boasts clusters of new McMansions with mirrored windows and cavernous living rooms. It has a Reebok store and coffee bars serving cappuccinos. For the first time in years tourists are commonplace.

Across Kashmir, cities and villages no longer slam shut at sunset. And yet . . .

The new Srinagar airport might boast soaring ceilings and cellphone kiosks, but it is also ringed by grim soldiers cradling automatic weapons. The state's opposition leader had a new official residence until recently—a feared military torture centre known as Papa-II. And while weeks can pass without major guerrilla attacks, sometimes a half-dozen Kashmiri villages are shaken by gun battles in one day.

Across Kashmir, more than 7,00,000 members of India's security forces remain on guard.

If support for the insurgency has withered, the Indian soldiers are still widely detested. Perhaps nowhere more than in the villages forced to bury the dead.

Atta Mohammed knows all about the nameless dead. The

seventy-year-old Bimyar farmer has buried 235 of them. He knows their bruises and their bullet wounds. He knows if they were burned so badly their mothers would not recognize them.

'I took mud from their mouths and ears. I cleaned the blood from them,' said Atta, a quiet man with rotting teeth and a neatly trimmed white beard. About twelve years ago, police began bringing bodies to be buried in a small empty field. They stopped only when there was no more room. All that time, Mohammed cared for the dead.

'The bodies started coming and coming and coming,' he said. 'Sometimes there were five bodies at once. Sometimes eight bodies.' 'We would ask the authorities: "Who are they?"' he continued, showing a visitor around the cemetery. 'They would just say: "They are militants."'

Then, as he always does when he visits the graveyard, he prays. He stands in the shadow of a mountain range speckled with pines and reaches out his hands in supplication. And his murmuring scatters across the graves.

This article was first published by the Associated Press, 6 December 2009.

The Wounds of Kashmir's Never-ending War

Ravi Nessman

The wounds of Kashmir's never-ending war are reflected in Arshid Malik's red, downcast eyes, in the tremble of the cigarette in his hand, in the self-inflicted knife scars gouged into his left forearm. Tormented by unrelenting memories of death and violence, he tried thirteen times to end his pain with suicide, sometimes slicing open his wrists, at other times swallowing fistfuls of pills, he said.

'I was crying inside, but there was nobody I could talk to because everyone was grieving,' the thirty-six-year-old said.

More than two decades of brutal warfare between largely Muslim separatist insurgents and largely Hindu Indian troops in this Himalayan region have left Kashmiris exhausted, traumatized and broken. The rate of suicide, once unthinkable in this Islamic society, has gone up twenty-six-fold, from 0.5 per 100,000 before the insurgency to 13 per 100,000 now, according to Dr Arshad Hussain, a Kashmiri psychiatrist. Drug abuse is epidemic. Depression, stress and mental illness are rampant. 'Directly or indirectly, everyone is suffering,' said Dr Muzafer Khan, who runs a small rehab clinic in Srinagar, the main city in the part of Kashmir controlled by India.

One man turned to drugs after seeing an uncle and two cousins shot in front of him; another became an addict after he was kidnapped by pro-government militia, Khan said. A third-grader wouldn't go back to school for two years after he watched gunmen break into his classroom, tie up his teacher and shoot him, another doctor said. Villagers accustomed to late-night searches by security forces have developed 'midnight knock syndrome' and are so jumpy they can't sleep without pills, Khan said.

For more than sixty years, the stunning Kashmir Valley has been a flashpoint for tensions and wars between rivals India and Pakistan, both controlling part of it and laying claim to all of it. Despite the fierce fighting, the tight-knit Muslim families of Kashmir formed a durable safety net. That fell apart when a separatist insurgency erupted in 1989. Children were caught in the crossfire between Muslim separatists and the pro-Indian government militia. Others were forced into informing on their families. Parents disappeared in the middle of the night, many into mass graves where their bodies were never identified.

An estimated 68,000 people were killed. Nearly every one of the Valley's six million people has been touched by violence. The conflict has created two lost generations—the teenagers of 1989 who saw their childhoods collapse into civil war, and the teenagers of today who never had a childhood at all.

About 19 per cent of Kashmiris suffer from depression, said Dr Mushtaq Margoob, a psychiatrist who has done extensive studies on trauma in Kashmir. Nearly 16 per cent have post-traumatic stress disorder. In the US, less than 7 per cent of adults suffer from depression and 3.5 per cent have post-traumatic stress disorder, according to the National Institute of Mental Health. 'They see someone get killed in their presence, some friend, some relative, and they get stuck in that moment,' Margoob said.

Kashmir's mental health network is overwhelming. Before the conflict, Margoob and other doctors at the psychiatric hospital in Srinagar saw 1,700 patients a year; now they see 100,000, he said. A newly opened psychiatric ward in a nearby hospital sees another 40,000. One-third of Kashmiris questioned in a 2006 Doctors

Without Borders survey said they had thought of killing themselves in the previous month. Most said they were nervous, tense or worried, were easily frightened and suffered from trembling hands. Nearly half had trouble sleeping and cried more than usual.

Children, inured to the violence, have become angry, aggressive and helpless, said Margoob. Worse, they don't fear death. It is this generation that picked up rocks in violent protests this summer, ignoring a crackdown by security forces that has killed more than fifty people. There is a complete breakdown of the social fabric, said Dr Wiqar Bashir, who is haunted by the nine-year-old he was unable to revive after the boy hanged himself four months ago. Children that young are simply not supposed to think about suicide, he said.

Drug abuse has become widespread. Kashmir, a traditional centre for mystical Sufi Islam, has a long history of opium and marijuana use in cultural practices. But now many are addicted to smoking heroin and hash, while others are taking codeine-laced cough syrup and prescription opiates from the rash of unregulated pharmacies that sell even morphine without a prescription. Teens regularly sniff glue, corrective liquid and even cooking gas. 'It's rampant here, it's really rampant,' said Bashir, who works at a small drug rehab centre in Srinagar that has seven beds and a waiting list of 150 people.

Ahmed Dar, twenty-five, came to the clinic last year, broken in mind and body. He had two crushed legs from a bus accident and convulsions from heroin withdrawal.

When he was seventeen, he had toyed with the idea of joining the insurgents for a month, but never picked up a gun. Then he went over to the side of the army and toyed with the idea of becoming an informant. He smoked hash and drank cough syrup to deal with the pressure, he said. When he met the militants again, they shot him three times in the arm and leg, sending him to the hospital for a month. Then a business setback sent him crashing into heroin addiction. 'Whenever I took the heroin, I never felt my wounds,' he said. 'I felt tremendous solace.'

With the help of the clinic, Dar has cleaned himself up. But Kashmir, which has only thirteen or fourteen psychiatrists in addition to a Doctors Without Borders therapy team, would need 200 psychiatrists and thousands of therapists to deal with the huge numbers suffering from trauma, doctors say. Malik, a Muslim, was fifteen when the fighting started. His school, run by Hindus who were largely seen as pro-government collaborators, shut down when the administrators fled. His Hindu friends ran as well. Check-points choked off his Srinagar neighbourhood. Gunfights broke out. Acquaintances got killed.

Then, on 20 January 1990, Indian paramilitary troops fired on a peaceful demonstration crossing the nearby Gawakadal Bridge, killing more than fifty people and sending thousands fleeing in terror past the teenaged Malik. 'People were running. Blood was rushing out. They were falling in the gutter. People were aghast. Women were crying,' he said. Malik wasn't physically wounded, but he would never recover. 'There was a deeper kind of hurt that passed onto me,' he said quietly, as his eyes welled up.

The ensuing years were filled with crackdowns on protesters, militant grenade attacks on government forces, and late-night police raids that forced his family and neighbours to sit in the winter cold for hours, 'not knowing what was going to happen next, and fearing,' he said. By the time he got to college, the playful, talkative boy who loved cricket and badminton had shut down. People were so busy burying the dead, tending to the wounded and trying to survive that no one paid attention to his suffering.

'It used to come in huge flows that would sweep me off,' he said. 'I used to think, let me get this over with.' One day as he studied quietly in his room, he swallowed hundred tranquillizers. His family got his stomach pumped. Three months later, he took more pills. Later he turned to knives. Some were serious attempts to end his pain; others were screams for attention, he said. His family and friends were furious. How could he be so selfish when so many were dying? His mother took him to a faith healer, who said he was cursed. His father burned his books, because he thought they were making it worse. Psychiatrists debated whether he was bipolar or borderline schizophrenic.

On the brink of being institutionalized, Malik decided he couldn't stand to cause his family any more pain. He suppressed his agony, got a job as a business executive, got married and had a son. But he suffers from headaches and stomach problems, and his emotional issues, though under control, remain unresolved, he said. 'I hardly talk to anybody about this,' he said. 'Nobody would be interested anyway.'

This article was first published by the Associated Press, 15 August 2010.

The False God of
Military Suppression

Gautam Navlakha

When post-colonial states deploy troops to bring a rebellious people, formally their 'own people', to submission, and hand over that area to the military, then in actual fact they act as an alien force. The relationship that ensues between the military force and the people is akin to that between a subject people and their imperial masters. The military force seeks to restore the authority of the state on a reluctant people, however long it takes to do so. When it comes to looking at such wars being fought amidst us there is a tendency to read them as somehow less than a war. The reason we do not perceive it as war is that it takes place within the borders of the nation-state, where the deployment of the armed forces of the union is somehow considered legitimate, even when it is engaged in suppressing our 'own' people.

The Indian Army's 'Doctrine of Sub-conventional Operations' asserts that sub-conventional operations have become 'the *predominant* form of warfare'. This doctrine conceptualizes the role of the armed forces personnel while fighting insurgency, or putting down rebellions within the borders of the nation-state. The doctrine says such operations are 'a generic term encompassing all armed conflict', and include 'militancy, insurgency, proxy war and terrorism that may be employed as a means in an insurrectionist

158

movement or undertaken independently' (p. 1). Therefore, the doctrine says, 'the military operations should aim firstly, at *neutralizing all hostile elements* in the conflict zone that oppose or retard the peace initiatives, and secondly, at *transforming the will and attitudes of the people* . . . The endeavour should be *to bring about a realization* that fighting the government is a "no win" situation and that their anti-government stance will only delay the return of peace and normalcy. Therefore, distancing from the terrorists is in their own interest and the only plausible course of action. However, the manifestation of *such a realization can take from a couple of years to decades as attitudes take time to form and to change*' (pp. 21–22) (emphasis added).

Remember, there is nothing non-violent about 'neutralizing hostile elements' or 'transforming the will and attitudes of the people': the latter more or less suggests a desire to break the will of the people. This type of warfare is a 'dirty war'. In this war casualties occur in the form now familiar to us: encounters, custodial killings, enforced disappearances, mortar shelling, search and cordon operations, arbitrary detentions, torture . . .

Apart from the regular units of the Indian Army, there is the army's counter-insurgency force, the Rashtriya Rifles (RR), the Border Security Force (BSF), the Central Reserve Police Force (CRPF) and several other paramilitary and state police forces. In a statement on the floor of the Jammu and Kashmir Assembly on 1 August 2006, the then deputy chief minister said that there were more than 6,67,000 security forces in the state. This is an incredibly high concentration of troops for an area whose total population is not more than ten million. In other words, the ratio of deployment is one soldier for every fourteen–fifteen people. By December 2010 their numbers would have been reduced by 40,000: that still leaves a force of 6,27,000.

More than half these soldiers belong to the Indian Army: on 17 June 2007 the general officer commanding-in-chief (GOC-in-C) of the northern command of the Indian Army, Lt General H.S. Panag, said while speaking with the press that there are 3,37,000 army personnel in Jammu and Kashmir. He tried to play this down by saying that only 25 per cent of this force was engaged in counter-insurgency, while 45–50 per cent were engaged in 'countering infiltration'. The rest, he said, were engaged in ensuring supply to the deployed soldiers. Given the Indian government's obsession with 'cross-border terrorism', countering infiltration must surely be seen as an integral part of counter-insurgency. And armies the world over traditionally retain 15–25 per cent of their troops to provide support to those deployed for combat. Support staff is needed when troops are fighting a war: they demit the area when the fighting force demits the area. In effect all the 3,37,000 army personnel were actually deployed in counter-insurgency operations.

Take a closer look at an example on the ground. The Pattan subdivision of Baramulla district of the Kashmir Valley has ninety-two villages. There are three police stations in the subdivision, at Pattan, Mirgund and Kreeri. But located among these ninety-two villages are four Indian Army brigade headquarters: Haiderbeig, Khaymbyar, Hamray and Tapper. There are twelve check-posts: those of the army and the RR are at Hamray, Malnah, Srwarpora, Tapper Bala, Tapper Pyein, Wangam Payech, Yadipora, Yakmanpora and Zangam. The CRPF mans Mirgund. Pattan and Babateng host camps of the CRPF, BSF and the special task force of the Jammu and Kashmir police. Each check-post has anywhere between 100 and 150 soldiers, although there are a few which have much larger numbers, sometimes over 300. Thus a cluster of roughly nine villages comes under one check-post. One brigade is available for operations covering twenty-three villages, whereas one police station caters to thirty-odd villages. Thus all movement to and from the village to fields, to market or town is monitored and accompanied by regular patrolling. The very nature of this deployment affects all the inhabitants. This is what occupation means in real terms: constant control over people's public and private lives.

Consider another example. The killing of two youths on 21

February 2009 at Bomai, Sopore, brought people out on the streets to lodge their protest. The army spokesperson, Colonel Uma Maheshwari, claimed that army jawans were not present on the scene and that 'some persons wearing army uniforms opened fire on the people'. The very same day the commanding officer 22 RR, Colonel Sanjeev, said that 'while jawans were searching the vehicle, two militants wearing pheran refused to alight from the vehicle. When troopers asked them to raise their hands, they opened fire, killing two persons' (*Economic Times*, 23 February 2009). The army subsequently stuck to this version, claiming that it fired only twenty rounds, although shells double that number were found. Protests by local people forced the state government to institute an inquiry. This state government report was presented relatively quickly, and the villagers were assured that the camp of the 22 RR would be 'relocated' within twelve days. But the Indian Army's response swiftly put paid to such proposals. Referring to the relocation of the camp, a senior officer of the northern command said on 6 March 2009 that a district commissioner has 'no domain over security issues and cannot dictate to us what to do' (*Greater Kashmir*, 7 March 2009). The army also refused to go by the investigations carried out by the civilian administration and refused to move against those responsible, saying it must complete its own independent investigation.

In the stand-off between the state government and the army, the chief minister had to persuade New Delhi to intervene. It became clear that the assurance given to inhabitants of Bomai by the state government about the 'relocation' of a security force camp meant little and that the authority to do so rested with New Delhi alone. Significantly, Bomai already has police and CRPF camps as well as four army camps nearby: one less would not have made much difference. Finally when New Delhi gave its consent to shift the RR camp, it was moved, but only two kilometres away. As for prosecuting the armed forces personnel accused of commission of this crime, the army challenged their arrest and trial by a civilian court: once the Armed Forces Special Powers Act (AFSPA) is invoked, and an area declared 'disturbed', all acts committed by security personnel are considered as taking place in course of 'active service'. The matter is entangled in the technicalities of whose jurisdiction it is to prosecute them.

In 'disturbed areas' the problem gets further compounded when an entire people are considered with suspicion, armed soldiers enjoy immunity, and *their* morale is accorded a premium. This is no exaggeration. In the Masooda Parveen case[1] the Supreme Court refused to allow the payment of Rs 50,000 as ex-gratia relief to the petitioner, whose husband was killed in a macabre manner while in the army's custody, because, as the honourable judge pointed out, such relief could 'demoralize' the security forces personnel.

Quite apart from conflict over the jurisdiction of civilian institutions for dispensation of justice, or the reluctance of the Indian judiciary to dispense justice to victims of crimes committed by armed forces personnel, the prolonged deployment of the military also results in armed forces wanting to remain in control and tending to interfere in matters related to the civilian domain. The most recent example is the statement issued on 30 November 2010 by the Indian Army's northern command headquarter, after an encounter in Srinagar's Qamarwari quarter a day earlier, in which three alleged militants were killed. Although the statement was later retracted and an apology tendered, the army's statement reveals how it perceives its role:

> The clamour to remove bunkers and thin out the police/ paramilitary presence from the urban areas had compelled the Omar Abdullah government to give in. Though it appeared to be a well considered decision, but the latest incident has raised many questions. While it may have pleased a few hardline separatists and their ISI handlers in Pakistan, but what about the common man in the Valley?

---

[1]Masooda Parveen versus Union of India & Ors (2007) 4 Supreme Court Cases 548.

The state capital has shifted to Jammu. Therefore, will the reduced security and visible absence of the security forces raise uncertainties, fear and doubt in the minds of the populace during the long winter ahead?

However, fake or genuine the encounter itself was, what is to be noted is the content and tone of the statement, which amounts to gross interference in the workings of the civilian domain. It is this that raises concern that even when armed forces of the union are ostensibly called 'in aid of the civilian administration' it tends to override the civilian authority and wants to call the shots. Incidentally, the argument over the 'thinning out' did not relate to the removal of bunkers manned by army personnel, but of a mere sixteen out of 400 bunkers manned by the CRPF and the police. Once it is brought in and empowered under AFSPA, the army considers that its opinion must prevail over that of the civilian authority.

So why does the Indian state need 6,27,000 troops in Jammu and Kashmir, and the sweeping powers of the AFSPA, when by all accounts militancy has reduced drastically, down to about 450 active militants? If the military is not there to control the civilian population, why are they crowding the densely populated valley and occupying valuable cultivable land? Even the leader of the pro-India People's Democratic Party, Mehbooba Mufti, has drawn attention to the huge presence of Indian security forces amid habitations, occupying, she said, 28 lakh kanals (3.5 lakh acres) of land (*Greater Kashmir*, 8 September 2009). The constant monitoring of the life of civilians affects everyone. It is a reminder that they are living at the mercy of a hostile military, which can act with impunity.

Military suppression has multiple fallouts. Apart from the violence perpetrated on civilians, the control exercised and the encumbrances placed on daily lives, it also aggravates livelihood issues and impacts the economic life of the society. There are reportedly 671 security forces camps in Jammu and Kashmir occupying 3.5 lakh acres of land and 1500 buildings. (These figures exclude those for

Akhnoor, Jammu, Kargil, Leh and Udhampur.) And the appetite for acquiring land continues to grow. In saffron-rich Lethapora in Pampore tehsil, where no construction is permitted under state laws, the CRPF has demanded 5,000 kanals for its group headquarters. The Indian Army is demanding 10,000 kanals for the expansion of their Khundroo Field Ammunition Depot. The Indian Air Force, which possesses 850 acres in Awantipora, has asked for an additional 763 acres of land. To get the army to vacate 139 acres of the Tattoo Grounds Garrison in Srinagar, it was alloted 212 acres in Sharifabad in exchange. (The army has taken possession of 100 acres at Sharifabad but refuses to budge from the Tattoo Grounds.) At the Cattle Research Centre at Manasbal, spread over 352 acres, the army first asked for permission to set up a few bunkers in 1990. It eventually built barracks there, and by 2005 laid claim to 252 acres of land. The former tourism minister of Jammu and Kashmir told media on 19 October 2007 that the army violated the Master Plan for Gulmarg and without requisite permission '(t)hey have occupied 400 acres of land on which they have raised huge concrete structures' (*Asian Age*, 20 October 2007). Finally, the 'Landmine Report 2007' states that about 160 square kilometres of land in Jammu and 1730 square kilometres in Kashmir were landmined.

In privileging the fight against armed militancy, and convincing itself that popular aspirations for freedom from India had waned in Jammu and Kashmir, the Indian state has become a victim of its own machination—so much so that it has been unnerved by the non-violent display of people's power and has begun to mete out 'collective punishment' for daring to express their desire to opt out of India. The Protocol Additional II (1977) to the Geneva Convention, 12 August 1949, relating to the protection of victims of non-international armed conflicts, under Article 4(b), prohibits collective punishment. Yet, a colonial custom whereby the British Raj used to mete out punishment to an entire group of people for daring to raise their voice against them continues wherever Indian military forces are deployed to restore the authority of the state.

Take a fairly recent example. The Indian prime minister, addressing a gathering of director generals and inspector generals of police on 15 September 2009, warned that '(s)ecessionist and militant groups within the State are once again attempting to make *common cause with outside elements and have embarked on series of protest movements . . .* We must not, and I repeat, we must not, allow such a situation to develop. It is imperative that these disruptive efforts are *contained, controlled and effectively checked.*' The prime minister's exhortation to the security apparatus to 'contain, control and check' protests was followed, and by 31 October 2009, Lt General B.S. Jaswal, GOC-in-C of the northern command of the Indian Army, the senior-most army officer in the Unified Command structure for Jammu and Kashmir, claimed that it is 'agitational terrorism', not militancy, which was the main issue in Kashmir. Here was an army general making a statement equating protests with terrorism. Protests against the atrocities of security forces were dismissed as being inspired and financed from across the border/Line of Control (LoC). And having elevated protests to the status of 'terrorism' it followed that targeting people, in particular the youth, would be a fallout.

Little wonder that by February 2010 authorities began charging stone-pelters for 'waging war', an act of high treason where the death penalty can be awarded—and began, in the name of fighting law-breakers, to demand strong action against stone-pelters, who it was claimed were provoking security forces. To justify this shoot-to-kill doctrine, this was accompanied with 'facts' such as reports of 'firing from within the crowd', 'instructions coming from across the border/LoC', and 'intercepts' shared with friendly journalists and channels. Each of these 'facts' eventually got exposed. But by then many people had already lost their lives.

If the success of the elections and a decline in the strength of militancy were projected as having reduced the appeal of separatists, as well as for the demand for self-determination, no one could explain why there is still so much anger in Jammu and Kashmir. The chief minister had said in February 2010 that young men pelting stones were paid by some 'forces'. He could not explain why young men would risk their lives to throw stones, even if they get money for it, when they know that their lives can be snuffed out for even less. In the make-believe world occupied by the rulers, cocooned by layers of security and fed the daily diet of intelligence briefings, the reality of the public mood, the sense of frustration at the shenanigans of an Indian military establishment which continues to maintain an iron grip on what they, for all practical purposes, consider a subject population, and that seething anger, are somehow not taken seriously.

Or perhaps it is. And that is precisely why the administration stepped up the attack on unarmed protesters. Stones are, after all, no match against the lethal weapons in the possession of security forces.

The attempt by authorities to pass off any crime as an aberration, attributed to some 'rogue elements' within the army, diverts attention from the impunity with which Indian security forces operate in Jammu and Kashmir (and for that matter in India's North-East too). This gets further legitimized because these killings are considered 'acts of service' which invite rewards and promotion. The five-month-long spree of killing in the summer of 2010 was triggered by protests against the cold-blooded custodial killing by security force personnel of Mohammad Shafi, Shehzad Ahmed and Riyaz Ahmed, residents of Nadihal in Baramulla district, on the night of 29 April 2010, three days after they disappeared. They were buried as 'unidentified militants' in the Kalaroos village graveyard on the LoC. The army officers received, without any hindrance, a reward of Rs 6 lakh. (Kalaroos also happens to be one of the graveyards investigated by researchers from the International People's Tribunal on Kashmir, IPTK, for their study of the phenomenon of mass graves.)

The IPTK report identified 2,373 unidentified graves in fifty-five villages of three districts: in thirty-three villages of Baramulla district there were 1,013 unnamed graves, in fourteen villages of Kupwara 1,278 graves and in eight villages of Bandipora eighty-two graves. The report was submitted in December 2009 to the Jammu and Kashmir state government as well as the Indian government. The report had urged the government to look into the matter, institute an inquiry, verify the facts referred to in the report and take steps to prosecute the perpetrators of the crime. Had the authorities taken the report seriously and investigated the matter they may have been in a position to prevent such incidents from occurring. In the first five months of 2010, thirty-six alleged militants have been killed on the LoC in so-called encounters. And the chief minister has even admitted that the Machil encounter has 'raised questions about several other encounters'. But he did not follow his statement with an investigation of the facts recorded in the IPTK report.

To 'transform the will and attitudes' of the people, apart from fear, humiliation too plays a role. Let me recount what happened when eleven boys were arrested on 27 October 2009 for pelting stones at security forces, a day ahead of the prime minister's Srinagar visit. When the boys were produced before the sessions court two days later, some of them narrated how they were forced to commit sodomy, how their photographs were taken by their torturers, and how they were warned to quit the movement lest these pictures were leaked out. The court-ordered medical examination confirmed that there were bruises on the victims' buttocks (*Hindustan Times*, 6 November 2009). Nothing happened thereafter.

It is necessary therefore to ask ourselves that if Jammu and Kashmir is an 'integral' part of India why has the Indian state and society been so cruelly indifferent to the violence inflicted on Muslims of Jammu and Kashmir by the Indian military? Is it because Indians look upon Jammu and Kashmir, and jealously guard it, as a trophy of war, a conquered, Muslim-majority territory won by India in a war with Pakistan in 1947–48? Why is it that the very same democratic voices which so courageously exposed carnages and massacres of minorities in India become mute when confronted with the role of the Indian state in Jammu and Kashmir? And why is it that a territory disputed since 1947, where a commitment was made for making a reference to the people for its resolution, was obfuscated by recourse to manipulation and unscrupulous wheeling-dealing?

We need to ask ourselves why and how India's constitutional democracy has been devalued, thanks to a war against a people who were treated as a subject population in order to deny them their democratic right to self-determination. It is only when we begin to raise these questions that we can begin to appreciate why Kashmiris feel that they are not safe living in union with India, that their future lies in opting out of India, and therefore demand that their right of self-determination be respected.

Languages of a Security State

Nawaz Gul Qanungo

'A tear-gas shell arced over a crowded street in Srinagar's Rajouri Kadal area.' Roughly in this manner, in the summer of what was going to be a much bloodied 2010, a piece of news analysis in one of India's best known, and respected, daily newspapers began. 'It landed, with surreal precision,' the essay went on to describe, 'on Tufail Matoo.' More graphic details seemed to be required and so were added: it ended 'ripping apart the seventeen-year-old's skull.'

As if those disgraceful, third-rate, mostly Hindi, 'news' channels—that feel no hesitation whatsoever in creating incredibly cheap sensation out of human tragedies—were not enough, a tragic death was now being given a sickening graphic treatment in a newspaper for no apparent reason, other than, well, cheap sensationalism. Mark the insensitivity with which the tragic death of Tufail Ahmad Matoo was described by the Indian media's intelligence expert Praveen Swami on 10 July 2010 in the *Hindu*: 'Four weeks ago, a tear-gas shell arced over a crowded street in Srinagar's Rajouri Kadal area. It landed, with surreal precision, on Tufail Matoo, ripping apart the seventeen-year-old's skull.'

Sadly, this is but just one example of such reportage, not to talk about the hackneyed analyses related to Kashmir doled out by the Indian print media not just this summer but over the years and even decades.

In 2008, former head of the *Hindustan Times*, Vir Sanghvi, wrote: 'Have you been reading the news coming out of Kashmir with a mounting sense of despair? I know I have.' ('Thinking the Unthinkable', *Hindustan Times*, 17 August 2008.) He was talking about the agitation in the Valley against the Amarnath land transfer. 'It's clear now that the optimism of the last few months—*all those articles telling us* that normalcy had returned to Kashmir—was misplaced. Nothing has really changed since the 1990s.' (Emphasis added). 'A single spark can set the whole Valley on fire, so deep is the resentment, anger and the extent of secessionist feeling,' he continued to his horror. It was the language of a layman that he truly is, for the remit.

Sanghvi's, along with some similar analyses around the same time, was considered by most in Kashmir as a reluctant admission by sections of the Indian media of the Valley's hard political realities. It wasn't. Sanghvi wrote in the next few lines: '[It] is true that we have rigged elections in Kashmir ... [But] ... nobody disputes that the last election was fair.' Several perplexities later over what needed to be done, he wrote: 'The short answer is: damn all.' It was to *trash* the legitimate demands of Kashmir rather than to recognize their basis and *allow* them in democratic fairness.

The seriousness with which one looks at such writings coming out of the Indian media is not to give it any respectability. But the point is just what informs the general public opinion in India on Kashmir, or any other subject for that matter. Sadly, it is the likes of Vir Sanghvi and Praveen Swami.

The Indian media has deliberately and persistently been using words like 'trouble-makers', 'mischief-makers' and 'mobs' for protesters in Kashmir despite the glaring fact that while the tool of resistance is at most just a stone, they are being answered with bullets fired to kill. The debate could well have been whether such public protests in the present times—against one of the world's largest military forces—could actually be on a par with Gandhi's non-violence. Kashmir remains the most densely militarized conflict zone in the world even today, several times more militarized than

Iraq has *ever* been under US occupation. Kashmir, however, has incredibly cut away from its more than a decade-old practice of armed violence. That, however, should not really bother a media that has long branded and dismissed its 'own' Naxals as a 'menace'.

What guides the majority of the Indian media to follow such a line? 'The task is to make money,' said the noted Indian commentator, Aijaz Ahmed, in an interview last year (*Greater Kashmir*, 23 October 2009). 'News is there to decorate the advertisement.' And then, he added: 'They have the viewpoint of the Indian upper class, the Indian liberal state and the Indian national security state. This is the framework within which they report anything.' Apart from being a willing tool for the Indian national security state as Aijaz Ahmed puts it, there is, however, a potentially much more dangerous factor out there, too: ideology.

Is it a surprise then that the moment the Indian home minister, Palaniappan Chidambaram, stated—with utter disregard to the ground reality—that there was a 'clear link' between anti-India protests in Kashmir and the Lashkar-e-Toiba, the Indian media lapped it up in breathless delight? Phone call 'intercepts'—claimed to have been acquired from top official sources in the Indian home ministry and supposed to be the talk of a plot between two extremists for staging demonstrations and instigating violence and killings in the Valley—were played, and played up. Asiya Andrabi— the head of a motley group of veiled women who was now suddenly being made out to be the central turbine of the movement—was 'sneaking her child out for overseas education' when schools back in the Valley remained shut due to the agitation. This, we were supposed to believe, was a horror.

Talking more about the 'Indian national security state', read M.J. Akbar ('Omar Must Know Army Is Not the Enemy'; *Times of India*, 19 September 2010): 'Why is the Indian Army the one-point target of those who want to break India? The answer is uncomplicated. The police, whether state or central, cannot defend the territorial integrity of India. The Indian Army can. It is therefore in the interest of secessionists and their mentors in

Islamabad to create discord between the Indian Army and the Indian state.' There is not a word of mention of the havoc the army, the paramilitary and police have wrought upon the people in Kashmir over the past decades. Not to talk about the spectacular surge in peaceful public protests in Kashmir since the last three years. That the so-called security of the state is what dictates this language is a given. Ironically, what stands at risk is the security of what has been called the idea of India.

But one of the most shocking, indeed preposterous, precedents was set by *Business Standard* in its editorial of 23 September 2010, when the agitations, and the killings at the hands of the Indian troops and the state police was at its peak: 'Those who harp constantly on poor governance in Kashmir must accept that there is nothing unique about either the so-called "human rights violations" in Kashmir, or the high-handedness of government and security forces. Millions of South Asians routinely complain about these problems all across the region. Improved governance, respect for the rule of law and plural and representative democracy are the only options open and that is as true for Kashmir as for any other state of India, or nation/region in South Asia.'

There is an absolute disregard for not just the political realities of Kashmir but even its history. And we are not yet talking about the dangers of having such an *editorial* being published in a major Indian daily which is respected most for its opinion, especially in the highest realms of policy-making in New Delhi. About the fact that an editorial ideally remains the most critically examined—and written at the highest level to begin with—piece of writing in a newspaper. And, also, about what it does to an organization from within, and to the reporters and editors that comprise it, considering that an *editorial* is not merely a position of an individual columnist or an employee but the position of the very institution that the newspaper represents.

Above all, to double-qualify human rights violations as 'so-called' as *Business Standard* does here is to be not human at all. As Mridu Rai—the author of *Hindu Rulers, Muslim Subjects: Islam,*

Rights and the History of Kashmir—noted, 'To suggest that protests in Kashmir, about the severe social, economic and educational deprivations, as well as the grave toll on mental and physical health and general morale, brought on by twenty years of living under military occupation amount to a "harp[ing] constantly" is not just plainly insensitive but also unprofessional in its rudeness.'

Fortunately, this narrative has also been punctured to some extent—however small that is, of course. And this has happened mainly at two places. One is where young journalists, including even the Kashmiris in India, have managed to enter the Indian media, seize the space of opinion and raise a voice *from within*. Najeeb Mubarki is a recent example that stands out. In fact, the *Economic Times* came out with some unexpected, favourable 'special coverage' of the current protests and killings in Kashmir ('Valley: Crisis Cast in Stone', *Economic Times*, 9 August 2010). The *Economic Times*, it must be conceded, however, does have a habit of coming up with such coverage, unusual for a business newspaper.

And two, of course, is the Internet, where almost the very institution of the media stands challenged. It was here where the real translation of the home ministry's phone 'intercept' was scrutinized in great detail. The translation was clubbed with a video showing the 'intercept' reports of various news channels superimposed with the correct translation of what was actually being spoken by the two persons on the phone. This spread like wildfire as soon as the tapes were played by the Indian media and within hours, the report had been pulled back by almost all the major news channels. Then, again, it was the Internet that helped spread the videos showing what was widely believed to be the local police parading and torturing Kashmiri youth forced to go naked.

However, all that a report in the *Hindu* could see in the whole phenomenon of 'e-protest' in Kashmir was what it called an 'ugly world of online rebels' (*The Hindu*, 24 July 2010). Of course, there's a lot of mediocrity on these web pages, some of which seems even dangerous. But there was hardly a mention in the *Hindu's* 'ugly world of online rebels' of the thousands of refined, informed and nuanced debates going on on various social networking sites, and which have left behind, and continue to do so, a massive body of significant short writings.

What seemed more important for the reporter—Praveen Swami, again—was to mention someone asserting about the Abdullahs that 'the Dalla [broker] family should be hanged publicly.' There was absolutely no mention of the fact that these were also the frustrations pouring out from the millions of young men, women and even children caged inside their homes for several months in a stretch under one of the most brutally enforced curfews in the Valley ever. Ugly online rebels! There was no mention of how *history* was being recorded right as it happened—history written up on online pages run by Kashmiris from across the world and filled by updates about almost each and every event written by young boys and girls in the Valley—*eyewitnesses*.

There are, no doubt, the exceptions. But, looking at the kind of response the writings on Kashmir of the likes of Arundhati Roy and Pankaj Mishra invite in the cyberspace, it is not too difficult to imagine how they are received by the Indian public. As for what the general response of an Indian layperson is when it comes to Kashmir, the answer is not too different from what, well, again, Vir Sanghvi asked himself in one of his more recent articles: 'Why do the Kashmiris hate us so much? And what is it that they actually want?' ('Our Secularism Will Stand Any Opposition', *Hindustan Times*, 19 September 2010.) Needless to say, he had no answers but, incredibly, he didn't expect the Indian people to have any answers either. All that there was, according to him, was 'bewilderment'.

Ideally, this scenario would have left the onus on Kashmir's own media, in whatever measure it could afford taking up. Unfortunately, the Kashmir-based media on the one hand sustain themselves on the exploitation of mostly young, mediocre and poorly trained reporters. And on the other, it thrives on corruption of the most ugly and rampant kind. How much, in any case, can it go against the establishment while itself existing on the mercy of the doles of that very establishment?

Still, where does all this leave the local media in Kashmir? In other words, what is in all this for the Kashmir media itself? Perhaps a lesson for what not to be. And also a need to recognize, and to learn from, the fact that the Indian media, so despised in the Valley, also carries a very significant part of the legacy that sought, fought for and achieved independence for a country from British imperialism. Its present notwithstanding, the Indian media is rightly proud of a history that boasts of the legacy of the likes of Mohandas Karamchand Gandhi and Bal Gangadhar Tilak. A legacy that Kashmir—be that its media or even its so called pro-independence political establishment—is clearly nowhere near to showing any signs of attaining.

This article first appeared in the *Kashmir Times*, Srinagar, 26 September 2010, and later on the website http://www.countercurrents.org.

Bub, Bunkers and Beyond

Sameer Bhat

There is an unseasoned mutiny in Mulk-e-Kashmir this summer. The boatmen in the Dal Lake have revealed to intrepid journalists—clad in bullet-proof vests—that the usually calm carp fish have been nibbling away at their oars of late. The defiance, it seems, has drained into the lake. A little ahead of the weed-infested Dal, an entire company of the Central Reserve Police Force (CRPF) with chestnut-coloured guns in their hands, fingers on the triggers, chased a few hundred street urchins through a tulip garden, completely squishing the flowers in the process. As a result the Zabarwan foothills are stippled with multicoloured floral boot-marks.

The only mills working in the city are the ubiquitous rumour mills, and the word on the street is that the Gregorian calendar will soon be replaced with a standard Syed Ali Shah Geelani calendar. Heck, Gregory XIII was anyway a pope! In the meantime, the newest chairman of JK Bank is mulling over the 2011 calendar with special green-coloured numerics for Hartal days and red-coloured numerics for Curfew days. Parleys shall be held with Geelani sahib when he is a little less angry, and with Omar, when Devinder, his chief of staff, goes, God willing, on a sabbatical and leaves him alone for a day or two. Besides, with the autumn fast approaching, there are chances that the chief minister may finally take his sunglasses off. Eye-to-eye contact is always better than an eye for an eye.

Kids, having had a field day till end-September this year (three months of unlimited holidays), thought in their juvenile abandon that the summer holidays (locally, fifteen *dohan hinz garma-chutti*) might stretch forever. Alas, it was not to be! In early October the education minister—clad in an ill-fitting suit—strode out of his Kokernag home to Srinagar, and called the media men—who assemble quicker than you can say Jack Robinson—to cut short the forever vacations. Uniforms not washed for 100 days went quickly into buckets, much to the chagrin of teenagers, and lo and behold, the lawyer-minister from Kokernag was giving student-attendance stats to media men—who assemble quicker than . . . (okay, the joke is stale now!)—the following evening. Only, his son didn't attend school, choosing instead to go by the now-famous Geelani calendar.[1]

Apart from the sad politics over body-bags in the last few months, there are glad tidings too. Out of more than 1,600 small and big bunkers located all over the province (mud and cement, brick and sand, trench and pillbox types—all unanimously ugly) sixteen bunkers shall be removed with immediate effect. Mostly unaesthetic, these sandbag formations pervade the mental landscape of people, apart from littering the stunningly beautiful (but seriously jinxed) geographic landscape of Kashmir. Called bankers by most locals, these bunkers have small slits for the gun barrel, serving a constant reminder to the hoi polloi that the Maginot line is not to be trodden upon in Kashmir. Sixteen such monstrosities shall go now! We must smile![2]

---

[1] Peerzada Syed's son skips school on Hartal day, as reported in *Greater Kashmir*, 28 September 2010 [http://www.greaterkashmir.com/news/2010/Sep/28/education-minister-s-son-absent-12.asp].

[2] Government starts dismantling bunkers in Srinagar, *Times of India*, 5 October 2010 [http://timesofindia.indiatimes.com/india/Process-of-removing-16-security-bunkers-from-Srinagar-begins/articleshow/6689368.cms].

A deadpan face-off is going on between Gupkar and Hyderpora. Betwixt these two residential locales in Srinagar the destiny of five million people is calendared—week after week. These days the young CM, fondly called BlackBerry Czar on the blogosphere, is at odds to break the deadlock set up by the padre of resistance, Syed Ali Shah Geelani. There have been numerous brainstorms and smear campaigns but nothing seems to be working. Be as it is, the government has now begun to fast forward Urs (Muslim saints' anniversary) holidays, originally scheduled for later this month to Hartal days.[3]

Talk of doing away with the Gregorian calendar, altogether.

---

[3]State government prepones Urs holidays, *Greater Kashmir*, 13 November 2010 [http://www.greaterkashmir.com/news/2010/Nov/13/holiday-today-32.asp].

This article first appeared on the website http://www.kashmirdispatch.com, 1 November 2010.

A Victorious Campaign

Arif Ayaz Parrey

In a beautiful small village perched on the hillside somewhere in Kashmir, anywhere in Kashmir, not so long ago, lived a *mott*[1] by the name of Azad. Like all those who had abandoned the realm of thoughtfulness in favour of mindless freedom, Azad the mott was revered as somebody who knew more about the world than ordinary unsuspecting folk could fathom. Parallel to this, it was also widely known that because his vision soared in spirituality, he was clumsy in the mundane affairs of life. The villagers therefore maintained an oddly dual posture towards him, they found his visible awkwardness in day-to-day affairs funny and could not resist patronizing him for it, but when caught up in situations beyond their control or understanding, they reposed a faith otherwise reserved for gods in his unorthodoxy. As he roamed around in his worn-out and torn-down pheran, heralded by the odour of his unwashed glory, people would invite him to have meals with them, to heal the sick, to fix the jobless, to concoct pregnancies, to bless the new-born or to simply drop down alms of wisdom on their pherans. He would absentmindedly oblige almost all, ostensibly oblivious to their bemused attitude towards him even in their hour of need.

---

[1] *Mott* translates into many words: mystic, mad, stubborn, etc.

His mouth was Jhelum. Words tumbled over his teeth as they flowed out in a continuous stream. The gibberish was a mixture of Kashmiri, Urdu, Farsi, Arabic, English, Sanskrit, Pashto, Hindi, Sindhi, Sheena, Balti and Punjabi languages, and quite often the combination of the words coming out of his mouth qualified as a legal sentence and sometimes even as wisdom; whether he consciously played a part in it or not, who is to tell. People listened intently to every word he uttered and every now and then a particular sequence of words would prove itself to be relevant and enlightening to one person or the other. The enigmatic nature of the message in those words meant that the recipient had to think long and hard about it. In this way, Azad's charisma allowed people to search their own souls for answers to the problems they faced. This most naturally led to small miracles every now and then.

Occasionally, somebody would organize a *wazwaan saal*[2] for the mott and invite friends and relatives for a rendezvous with him. Before and after eating, people would flock around Azad and out of a genuine need for advice, or reverence, or curiosity, or mischievousness, would ask him all sorts of questions. On such occasions, the expression on Azad's face testified that beyond the slight variation in tone when a question is being asked, not much registered in the impenetrable vastness of his mind. Therefore, how his answers managed to connect themselves to the questions was nothing short of a marvel. For example, Azad was in the habit of collecting all sorts of rags and bits and pieces as he wandered around the village. He would then deposit all these in a small abandoned hut situated at one corner of the village which smelled more like Azad and less like rubbish. He even burned some of the junk in the evenings, and the play of the flames in the failing dusk made him jump around in joy like a child. Once, during the course of a wazwaan meeting, somebody asked, '*Paane chukh yoat*

---

[2]A traditional Kashmiri feast with many courses, mostly meat, but also some vegetarian food.

mokur rozaan, telle kyazi chukh jande jamma kareth gaam saaf karn? ('You keep yourself so unclean, then why do you tidy the village by scavenging for rubbish all over the place?') Azad stopped his babble for a second, as if considering an answer, and then replied, '*Wojood chuh paanas wareay soarey kenh. Yelle su saaf, telle bu saaf.*' ('Existence is everything other than self. When that is clean, I'm clean.') At another time, somebody wanted to know when Kashmir would get Azadi. Azad reacted, '*Poien chuh waarewaar baalas gaalan. Weinne te cheh duniya wuchen.*' ('Water slowly brings down the mountain. The world has a world to see yet.')

Azad was politically very conscious and his continuous murmur was filled with the language and understanding of politics. '*Hendustaanun neu eabee awwal, Paekistaanun neu eabee dowomm, Kosheren paatheay gaas-charaey,*' he often repeated. ('India takes the best [land] from Kashmir, Pakistan gets the second best [land], Kashmiris are left with the waste [land].') Another motif he was very fond of was the motif of zaal or net. Zaal for him was the underlying schema, the structure of a phenomenon. In an astonishingly long reversion to sanity, he once said, '*Yelle shikaer zaal chuh trawaan, haput te hirran, shaal te khargosh, saeree fasan. Patte yelle haput hirranes kaed wothan te shaal khargoshes zaagaan, aes diwaan haputas leakke te shaalas shalak, zaal chuh gatsaan mushite.*' ('When the hunter lays out his net, the bear and the deer, the jackal and the rabbit, all are caught in it. Then, when the bear breaks the neck of the deer and the jackal prowls on the rabbit, we curse the bear and beat the jackal, but forget the net which lead to everything else.')

Azad had a habit of climbing the hill every morning before sunrise. He would sit on the hilltop till about nine or ten in the morning and then would climb down back to the village. When asked why he went through this routine he would reply, '*Bu gatsaan gaash chhalni.*' ('I go to wash light.')

One early July morning, *mintary* started to arrive in large numbers in the village. They had not been in the village for quite some time so people were a little startled by their sudden arrival.

The *moqdam*[3] inquired whether he should make the oft-repeated announcement of *crackdown* from the village mosque. The officer-in-charge told him not to bother because they had come to stay; they were going to set up a camp just outside the village.

However, the people had already, out of habit, started to assemble in the school-ground. The *mintary* picked up young men from the gathered villagers to build bunkers, barracks and walls for them, and to lay the barbed-wire fencing around the camp. The newly enslaved youth were made to toil hard which ensured that all the constructions in the camp were complete within a week.

Now the camp was strategically placed on the hillside, just above the village, and this fact meant that villagers going uphill to their fields or the forest had to pass through the camp. In the first few days itself, there were allegations of harassment, beatings and molestations. Besides, the establishment of a permanent camp meant that people started to get used to the *mintary* and dropped down their guard. The huddles in which the villagers went around began to become smaller and smaller till they were reduced to groups of two and three, and sometimes not even that. The *mintary* made its random patrols. Allegations of rape and disappearances began to surface and the villagers protested by performing the rituals of a few hartals but who in this wide wise world listens with any degree of seriousness to a few complaining hillbillies. The rituals of the people were matched by the state with its own rites and, as always, the magical exercise of inquiry revealed nothing.

Threats to life and honour meant that villagers only noticed certain other things but did not deem them important enough to protest against. The forest above the village began to thin visibly. The *mintary* vehicles which went down the hill were covered well, but the unpredictable Kashmiri winds sometimes gave people glimpses of the timber being transported in them. Then, all of a sudden, a band-saw was established in the village, run by a few individuals considered close to the *mintary*. People only began to

---

[3]Village headman.

groan when some of their walnut trees were cut to feed the
voracious appetite of the blades at the band-saw.

In the meantime, Azad had a few confrontations with the guards
at the camp. They asked him the purpose of his uphill visits, so
early in the morning, and he replied, '*Roshni dona hai,*' whereupon
he was heartily ridiculed. Who for God's sake would want to climb
a hill to wash light! On one occasion, the moqdam intervened,
'*Yeh mott hai na, Azad, duniyahich khabar nahi hai. Mott hai
bechara, ijaazat dou,* please.' ('This mott, Azad, knows nothing of
the ways of this world. He is only a pathetic mott, please allow
him.') But the guards would not let him pass through. On their
way back to the village, the moqdam admonished Azad, '*Tse kyazi
karn hajje katha? Soed paeth banne na katha wanin?*' ('Why do you
talk obliquely? Can't you say a thing or two in a straightforward
manner?') To this, Azad replied, '*Danish dardastey qabelayea
sitmgaraan dirham ast. Pi aasne neshe fikre tarun setha jaan.*'
('Knowledge is the currency of the tribe of oppressors. Understand
more, even at the cost of knowing less.')

Azad kept arriving at dawn, crawling under the barbed-wire and
banging the loud iron-gate. The attitude of the guards turned
from bemusement to indifference to open irritation and hostility.
'*Saaley, tere maa ki . . . teri behen ka . . . subha subha aa jaata hai
disturb karne, dobara aaya toh goli maar dengay.*' ('Fuck your
mother, I'll fuck your sister . . . Disturbing us so early in the
morning; if you come here again, we'll kill you.') The next day,
Azad appeared at the gate. The guards opened the gate and took
him in—straight to the room they simply called 'Cell No. 2'. Azad
was tortured for five days. Electricity was passed through his body,
one electrode in his mouth and the other in his anus, rollers were
moved over his legs and chest, fracturing his bones, chilli powder
was inserted into his rectum, penis, eyes and ears. Salt was rubbed
into his wounds. It is said that his reply to their questions was,
'*Innal insaan lafee khusr,* is it God's position or man's?' ('Without
doubt humankind is in loss[4] . . . is it God's position or man's?')

---

[4]Al-Quran. Chapter no. 103, verse no. 2.

They did not understand—did not want to understand, did not need to understand—that the worst torture could not stop him from responding to their queries with, what they thought was, gibberish. After they got tired, they threw him outside the gate.

The villagers picked the mass of pulp which was Azad and brought him back to the village. The whole village got together to tend to him. The combination of so much care and the resilience of his invincible spirit ensured the commencement of a recovery even from such a state of mutilation.

A few days later, some young boys of the village had an altercation with the soldiers at the gate over their right to pass through the camp. Matters heated up and ascended onto the slogan of Azadi. The soldiers fired upon the group. Four boys died on the spot. Three more succumbed to their injuries on the way to the hospital. The grey ash of grief spread over the village.

When Azad had recovered enough, he heard about the news of the killings in the village. He directed a young girl to get him some nettle. It was promptly brought to him. He took it in one of his still-bandaged hands and caressed it. Then he said, '*Soi, soi, watte khawoo.*' ('Nettle, nettle, path-eater(s).')

Presently, strange events began to occur inside the camp. The villagers reported that the *mintary* slept inside their barracks and tents, but found themselves outside when they woke up. There were many poplar trees in and around the area which had been converted into the camp. These poplars mysteriously began to fall down on the bunkers and barracks, injuring many soldiers and killing at least five. The largest barrack in the camp, which also housed the canteen, was built around a young chinar tree. The chinar suddenly opened up its branches, tossing the bricks and corrugated iron sheets all around. These reports were confirmed when the decision to abandon the camp was conveyed to the thrilled villagers through the moqdam. The villagers saw it as divine retribution. One crone screamed, '*Yemmav loi Azad mottes, khuda-dostas, yemman karri parvar-digaar neast te nabood!*' ('They beat up Azad the mott, friend of God; the Sustainer with the most watchful eye will annihilate them!') To this, her brother rejoined, '*Ahanhe, yem marikh, yemman sataevekh, tuhund khoon hay-hekh na badle.*' ('Yes, of course, the blood of those who were killed and oppressed will return to torment them.') As the *mintary* left the village, a few stones followed them downhill.

The officer-in-charge still maintains that the decision to remove the camp was a strategic one and had nothing to do with the 'seemingly supernatural' events which preceded it. He even has explanations for those events. 'Look, we were based on a hillside, so it was quite natural that when we slept, sometimes we rolled out of our beds down the slope; and the poplars, maybe some of the jawans urinated under them which made their bases weak and they got uprooted. Same is the case with the chinar; it must have been getting more nutrients than usual because of the biochemical waste from our canteen.'

But the people of the village are in no mood to listen. A fragrance has been released in the air, the fragrance of Azad; an idea has been planted, the idea of victory; and the categories of madness and civilization, power and helplessness have been rendered problematic for all times to come.

This short story first appeared in the *Honour* magazine, Srinagar, August 2010.

A Place of Blood and Memory

There cannot be any dialogue inside an army camp.

Yirvun Kreel

Kashmir
A Place of Blood and Memory

Nitasha Kaul

Parts of present-day Kashmir are occupied by India, Pakistan and China. When you try to locate the territory of Kashmir on a world map, you will find it partitioned into Pakistan Occupied Kashmir (POK, called 'Azad Kashmir' and 'Northern Areas', in Pakistan), India Occupied Kashmir (IOK, called 'Jammu and Kashmir' including 'Ladakh', in India), and areas such as Aksai Chin and Shaksam Valley under Chinese control (part of the 'Xinjiang autonomous region' in China).

Yet, even as it is devoured by the big states that surround it, Kashmir cannot be understood through the simplistic framing of 'India versus Pakistan', 'Hindu versus Muslim', or 'China-allied-with-Pakistan versus India'. Instead, Kashmir should be seen as a vital link in the Himalayan mountain chain—a historic part of the Silk Route, that is now a violent battleground. Why? Because none of the people in these three regions primarily identify themselves as Pakistani, Indian or Chinese. And neither should they be forced to.

Cartography might lie, but topography and cultural geography does not. Kashmir is not India. Kashmir is not Pakistan. Kashmir is not China. Kashmir is the boundary zone of India–China–Pakistan. But it is distinctively Kashmir. And its people—whatever their religion or national identity—are Kashmiris. In the guise of crude nationalist narratives, peddled by the surrounding postcolonial states for internal politicking and international leverage, the history of the Kashmiri people is being stolen from them. Wherever in Kashmir they are, their options boil down to bullets or ballots— bullets if they protest to being co-opted into the big country which is *not* their homeland, and ballots if they agree to being co-opted into the big country which is *not* their homeland. How can a Kashmiri live under this perpetual erasure of his or her identity? The same way that every colonized people has survived through the ages: by interpretation and by insurrection. Interpretations enable a re-understanding of the identity choices available to a person, and insurrections allow a collectivity to challenge unjust dominance by force.

In the last few years, regions of the POK saw nationalist Kashmiri protests against Pakistan (for example, in Muzaffarabad in December 2009), and, at the moment, nationalist Kashmiris in IOK are witnessing a harsh repression at the hands of Indian security forces. On average, a person a day has been killed in the last two months since June 2010, and nearly half of them have been teenagers. My focus is IOK, in particular the ongoing brutality in the Kashmir Valley, and the various erasures of blood and memory that surround it. Some in IOK give rallying cries in support of POK ('Muzaffarabad Chalo'), and in turn others in POK warn that they will cross over to 'help their brothers in IOK'. Moreover, even during periods of so-called 'normalcy', people in both POK (some being Shias who live in Sunni-majority areas) and in IOK (being a Muslim-majority region in a Hindu-majority India) often live with severe restrictions on their freedom and face multiple levels of discrimination. No wonder Kashmiris who live under occupation feel solidarity for their kind across the boundary lines.

The story of the mountain peoples of Eurasia is, by and large, a tragedy. Run your finger on the multicoloured land surface of a modern-day political world map, and you will see how many 'problem areas'—some states, some sub-state entities, some overlapping zones of displaced peoples—were thriving zones of contact between diverse communities that traded goods and exchanged ideas along the arteries of the 'Silk Route': Tibet, Kashmir, north Pakistan, Afghanistan, Kyrgyzstan, Uzbekistan, Iran, Iraq, Syria. Like many of these other places, Kashmir, a Himalayan zone of contact between diverse peoples in history, has become a zone of conflict, largely due to modern boundary-making processes which evolved to accommodate economic privileges and political trade-offs with rivals that were necessary for European (especially British) colonization of the region.

In the case of the Himalayan mountains, the British never saw much advantage in direct control. They calculated that the administrative, policing, and transportation costs were too high and the returns not worthwhile when compared to the fertile and bustling plains. Instead, they preferred to follow a stated policy of 'controlling the hills from the plains', for which a system was set up during colonial times—the bureaucrats at the Centre would be the administrators and policy-makers and they would cultivate local aristocratic, political and business elites in the peripheral regions. To this day, the Indian state manages its peripheries in this way. Both Kashmir and the 'North-East' are examples.

Why does this matter?

Because it sets up structures of power and responsibility that do not overlap meaningfully. The bureaucrats and politicians at the Centre do not have direct interaction with the regions; their interest is only to have a 'reliable' power base in the periphery. Equally, the local elites in the periphery exaggerate reports of their influence over 'their' people in order to gain maximum advantage from the Centre. This pattern—which I would call the 'Mandarin–Machiavelli interaction'—has characterized the relationship of India with Kashmir (or rather of New Delhi with Srinagar). Neither the Centre nor the periphery has any interest in being genuinely concerned about the people in whose name they wield power and exercise authority. What is more, in such a scenario, there is enormous potential of corruption as long as it doesn't harm the ruling interests of both ends of the chain, and any dissent will only be tolerated if it can be channelled for political gains. Otherwise, those dissenting or seeking change will be punished and brutalized. This is exactly what is happening in IOK today.

Kashmir as India's disputed 'integral'

IOK has never been an indisputable part of India. Paradoxically, presenting this historical fact invariably causes most Indians to assert even more vigorously that Kashmir is an 'integral' part of India. Why? Why is Kashmir so fundamental to the Indian psyche?

The average Indian insists that Kashmir is an indisputable part of India, to be held by force when necessary, in the same way that the Indian state insists that Kashmir is an 'integral' part of India while occupying it by military means. Indians and the Indian state find it necessary to affirm this repeatedly because they know that Kashmir is *not* actually an indisputable part of India and this galls them.

It is no coincidence that Kashmir and the North-East were two of the least involved regions during the nationalist freedom struggle which led to India's independence, and it is these regions which have remained least understood in the mainstream nationalist imagination. In Kashmir, for example, in the 1930s and 1940s, it was the Kashmiri Nationalists (led by Sheikh Abdullah) and the Kashmiri Communists (both Hindu and Muslim) who shaped the pre-1947 political landscape by their opposition to princely rule (of the unrepresentative Dogra monarch); integration with India was an 'unintended consequence' of their progressivist leanings. With time, their faith in India was rudely jolted—independent India came to fear two things most: Muslims and communists. Kashmir had both.

The way Kashmir is viewed in the mainstream Indian imagination is linked to the wider evolution of Indian self-perception in the decades after Independence and, more specifically, to the quantum shift in the political and economic structure of Indian society in the late 1980s and early 1990s.

The Indian nation, born in the wake of the Partition with idealistic anti-colonial promises, saw its first national event in the assassination of its biggest moral voice, Mahatma Gandhi, at the hands of a fanatical Hindu extremist. The successive decades saw an undoing of the social, political, economic and moral ideals which had motivated the people in their anti-colonial independence struggle. The two biggest, and significantly reactionary, transformations that India has seen since Independence became most visible in the late 1980s and early 1990s—the rise of economic and religious fundamentalism: neo-liberalism and Hindutva. From the late 1940s to late 1980s (with the exception of the rather telling 'Emergency period' and its aftermath), electoral politics in India was dominated by the traditional elites. Within such a system, there was a continued 'capture' of the Indian state by the privileged, and the only route into the political imagination left for others was through asserting 'identity politics', especially caste-based identities, as in the case of the Bahujan Samaj Party (BSP) and the Mayawati phenomenon.

The founding myth of the postcolonial Indian state was that of a 'sovereign democratic republic' (as stated in the original preamble to the Indian Constitution). Later, it was amended to 'sovereign *socialist secular* democratic republic'. The same amendment (the forty-second amendment to the Indian Constitution in 1976) that added the words 'socialist' and 'secular', also inserted the word 'integrity' in addition to the 'unity' originally mentioned; the changed preamble went from 'unity of the nation' to 'unity *and integrity* of the nation'. It is of crucial importance that the labels confirming India as 'socialist' and 'secular', and the pledge for 'integrity' came about in 1976 during the Emergency era (1975–77) which witnessed a general curtailment of the freedoms of most ordinary Indians, especially those such as religious minorities and the economically deprived.

In other words, by the 1970s, India's founding myths were already severely challenged, and therefore needed to be proclaimed as an exercise in self-justification. There was discrimination against religious minorities (for example, as an unstated rule, Muslims were never placed in 'sensitive' government positions—and this has never changed), hence India needed to call itself 'secular'. There was growing inequality and continued widespread poverty, and so India needed to call itself 'socialist'. There was justified alienation in various parts of the country due to ignorance and corrupt misgovernment enabled by the Mandarin–Machiavelli relations (while the 'integrity' of India's neighbour, Pakistan, had been challenged with the creation of Bangladesh in 1971), thus India's 'integrity' needed to be affirmed.

From 1947 onwards, postcolonial India saw itself as an inheritor of the British imperial mantle in the region. Indian leadership, while aware of the negative legacies of the empire, also inherited its realpolitik attitudes, which were made worse by the euphoria of emergent nationalism and self-righteousness. In the years following Independence, India refused to negotiate with China on the boundary issue (while simultaneously following a less-than-pragmatic policy on Tibet) and pursued an ill-advised 'forward policy' in NEFA (North-East Frontier Areas), while Nehru—a Kashmiri himself and fond of Kashmir—promised Kashmiris a plebiscite to determine their future.

In the middle of the twentieth century, my grandfather, then a young man, stood among the crowd at Lal Chowk in the centre of Srinagar, listening to Nehru make a rousing speech to the people of Kashmir—'*Kashmir ke log koi bhhed-bakri nahin hain ki hamne kaha yahaan chalo ya wahaan chalo . . .*' (The people of Kashmir can't be led by us like goat or sheep in one direction or the other . . .)—in which he promised them a choice to determine their identity, specifically a plebiscite to determine their own future. In later years, my grandfather would often recall those words of Nehru apologetically. This Nehruvian promise came to naught as India's stance on Kashmir became ever more legalistic.

Recently, my grandfather passed away and I went again to Srinagar to mourn for him in his birthplace, the land of my lost memories.

India's claim that Kashmir is 'integral' to the country only seeks to confirm its secular credentials (being the only Muslim-majority state in a Hindu-majority India). This assertion is ironic, considering that India's secular credentials (being an afterthought as the 'Emergency' time amendment shows) were not 'integral' to the Indian state at its founding!

Internationally, the Indian state has thrived by trading on its publicized self-image as democratic, secular, and peaceful. The comparison has always been with neighbours like China and Pakistan—one communist, the other theocratic. To the wider Western world, nothing could be worse than someone who is a 'Commie' or 'Islamic'. The world at large has been fooled for too long by the articulate, if not argumentative, Indian upper-class governmental and corporate elite and their publicity machines. So successful is this illusion about India, that the world media consistently under-reports the Indian state's brutality when it comes to Naxalites, the 'North-East' (the only part of the country which is referred to by geographical co-ordinates—a telling synecdochic use of the generic term 'North-East' to refer to one or all of the seven different states together), and Kashmir.

India is demographically a Hindu majority state, and for all its talk of 'unity in diversity', it is intolerant towards its minorities. That discrimination and intolerance flourishes in Pakistan or China or the West is no justification for ignoring this fact in India. For instance, there is a violent ongoing repression of the tribals, there is recurrent and extreme state brutality in Kashmir, there have been orchestrated pogroms against the Muslims (Gujarat 2002), violence against the Sikhs (Delhi 1984), the Christians (Orissa 2007–08), in addition to which there is constant discrimination against people in terms of their religion, caste, class, gender, sexuality. The people who fit India's self-narrative best are affluent Hindus.

In so many regions and in so many ways, the project and vision of post-colonial India is coming apart at the seams. The same old routine use of the narrative of 'national integration' and 'outside infiltration' (Pakistan-trained terrorists in Kashmir, China-trained Maoists in eastern India) cannot inoculate a country that is failing its people economically, politically and socially.

The Indian political class is superbly corrupt. Entry into politics is seen as a route for upward class mobility by enabling wealth accumulation; generally only the sons and scions of those with pre-existing political connections rise through the ranks, unless one is a goon with a criminal record! Indian bureaucracy has a reputation for being tremendously arrogant. It is a truism that Indian bureaucrats are generally smug and supercilious, unwilling to learn or exchange ideas from any but the most hawkish and pro-establishment intellectuals. The large swathes of the Indian middle classes are stuffed with intolerance, unthinking mass entertainment, and overconsumption—fed by a corporatized media that 'manufactures consent' in a textbook Chomsky way. The mix of ignorance and blustery self-confidence that one encounters in middle-class Indians rivals Americans (they share this 'superpower' trait!). All of the above—a corrupt political class, a smug bureaucracy, an unthinking and avidly consuming middle class— makes India a wonderful 'market' globally. This is the reason why the world keeps silent when the Indian state commits or abets violent atrocities, both inside its boundaries and outside.

In such an environment, proper political consciousness is rare. Indian people are fed the 'national integration' mantra and they lap it up, unable to perceive the way in which people such as the Kashmiris are being dehumanized. The average middle-class Indian is intolerant of Pakistan, suspicious of China, unwilling to commingle with Muslims or 'lower castes', and wilfully blind to the poverty that surrounds them—s/he is focused on making money, spending money, and occasionally, redemption through self-help. Kashmir is a distant nightmare for them.

Indian politicians ultimately don't care for Kashmir. When the situation looks extremely grim, as now, they make a few statements, a few changes happen at the state level, a few lies are spun, and some schemes are floated to keep public opinion on board. The leadership is, by turns and at different levels, dull, corrupt, and lacking in morals.

Most importantly, the compulsions of India's domestic politics ensure that there is no real potential for dialogue and understanding on Kashmir. The entrenched national narrative is so strong that any move forward is seized by the opposition as 'compromise' and 'betrayal'. Given the circumstances, even the most measly statement made by government representatives that recognizes any problem in Kashmir, or questions the Hindu right-wing, is challenged by the xenophobic, intolerant right-wing politicians (Bharatiya Janata Party [BJP] and their ilk) and exploited for political gain (for instance, the BJP asking the home minister to apologize for commenting on 'saffron terror', and the BJP challenging the prime minister for his statement on autonomy for Kashmir).

Furthermore, India's political, military and bureaucratic interests in Kashmir are not coherently aligned, and are subject to the varying intensity and profitability of India's strategic international alliances. The strength and honesty of the Indian government's political will on Kashmir then becomes a pawn in line with India's interests in Afghanistan, and in turn hostage to US policy on 'Af-Pak'.

Finally, India's defence sector is rapidly modernizing and is, therefore, currently very lucrative internationally. At the same time, there is an excessive use of force in the occupation of Kashmir. Such conflict then unleashes its own perverse incentives such as the increased expenditure on arms, thereby debilitating the initiatives for peace. In any case, the militarization of security in India is a dangerous development for the dehumanizing violence it enables (some Indian military tactics in Kashmir are excessive even for the Israeli Defence Forces [IDF]).

Kashmir can be called India's disputed 'integral'. In fact, as I have argued, the Indian attitude to Kashmir can only be understood in the wider context of the failed political, economic and social promises of post-colonial India. In the name of 'national integration', India is occupying a region against the will of the people who live there. Kashmir is 'integral' only to the lives of Kashmiris.

The tragedy of Kashmir

The distinctive identity of Kashmir was shaped by multiple influences and rulerships. Kashmir's history is a knot of contested interpretations made worse by ignorance. The biggest myth of recent times is that of seeing Kashmir historically in terms of Muslims *versus* Hindus, instead of Muslims *and* Hindus.

Kashmiris did not see themselves in these terms until they were classified as such by the political games of the later part of the twentieth century. The centuries-old tradition of '*Kashmiriyat*' bears testimony to the identity of Kashmiris as a people who did not let their religious affiliations overwhelm their ethnic and regional commonality. Contemporary Hindu religious extremists often try to extrapolate selective facts from Kashmir's rich history to push their communal case—citing especially the forced conversions to Islam, and the 1989 exodus of Kashmiri Pandits (minority Hindus) from the Valley as having been forced by Kashmiri Muslims.

Kashmiris were a people who were somehow 'bargained' into nationhood when the British left the region. From the mid-nineteenth century onwards, the practice of statecraft and governance came to be tied closely to statistics, enumeration and classification. In the colonies too, the British tried to stabilize and centralize channels of power by classifying their subjects and dealing with them in terms of race, genetic stock, community leaders, and religion. Hindus and Muslims were two important lenses through which people were perceived, roused, and then divided during the Partition. In the case of Kashmir, this British formula was bungled—the Muslims were the majority in Kashmir, but the ruler (Hari Singh) was not Muslim; the Indian PM Nehru was a Kashmiri Hindu but close to Sheikh Abdullah, the most prominent Kashmiri leader, a Muslim. Plus, the entire Himalayas, including Kashmir, had been constructed as a strategic geopolitical buffer in the imperial trajectory till then; the 'Great Game' was a kind of proto–cold war. When India and Pakistan were being carved up, Kashmir was coveted on either side. This manic struggle over possessing Kashmir has led to multiple wars—in 1947, 1965, 1999—between India and Pakistan, both of whom use Kashmir as a propaganda pawn for their opportunistic and hypocritical purposes, as well as a continued boundary stalemate.

In so many ways, Kashmir was 'special'. The Kashmiri political voice and consciousness was different from that of the rest of India. The Kashmiris of an earlier generation (up until the 1980s) saw themselves as 'Kashmiris', in spite of everything. Kashmiris as a people have historically shared language, mannerisms, speech inflections, customs and even some festivals (such as the springtime '*Badaamwari*'). Today, very little understanding of this commonality remains. Why?

Because mainstream India (and Pakistan) never understood Kashmir nor cared for Kashmiri people.

When Pakistan and India came into being, Kashmir was attacked by one side to obtain it by force while its unrepresentative ruler was compelled by the other side to sign an 'instrument of accession' as a condition of providing help in repelling the attack. Where were the Kashmiri people's aspirations accounted for in all of this? In India, they were promised self-determination, but the subsequent decades witnessed a tug of war between the Centre and periphery during which governments in Srinagar were removed from power, puppets were installed, and elections were rigged. India saw the people of Kashmir as inherently 'alien' and 'untrustworthy', and somehow forever 'tainted'.

The progressivist aspirations of Kashmir's leaders and their openly communist leanings from the 1930s onwards did not help either when it came to the fast-polarizing ideological alliances between states in the cold war era (other larger factors were salient in this framing also, such as the Dalai Lama's exile to India, and

Z.A. Bhutto forging the alliance with communist China). The communists of Kashmir had surnames that were both Hindu and Muslim. The intellectuals of Kashmir had vivid memories of pre-independence Lahore, a centre of gravity in those times. But, most people in India have never heard of Kashmir and communism together in the same sentence.[1] The currently evolving Chinese stance on Kashmir (China denied a visa in August 2010 to an Indian general posted in Kashmir) is news only to someone who doesn't know of Sheikh Abdullah meeting Chou-en-Lai in Algiers in 1967.

Do those non-Kashmiri Indians—who spew hateful anti-Muslim rhetoric today and claim Kashmir as an undying part of India—know of one festival or tradition of Kashmiri Hindus, let alone of Kashmiri Muslims? But, why speak of festivals? Ask the average Indian what happened in Kashmir in the late 1980s. Some might know about the exodus of Kashmiri Hindus from the Valley from 1989 onwards (only some, for mainstream India does not actually care for Kashmiris, either Hindu or Muslim; they care for their own existential need to control and possess Kashmir). But they are unlikely to know about the elections of 1987, by which time India was acting desperate, which were rigged to prevent the Kashmiri people from electing anyone but those 'approved' by New Delhi.

---

[1] I recommend Andrew Whitehead's recent article 'The People's Militia: Communist and Kashmiri Nationalism in the 1940s', *Twentieth Century Communism*, issue 2, 2010, pp. 141–68; it discusses the radical 'New Kashmir' manifesto of 1944 and the drastic land reforms, the 'Quit Kashmir' [note *not* 'Quit India'] cries of 1946, the Kashmiri women militia of 1940s who were the first women in India trained to use rifles during the late 1940s, and the subsequent worries about the spread of communism in Kashmir, both in India and beyond. Whitehead quotes the diplomat Josef Korbel's words from the 1954 book *Danger in Kashmir*: 'Kashmir might eventually become the hub of Communist activities in Southern Asia'. Korbel was the father of Madeleine Albright and the mentor of Condoleezza Rice, both former US secretaries of state.

Every grievance of the Kashmiri people (who are largely Muslim) was seen through the anti-national lens. Is it any surprise then that some of those Kashmiri Muslims, frustrated and pigeonholed by India for decades, actually turned to radicalized political Islam, given the role of the Pakistani Inter-Services Intelligence (ISI), the wider dynamics of the closing cold war, and the Afghan and central Asian scenario at the time?

In the 1980s, radicalized Islam rose in Kashmir. But let us not forget the figure of Jagmohan, the governor of Kashmir in the 1980s (1984–89, and again in 1990) who played a prominent (though not exclusive) role in instigating the departure of Kashmiri Hindus from the Valley. A communal right-wing Hindu who later joined the BJP, he was the representative of the Centre in Muslim-majority Kashmir in those turbulent years which included the 1987 election-rigging.[2] Much more needs to be written about his terrible tenure in Kashmir in the 1980s.

Still, as Pankaj Mishra details, 'Jagmohan's pro-Hindu policies in Kashmir, and the lack of economic opportunities for educated Muslim Kashmiris, drove many Kashmiri youth to support Islamist parties that were gaining influence in the state'.[3] These Islamist parties, he adds, were 'helped by the growth of *madrassas*, the privately owned theology schools which were often run by Muslims from Assam in eastern India, over a thousand miles away, where mass killings of Muslims in the early 1980s had forced their

---

[2] Jagmohan's main achievement there was renovating the 'Vaishno Devi' Hindu shrine; in 2010 he wrote a book titled *Reforming Vaishno Devi and a Case for Reformed, Reawakened and Enlightened Hinduism*, which was favourably reviewed in some media with much praise: 'Among the many reasons I admire Jagmohan, the former BJP minister who sadly, seems to find no place in his party these days, is because he has no hesitation in talking about Hinduism.' [http://www.hindustantimes.com/A-pilgrim-s-progress/Article1-576805.aspx]

[3] See Pankaj Mishra, 'The Birth of a Nation', the *New York Review of Books*, October 2000 [http://www.nybooks.com/articles/archives/2000/oct/05/the-birth-of-a-nation/].

migration to Kashmir'. During Jagmohan's tenure, the elected government of Kashmir was dismissed twice, the number of Muslims being recruited in government service went down, non-Muslims were encouraged to work in Kashmir. He also sought to impose 'a peculiarly Hindu modernity' on the state, permitting unrestricted sale of alcohol but forbidding Muslims to slaughter sheep on a Hindu festival day. Jagmohan was removed in 1989, but reappointed in 1990 (at which the state government resigned in protest) to govern Kashmir directly under Central rule and deal with the militants.

Patricia Gossman writes, 'In response to widespread threats and targeted attacks and killings by militant groups, many Hindus had fled. Jagmohan's government ultimately assisted some 90,000 Hindus in leaving the Kashmir Valley for camps in Jammu and New Delhi.'[4] What of those Kashmiris (mostly Muslim) who remained in the Valley? Gossman further says, 'In the weeks that followed, Indian Army and security forces opened fire repeatedly on unarmed protesters, in some cases shooting to kill wounded prisoners. These killings constituted a serious violation of international humanitarian law. Foreign journalists were expelled from Kashmir for several months, and new laws enacted granting the security forces increased powers, limiting defendants' rights, imposing restrictions on public gatherings, and prohibiting virtual any public expression of dissent.'

Many Kashmiris and others[5] in India believe that he envisaged a 'total solution' for Kashmir, and the reason he aided the exodus of Kashmiri Hindus was because he planned to isolate the Kashmiri Muslims from the Kashmiri Hindus and then 'deal' with them by violent means.

---

[4]See Patricia Gossman, 'Kashmir and International Law: How War Crimes Fuel the Conflict', The *Crimes of War* Project, July 2002 [http://www.crimesofwar.org/onnews/news-kashmir.html].

[5]Vir Sanghvi, the reviewer of Jagmohan's book, disparagingly calls them 'secular journos'.

In a way, this has already come to pass. In a more fundamental manner than theocratic Islamic Pakistan could ever manage with all its cross-border airwave propaganda and infiltration, a democratic India with its bungling Hinduized outlook has managed to convert Kashmir into a sorry communal battleground. The proliferation of the politics of hate has meant that the rise of Hindutva in India has been mirrored by the growth of radicalized Islam in Kashmir.

The Kashmiris are alienated evermore each day. In the last two decades, the Kashmiri psyche has been surgically cleaved into Kashmiri Hindus and Kashmiri Muslims. An entire generation of Kashmiri Hindus have grown up outside Kashmir in India where they have learnt to identify themselves as Hindus before Kashmiris, in accordance with the right-wing Hindu sentiment of mainstream India. This generation of young people is a recruiting ground for Hindu extremists for the Rashtriya Swayamsevak Sangh (RSS), Vishwa Hindu Parishad (VHP), BJP and their kind. Their justified nostalgia for their homeland is condensed into narratives of anti-Muslim hate which can be exploited for political vote gain. Equally, an entire generation of Kashmiri Muslims have grown up inside Kashmir where they have learnt to identify themselves as Muslims before calling themselves Kashmiris in the environment of militancy and a brutal Indian military occupation who view them only as latent Islamic fundamentalists. Their justified aspirations of life and livelihood are daily denied by severe discrimination and lack of representation. In their imagination, Kashmiri Hindus are a traitorous pro-Indian minority, linked to the oppressive Hindu Indian majority. Often, even the Valley leaders who supposedly represent them are self-serving, corrupt, and manipulate their sentiments for political gain.

This two-fold *absence*—of Kashmiri Hindus whose memory is wiped clean of Kashmiri Muslims as being Kashmiris and who have had to strike roots outside their homeland and adapt to mainstream India, and of Kashmiri Muslims who have lived under militancy and an Indian military occupation without the memory of Kashmiri Hindus being Kashmiris and who are tired of being scapegoated for machinations beyond their control—is the grafting of a virtual partition of Kashmir's history and identity.

Until the 1980s, a Kashmiri—whether Hindu or Muslim—might say, we the people of Kashmir, do not belong to India, we are Kashmiri. Beyond the Banihal tunnel (Jawahar tunnel) was the land of Lipton tea, not Mogul chai. India was an 'other' to a Kashmiri as much as a Kashmiri was an 'other' to an Indian. Now, a Kashmiri will, in all probability, speak in line with their location and their precise suffering will systematically depend on their experience of where they spent the last two decades—within the Valley or outside it.

The sheer toll on Kashmiri people has been staggering. Over 1,00,000 Kashmiri Hindus left their homeland, several hundred were killed, numberless young people have grown up in refugee camps. Especially for those who were poor and from rural areas of Kashmir, it has been a journey of ruin and devastation. Having lost home and homeland—living on handouts in the festering, sweltering chaos of refugee camps in India; peddling wares; being discriminated against—they have no political voice other than the high-pitched shrill of the right-wing Hindu leaders. The Indian state consistently downplays their situation and thus helps to channel their frustrations into Hindu extremism by having no vision for their future, ignoring their specific plight on the one hand, and by being generally Islamophobic, on the other.

The arithmetic gets really, truly miserable when it comes to the Kashmiri Muslims in the Valley. Their tragedy is to live their life under constant threat of militancy and an Indian military occupation of hundreds of thousands of security personnel. Since 1989, over 60,000 people in Kashmir have been killed, over 7,000 have gone missing, several hundred thousand have been maimed, tortured, and psychologically damaged. In addition, there are thousands of unmarked graves, thousands of women have been raped, tens of thousands widowed and children orphaned. In the crazy count of violence, numbers lose meaning. And the atrocities—murders, rapes, torture, extra-judicial killings, forced disappearances—

committed by the Indian security forces in Kashmir are never investigated properly (as in the recent Shopian rape case of 2009).

The people living in Kashmir for the last two decades have only seen the inhuman face of an occupying force which degrades and kills people if they dare to raise their voice, which rapes women, kills young boys, and slaughters beggars in fake encounters. Under such circumstances, it is the paramount duty of mainstream Indians to stand up and be counted, to convey the message to the Indian government that such atrocities cannot and should not be committed in their name.

Instead of rabid anti-Muslim hate-mongering and chanting how Kashmir is 'integral' to India (which can only produce mirror responses of hard-line intolerant Islamist ideologues inside the Kashmir Valley), the Indians have a duty to recognize the rights of Kashmiris as a people. Yes, the Kashmiri Hindus had to leave their homeland, but how will the perpetuation of violence and hatred help their cause?

Kashmiri Hindus themselves have been used as pawns by the Indian state. Their story is one of a small but educated and comparatively elite, affluent minority in a Muslim-majority state who had close connections with the Indian establishment and were always targeted and cultivated by Indian intelligence machinery as agents of RAW (Research and Analysis Wing), IB (Intelligence Bureau) and the Indian state. Such machinations over the decades since independence have only served to widen the gulf between Kashmiri Hindus and Kashmiri Muslims.

The Indian state has failed both Kashmiri Hindus *and* Kashmiri Muslims, failing to account for the aspirations of both communities; it has however, succeeded in dividing them in a fundamental—though hopefully not irreversible—way.

What Kashmiris want

With Kashmir becoming a war zone from the 1980s onwards, successive Indian governments have let Kashmiris down. In its negotiations with the leaders of Kashmir, India has been more willing to recognize the 'politics of their struggle' (who represents what voice, can be played off against whom to what effect) as opposed to their essential 'political struggle'.

The demand of the Kashmiri people is 'Azadi'. *Freedom.* Freedom to be themselves, to choose their national destiny. *We are not Indians. We are Kashmiris. We have a history, a language, a culture that demands recognition.*

Instead of recognizing this gut-wrenching, existential cry of the Kashmiri people, the Indian state sends in more guns, more troops, more rolls of barbed wire, more bribes, more bullets. When this does not work and the Kashmiris scream 'Go India Go', they send in a battery of words—Development, Employment, Infrastructure, Laws, Training, Security, Curfew. The big words fall flat and disappear without trace between the folds of the pheran, in the wrinkles on the face, on the marks on the graves, and in the flow of Kashmiri blood.

Here's a valid question to ask Indian political leaders, bureaucrats, army chiefs, right-wing extremists, the ignorant layperson: *Are you blind? Can you not see that we want a recognition of our identity as a people?*

Burn your Bollywood movies. Come to Kashmir. Walk through our cities. The bridges. The ruins. The graves. Look at what we eat. Look at our buildings. Our shrines. Our architecture. Our speech. Our history. Speak to us. See how we live.

We are not you. We have never been you. We don't want to be you.

Freedom cannot be denied finally. Borders do sometimes get realigned. Small states can manage to survive in the middle of large ones—I am in one: Bhutan.

For over fifty years, every schoolchild in India has been fed lies—shown an incorrect map of Kashmir that they only recognize as being false once they see a map printed outside India.

What do Indians know about Kashmir anyway?

1. Exotic tourist version/Kashmir the beautiful (from holiday photographs)

Kashmir is a picture postcard beautiful land crowned by the lofty Himalayas and marked by clear running streams. Old romantic ruins, walnut trees, apple orchards, wooden houses and rare flowers populate the region. There are people huddling with cups of almond kahwa over the kangri embers in winter, reflections of red chinar leaves on the Dal Lake in autumn, bustle in Srinagar's Lal Chowk in summer, and some landslides when it rains. The children are excited for months before the big festivals and pretty women in embroidered pherans are everywhere. There are shikaras and houseboats, unrivalled wood carvings, intricately decorated papier-mâché boxes, and of course, the shahtoosh, cashmere and pashmina woollens.

2. Security problem version/Kashmir the cruel (from media photographs)
The place on maps with the name Kashmir is a conflict-riven divided territory where bloodshed has not ceased for decades now. In the name of separatism, insurgency, militancy, freedom-struggle, territorial integrity, occupation or terrorism, this bloody valley has seen people dying, endless grieving and lost orphans. Kashmir is the name for a problem—like Palestine. Curvy newsprint alphabets indifferently remark the deaths in the Valley; some number shot by soldiers, shot by militants. People read and often forget.

The political and public perceptions of Kashmir vary at the levels of the Indian state and the Indian individual. For most Indians, Kashmir is an exotic place, unreal and wholly imaginary. In the time-honoured manner of stereotyping, the Kashmiris are not seen as real people, they are 'the other'; represented to suit the self-image of mainstream Indians. In the pendulum swing between Bollywood movies and Islamophobia, typically, Kashmir is either filled with an entire assortment of enchanting people and precious things (rosy-cheeked fair girls, apples, walnuts) or a dangerous place filled with repugnant, ungrateful and violent Muslims and almost-Muslims.

But this 'wrecked paradise' of Kashmir is inhabited by real people with real lives and aspirations. The longer India occupies Kashmir instead of understanding what the people there want, the more it will pave the way for the influence of hard-line intolerance in the Valley. Already, a land with famous women poetesses like Lalla Ded and Habba Khatoon is becoming known for women like Asiya Andrabi, the head of the Dukhtaran-e-Millat, or Daughters of the People, which seeks to promote compulsory veiling for women and attempts to enforce rigid Islamic values hitherto alien in Kashmir's syncretic culture.

Protests by stones and phones

Nearly half of those killed in Kashmir in recent weeks were teenagers, one butchered on his way to the hospital in an ambulance. Another eleven-year-old is killed as I write. The wider world, especially the West, is 'careful' in how it reports Kashmir, always stressing that the police were 'provoked', that the protesters were 'anti-national'. Far away from the raw fury of Kashmir, commentators in Delhi muse on twitter 'NOT condoning death: but WHY wd parents allow 11yrolds to protest'.

Why would parents allow a child to protest?

I want to ask the stranger back: have you ever been to a war zone? The rules of normal life are suspended in a place where brutality abounds. Middle-class parents in comfort zones 'allow' their kids action in line with what is good for them. In Kashmir where bullets zip past and people endure daily humiliation, children too (as in Palestine) become cannon fodder. By the time you read this, more will have died. What image does the Indian state have of these children and teenagers—child terrorists? Child soldiers? Or brutalized young people who only have the weapon of the defenceless: a stone?

Kashmiris are not allowed to protest, and are denied freedom of assembly, even as they are under occupation by a democracy. When they shout 'enough', they are shot at by 'security' forces.

The Indian state announces that it will create jobs, sends in more troops, announces a billion-rupee propaganda fund, places political leaders under house arrests, mulls over 'non-lethal ways of crowd control' and intelligence-gathering in local languages. It does everything that confirms it as an occupying force—it will spend money, it will send moles, but it will not recognize the basic reason why people are fed-up to the extent of throwing stones: their need for freedom.

Of course, the people of Kashmir are economically deprived, there's poor infrastructure, and the lack of even basic necessities like electricity—prolonged power cuts in severe winters are a routine feature. On this latter occurrence, the standard Indian answer is that there's a lot of power-theft in Jammu and Kashmir, but as a poet humorously wrote, burning dinner is not incompetence but war. There are reasons why disenfranchised people don't pay bills—for example, the lack of identification with the authorities, as in the case of apartheid South Africa.

But the experts analysing Kashmir in terms of the development critique forget that a prinked cage is still a cage. If a people have been alienated over decades and truly yearn for freedom, then they cannot be bought with promises of jobs.

By focusing on the stone in the hands of the Kashmiri, the Indian media manages to erase the brutality of the pointed gun in the hands of the soldiers who face them. The extreme methods of repression that India is trialling in Kashmir will gradually find their way into the standard procedures for dealing with protesters elsewhere too.

Moreover, the protesters of today have a way to document the atrocities perpetrated on them—YouTube, Twitter, Facebook. The world may not be Twitter-trending Kashmir at the moment, but someday it might. In the meantime, there are hundreds of videos and pictures online that show exactly the kind of attitude the Indian forces have towards the residents of Kashmir—charging at women, beating up children, damaging private property, and being very violent towards young men.

It is an irony of the 'security situation' in Kashmir today that the security forces who are supposed to 'secure' the people, stand barricaded behind razor-wire rolls and camouflaged walls (adorned with slogans like 'Help us to help you') wearing body armour.

Who are these soldiers? The average face of Indian terror in Kashmir are uniformed men of the security forces who hail from poorer economic classes of towns and villages in the plains of India—they have to serve in the tough conditions of a Himalayan valley where they *are* the face of the occupation. They live under rough barricaded conditions, feel hemmed in by the mountains; the food, climate, society is nearly entirely alien to them. They have little knowledge of Kashmir's history, language, or culture (the wisdom of Indian defence seems to be that soldiers who are able to empathize with people in the areas in which they serve, cannot be effective). Many of them are devout Hindus—some posted at a temple in Kashmir complain that they are pelted with stones, that temple bells are unfastened, that land is encroached upon. They are ill-informed about the objectives of the Indian state or the grievances of the Kashmiri people. Quite a few of them turn hostile to the local population under such circumstances.

On a recent visit to Srinagar, I was talking to an Indian Central Reserve Police Force (CRPF) soldier at a prominent civic location in the city who lamented to me that: 'Kashmiri people are dogs. We do so much for them and they are ingrate curs.' I disagreed, mentioning later that I was Kashmiri myself. He was a young man, far from home, trapped by circumstances, who dreamt of a place called Italy. Periodically, in the middle of conversing, he or one of his colleagues would randomly shout at local Kashmiri passers-by; rudely, brusquely, asking them to stop, search them, call them names, shoo them away. The interaction was obviously power-laden and inhuman; the Kashmiris around him were nameless, faceless bodies. Soon after I left, I read in the papers that there had been a blast at that site in which a soldier was also killed. I always wondered whether he had been the same man I had spoken to; the one who could not wait to get out of Kashmir.

In Delhi, earlier this year, a Kashmiri Hindu stood posted at the gates of the 'Kashmir Expo' (a handicrafts fair selling Kashmiri clothes) and confidentially whispered to me that he was there to 'keep an eye' on the Kashmiri Muslim sellers inside. Elsewhere, in Srinagar, in the midst of playing cricket, small Kashmiri boys belted out slogans about 'Azadi', reminding me of East Jerusalem or Ramallah. An elderly craftsman uttered the precise and profound loss of the 'kalam', the pen, writing, but also perhaps what it enables: story, art, tradition.

Nostalgia for the future

Kashmir is daily witnessing an attrition of its culture, literature, architecture, psychology. The ruin of the Palladium Cinema, which stands at the centre of Lal Chowk, shows how the once thriving cultural buzz of Kashmir has been decimated in the wake of the last two decades of mindless violence and cultural repression. Even the last surviving cinema in IOK is under threat of closure. This destruction of cultural objects in wars is continuous throughout the history of the world.[6] On the first day of New Year 2010, when the near-full moon rose over the Zabarwan mountains at night, very few Kashmiris were out to see the copper-coloured miracle. There were no public celebrations at midnight. The city has been ghosted by oppression, violence, and terror perpetrated by the military/militants.

The Kashmiri Muslims being killed, raped, tortured, maimed in Kashmir are my fellow country people. The Kashmiri Hindus displaced in India are my fellow country people too—even as they classify me for my Kashmiri Pandit Hindu surname 'Kaul' and curse me for expressing the views I do. Other non-Kashmiri Indians insinuate treachery when I call myself 'Kashmiri' instead of Indian. Never mind. I am Kashmiri. I belong to Kashmir: my fatherland bequeathed to me by a father now dead. My ancestral home by a river is a carved wooden house with many floors and

---

[6]See Robert Bevan, *The Destruction of Memory: Architecture at War* (Reaktion Books, 2004).

stairs leading up to an attic in a street named after a fifteenth-century sultan who could read Sanskrit, Persian, Tibetan. The meta-narratives of big states have eaten up my history, my identity, my notion of a 'home'. And it is the same for every Kashmiri. I am alive, and for now, away. Those Kashmiris dehumanized and dying in the Valley do not have the luxury of reflection.

Indians should stop firing at those who pelt stones. Instead of the task force on crowd control, they might think about the meaning of the endlessly gathering crowds, the message in the parched heart of each stone. Any political movement always has multiple strands within it, multiple aspirations, which is where leadership comes in. But the freedom of Kashmiri people to elect political representatives into power was the most dangerous thing to tamper with in a democracy. Messy political accommodation may delay, but will not cure, the raw fury of the Kashmiri people who, at the moment, face indoctrination or liquidation.

Every year in the middle of the month of August, on Independence Day, Indians repeat the momentous 1947 midnight freedom speech of Nehru: 'Long years ago we made a tryst with destiny, and now the time comes when we shall redeem our pledge, not wholly, or in full measure, but very substantially . . . A moment comes, which comes but rarely in history . . . when the soul of a nation, long suppressed, finds utterance . . .'

Let these magic words be true for the nation of Kashmir too. Redeem the pledges, if not wholly and in full measure, then very substantially.

Understand Kashmiris instead of attempting to 'solve' or 'resolve' Kashmir. Conventional strategists don't always know best: demilitarize Kashmir. Repeal the draconian laws. End the mistrust of the Kashmiri people. Work with Pakistan and China to open borders and make the nation of Kashmir a reality for Kashmiris. Freedom cannot be realized without the capacity to conceive of the freedom of others.

This article first appeared on the website http://www.opendemocracy.net, 31 August 2010.

Kashmiri Marginalities
Construction, Nature and Response

Gowhar Fazili

To start the argument, we could club the dominant discourses around Kashmir into three broad categories: the Indian, the Pakistani and the Kashmiri discourses. The Indian and Pakistani discourses accommodate Kashmiri people, and the history of their collective struggles, only when (and if) these buttress their respective positions. The Kashmiri discourse is quintessentially about these struggles, and in turn the dominant Kashmiri discourse simplifies the sub-struggles and the fragmented politics that exist within, and the connections these have with the outside world. These dominant discourses of political history are a quagmire of claims and counterclaims. For those who have not borne the immediate brunt of the conflict, these generate excitement and passion, and the discourse is consumed through various media much like a one-day cricket match.

The Indian state, and the nationalists of many hues (including Hindutva, leftist, liberal, secularist) unanimously deploy various moments of Kashmir's history, including the accession signed by Maharaja Hari Singh, the elections held, the wars won, the leaders bought over, the subsidies given, the development achieved, the investments made, and so on, as indicators of Indian legitimacy and control in Kashmir. Kashmiri alienation, and separatist movements, figure in this narrative, if at all, variously, as consequences of external interference, uneven development, appeasement, the result of one-off political mistakes made by previous leaders, etc. These are to be corrected in due course, as and when Indian democracy matures. This discourse denies Kashmiris any intelligence or capability for autonomous political behaviour. It betrays amnesia around the rich history of struggles in Kashmir that preceded accession in 1947 and which still continue to inspire the people.

The Pakistani discourse emphasizes the 'Muslim connection' and dwells on the disputed nature of Jammu and Kashmir, which should have been Pakistan's by the logic of Partition. It focuses on the denial of self-determination to the people, and disregard of the UN resolutions calling for plebiscite in the region. It recounts the valour with which Azad Kashmir was won, and their view of the continued support and affinity that the majority of Kashmiri Muslims feel towards Pakistan. Though Pakistan lends moral and diplomatic support to the current 'separatist' movement in Kashmir, it devalues the nuanced engagement and struggle Kashmiris have held with the Indian state over the last sixty years, largely independent of Pakistan.

The dominant Kashmiri narrative, obviously at a marginalized position with respect to the other two discourses, imagines itself to be at the centre of the current political struggle. It draws from a long history of marginalization that predates modernity, tracing Kashmiri dislike and resistance against foreign occupation to the Mughal invasion in 1588 and the subsequent progressive emasculation and dispossession of Kashmiris by the Afghan, the Sikh, the Dogra and, in the same league, the Indian regime. It leverages dates like 16 March 1846, when the Amritsar Treaty was signed, and Kashmir was sold by the British to Maharaja Gulab Singh for 75,00,000 Nanakshahi rupees. (And in addition to this, six pairs of pashmina goats and three pairs of Kashmiri shawls annually). This was followed by excessive taxation to recover this money, and led to the famine of 1877–79, in which a large number of Kashmiris died (or were drowned by boatloads); the systematic denial of basic rights and dignity, and the discrimination on the basis of religion and region under the Dogra regime; the 13 July 1931 uprising against the maharaja and the massacre that followed. There is the year 1953 when Sheikh Abdullah, the first democratically elected prime minister of Kashmir was deposed and imprisoned by India on charges of conspiracy and sedition, arresting along with him the wide-ranging socio-economic revolution that was underway. It presumes the subsequent elections—held while Abdullah was in custody for twenty years—to have been rigged, and the period to have been marked with extreme suppression, corruption and co-option. The attempt to bring Kashmir closer to the Indian union though changes made over the years to extend provisions of the Indian Constitution are seen as the bulldozing of the residual safeguards against assimilation. It cites the failure of India to make progress on the various agreements and accords calling for plebiscite, for restoration of autonomy, and so on, as illustrations of India's '*chanakya neeti*'.

The significant moments in recent history, like the 1984 hanging of the Jammu Kashmir Liberation Front (JKLF) leader, Maqbool Bhat, the rigging of the 1987 elections, the mass uprising for Azadi, and the repression that began in 1989 when Kashmiri youth took to arms against the Indian state—these form the key markers around which the narrative of dispossession and valour is woven. Not surprisingly the Indian national days are designated as black days (including the day the Indian Army landed in Kashmir) and are marked with protests and blackouts. The narrative erases the moments of relative calm that Kashmiris have enjoyed in spurts in the intervening years, creating room for the rise of the educated middle class, which is now spearheading the separatist movement.

Much of the writing on Kashmir prior to the year 2000 concerns debates around these discourses as they emerged from the respective camps. Spokespersons, scholars, 'strategic' think tanks and a significantly large number of literate and illiterate Kashmiris are socialized into the importance of each of these claims, and possess the ability to manoeuvre through controversies to establish their political claims.

These positions are entrenched and provide for little flexibility. The dominant narratives have also found their way into the colloquial language, and abuse, frustration and humour are often expressed with reference to these moments. To mention just one: *'Ye nai Sattejihas yeeha balaay',* (Had forty-seven not been accursed), refers to 1947, the year the Indian Army landed in Kashmir, and the maharaja signed that ill-fated accession. The expression is used to let out everyday frustration, or to poke fun at someone's undue claims, or to lampoon some unworthy person's rise to power, wealth or fame through corruption.

While the Kashmiri self is torn between commitments to multiple, overlapping and contradictory identities and interests (like people anywhere else), the fact of being born in a territory where the conflict around its disputed nature has raged, in varying degrees, for over sixty years, complicates and intensifies concern for some identities at the cost of others. The political uncertainty impacts different members and groups differently, as they choose different strategies to deal with the onslaught from within and without.

To grossly simplify one example, a large majority of Pandits have moved out of Kashmir and many have allied themselves with Indian Hindu right-wing parties. Kashmiri Shia and Sunni Muslims largely identify with the broad contours of separatist politics, Pashtoons are invisible, Gujjars maintain an ambivalent position depending on where they are physically located. People in Gurez, Karnah and Uri, geographically isolated from the valley and living in close proximity with massive security garrisons, do not manifest sympathy with separatism, or at least not overtly, for obvious reasons. Within the state of Jammu and Kashmir, people of Doda, Poonch and Rajouri ally with Kashmir or Jammu depending on which of their interests and identities are threatened at a particular moment. People of Kargil gravitate towards Kashmir if and when the Buddhist majority discriminates against them. Hindu-majority areas of Jammu, and Buddhist Leh, have consistently favoured India and alleged discrimination by Kashmiri Muslims and their appeasement by the Indian state.

Kashmiri society is variegated along caste, class, community, gender, region, religion and political orientation. These identities contract within, and extend beyond, the geographical boundaries of Kashmir in different situations and along different questions. Yet it is the collective experience of a shared geography, history, language, culture and meanings that make Kashmiris conversant with each other in a special way, rendering others as outside. The identification with the dominant Kashmiri narrative presented above, which at this moment has a favourable bias towards the masculine, Muslim majoritarian identity, depends on where one is located within the cross-cutting mesh of identities, experiences and intellectual trajectories.

In India, Kashmiris are marked, irrespective of their other identities, by race, religion and language. Physically, they do not look, sound or behave like stereotypical Indians and are often harassed and made to prove their nationality at the ticket counters or wherever nationality applies. Outside Kashmir, given the context of the twenty years of armed conflict, and the consequent stereotyping of Kashmiris as terrorists, they face difficulty in finding accommodation and are forced to inhabit Muslim ghettos; they receive stares and unwelcome comments while travelling; they are easy prey for the security agencies seeking instant suspects for terror attacks; they cannot stick their neck out too much in day-to-day struggles so as not to risk being falsely reported; and cannot easily get visas to 'civilized', aka non-Muslim, countries. (For being a Muslim is bad enough, but being a Kashmiri Muslim, with the word 'Kashmir' on the passports, makes them doubly illegitimate.)

For the majority of the over 6,00,000 armed forces dotting neighbourhoods in the Valley, Kashmiris are potential Pakistani terrorists, who deserve to be eliminated, incarcerated or insulted on the flimsiest excuse. Kashmiris are targets for ready retribution in the wake of militant attacks. Homes can be searched, vehicles are stopped, people made to disembark, and are detained any moment and without explanation. Laws like the Armed Forces Special Powers Act (AFSPA) permit the security forces to shoot people as a preventive measure against possible future terror attacks. The Public Safety Act provides for preventive custody without trial even before one engages in 'objectionable' activity. Men, women and children are susceptible to sexual assault and torture and other forms of humiliation. Since the above experiences do not vary significantly among different segments of the Kashmiri population, they reinforce the collective marginalized identity.

The militant violence against the security forces, and the consequent deaths of Kashmiris in the conflict caused by militants or in crossfire, the killing of assumed or real Indian agents, the damage to personal property, cultural and religious places, though used as firewood for Indian propaganda against the separatists, enhances the collective sense of victimhood. In some it has also resulted in abhorrence for all forms of violence emanating from anywhere. Others hold Pakistan or foreigners or religious fundamentalists responsible and dislike them for this reason. Still others have turned overly apologetic, servile and defensive. But curiously it has not resulted in increased love for India among many.

The violence in the society has also resulted in intolerance towards those who for various reasons do not subscribe to the dominant narrative of victimhood, or those who try to channelize their anger and energies differently. Identities which are in-between, or fall outside the markers of dominant Kashmiri identity and victimhood, are rendered invisible or sought to be assimilated or, in extreme cases, eliminated. This is in consonance with how radical identities often turn upon their own people, on those who may choose divergent strategies or cannot fit within their grand 'emancipatory' project.

The dominant Kashmiri narrative is augmented with the indices of development like poor representation in civil services, academics, armed forces; backwardness of the region in terms of industrial development, educational infrastructure and employment opportunities within and outside the state. It also draws from the narrative of regional discrimination, establishing how India has favoured development in Jammu and Ladakh at the cost of Kashmir.

In the years prior to the 'liberalization' of the economy, as the only source of funding the Centre could offer financial packages to loyalists and compromisers, and punish those who tried to deviate, or rose in opposition to the Centre's hegemony. This practice continues. In the present times multinational private enterprise or funding cannot move in due to 'instability' and 'disturbance'. But irrespective of this, deals have been struck by the government with foreign companies. For example, power projects, are often complete sell-outs, helped by the fact that people are alienated from state-sponsored politics, and too busy fighting the separatist cause. The stunted development, wilful or incidental, adds to the alienation.

Kashmiri responses

How do the marginalized respond to the state of being marginal? Marginality, to borrow a phrase from Robert Park is a 'state of limbo' between at least two cultural worlds.[1] Being barred by prejudice from fuller acceptance into the dominant group on equal terms, the marginalized find it impossible to return to the original state, having transformed irredeemably in the process of interaction with the dominant culture. Park's understanding is drawn from the experience of migrant groups who fail, or are prevented from getting integrated into the dominant society. The social and psychological rupture is even more acute when marginality does not accrue from rejection or discrimination against a group seeking

---

[1]Robert E. Park, *On Social Control and Collective Behavior* (Chicago: University of Chicago Press, 1967).

to be assimilated, but is a result of forced assimilation of an unwilling population under occupation.

Such a population may reject assimilation, but be forced by circumstances to partially live and imbibe the elements of the very structure it resists. Its responses may appear to be erratic or even schizophrenic but they are guided by a definite logic and pattern. Adam Weisberger establishes marginality as 'a structure of double ambivalence—ambivalence toward the marginal person's native culture and ambivalence toward the "host" culture'.[2] For him, marginality yields four theoretically 'pure' responses—always somewhat mixed empirically—which he terms as poise, return, transcendence and assimilation. 'These responses represent attempts by the marginal person to resolve (or not to resolve) his or her complex ambivalence.' Let us examine what each of these implies and could represent in our context.

Assimilation, in his words, denotes 'the marginal person's absorption of the host's cultural standards, in the course of which he or she may sacrifice the practices and beliefs of the original culture, especially when the members of the host culture are inimical to the newcomer.' In Kashmir, the assimilationist tendency is largely exhibited by the co-opted upper class of politicians, bureaucrats, police officers and sections of the civil society and media invested in and working closely with the establishment. This should not be understood merely as a measure of convenience, but may, in fact, have a deeper ideological basis in seeking resolution of one's ambivalence. The political class that tried to negotiate a degree of autonomy within the existing political arrangement over the last sixty years did flirt with the idea of assimilation in some measure, though it was never acceptable to the masses and could not be openly and comprehensively advocated in the larger Kashmiri society.

---

[2]Adam Weisberger, 'Marginality and Its Directions', *Sociological Forum*, vol. 7 (September 1992), pp. 425–46.

Poise, on the other hand, represents 'a simultaneous rejection and acceptance of both cultural fields: rejection because neither culture is joined, and acceptance because no attempt is made to transform them from within.' Large sections of the Kashmiri middle class and upper middle class have exhibited poise, by neither imbibing or accepting the Indian mainstream political culture, nor actively seeking disengagement with it, or asserting a politically conscious counter-identity. For a greater part of its recent history, they have largely maintained silent compliance, or a distance from everyday political struggle on the streets of Kashmir. Though people, irrespective of class, have harboured resentment against the process of forced assimilation, they have risen in mass revolt only intermittently and in spurts, even while passively resisting it by not embracing the Indian identity.

In the stance of return, 'the marginal person may double back to his or her original group after confronting the host culture. The return actually results in a reconstruction, as the one who returns, changed by his or her exposure to the host culture, interprets the original culture in new terms ... The one who returns often exhibits an overzealous identification with his or her own group.'

The equivalent of this phenomenon in Kashmir would be those who portray themselves as more Muslim than Muslims or more Pakistani than Pakistanis or in case of Pandits or Dogras (if we were to consider the state as a whole), as more Hindu than the Hindus or more Indian than Indians. The recourse to religious fundamentalisms, parochial chauvinist nationalisms, extreme forms of cultural assertion have also been around in Kashmir all along, though not unmediated by the social engineering by the Indian and Pakistani establishment who have played different groups against each other to their own respective advantage. Both Pandits and Muslims have taken recourse to the invention of exclusivist pasts and have, at various moments in history, adopted rigid identities taking selective recourse to history.

Transcendence constitutes adoption or identification with ideologies and identities that may not necessarily spring from one's personal victimhood and seek one's redemption in emancipation from say, feudalism, colonialism, patriarchy, caste or other forms of exploitation through recourse to ideologies such as liberalism, socialism and secularism. The post-1938 Kashmiri liberation movement, the Naya Kashmir document, various trends in Kashmiri poetry and theatre enshrine such transcendence in ample measure. In contemporary times Kashmiri artists, poets and intellectuals have taken recourse to deep nationalism, drawing from spiritual traditions, translational liberation ideologies, accommodative varieties of neo-Islamism, humanisms, human rights discourses, left-leaning emancipatory movements, and postmodern identities of various hues.

Through history Kashmiris have, with varying degrees of success, pursued various directions in order to overcome their personal and collective sense of marginality. If we were to coalesce the four directions in which the marginalized react as suggested by Weisberger—namely assimilation, return, transcendence, poise—we can find parallels for each in different time periods, groups, institutions, individuals, or even simultaneously present as contradictory tendencies in a single entity or individual. (It would suffice to mention the lives of just two individuals: Sheikh Mohammed Abdullah and Prem Nath Bazaz). Kashmiris have also produced a wide range of political, intellectual and strategic responses that range over many categories: separatists, autonomists, Islamists, secularists, loyalists, anarchists, humanists, spiritualists, apologists, radicals, pacifists, and a myriad other responses (including self-loathing) and many still nascent and yet to be born.

Indian responses: encouragement of marginalities within

Indian civil society has looked at Kashmir interchangeably with empathy, apathy or disdain. The Indian mainstream has largely been silent on, or apathetic towards, Kashmiri suffering, perhaps because they do not share blood-ties, or see commonality of interest with Kashmiris. Those who empathize have their empathies conditioned by their location within the mainstream Indian politics. Indian intellectuals have tried to read Kashmir into their own respective projects, unidirectionally, rather than looking at the Kashmir problem from the viewpoint of Kashmiris and their own historical narrative. (Or conversely, to look at themselves or Indian politics through the Kashmiri prism.) Similarly, Indian Muslims and their sympathizers look at Kashmir as a minority problem, and expect Kashmiris to behave in a manner that does not threaten the survival of Indian Muslims through a 'backlash', which would in turn harm the fragile secular polity. The left (at least the co-opted statist left) sees it as a class problem, or at best that of regional imbalance, and because of false consciousness and undifferentiated class structure, unfit for class struggle and revolution. Large majorities in India, under the influence of the media with its nationalist bias, look at Kashmiris with disdain as they see them as anti-nationals who share cross-border loyalties and are mostly terrorists and fanatics.

Indian civil society groups have tried to identify or create their respective constituencies by promoting various sub-marginalities. Since funding to NGOs is channelled through the Indian elite, largely based in Delhi, they exercise substantial influence on how 'civil society' in its NGO avatar develops in Kashmir. The initiatives presently active in Kashmir have diverse ideological backgrounds. If we leave out the covert intelligence operations dressed in the form of NGOs, we can cite at least three: the Gandhian, the left leaning, and the feminist. Each sees the central problem in Kashmir to be that of fissuring of the community due to communalism/violence, feudalism and/or patriarchy respectively. While these faultlines exist, to see them as detached from the nationality question does violence to Kashmir. This is akin to British colonialists delegitimizing the Indian nationalist struggle on account of India's backwardness, male chauvinism or caste oppression.

Right-wing nationalists block any positive moves by the state towards a negotiated solution or reconciliation by branding the seasonal olive branch overtures by the state as 'Muslim appeasement', while at the same time cultivating a constituency among Pandits, and caste and class groups among Hindus of Jammu. They also use Kashmir as a spectacle to shore up their Hindutva constituency in India, by calling for abrogation of Article 370, or through flag-hoisting missions to Lal Chowk, and other such spectacles.

Since 1989, the state has responded largely with repression through violent means. Talks are offered and withdrawn, often at the peril of those who come forward, and end up being disowned by the community for the fear of failure and embarrassment (JKLF, Al-Jihad, Muslim Janbaz Force and so many others who renounced violence and entered dialogue at various stages of the struggle are cases in illustration).

There is also an unceasing ideological onslaught that sees Kashmir merely as a problem of development exacerbated by the ever-present 'foreign hand', that portrays all protest as political intrigue and at best a result of internal power struggle for control over resources. But if one were to follow the dialectics of politics in Kashmir over a longer period, it follows predictable, Sisyphean cycles of eternal return—of protests, repression, compromise, corruption and back to protests.

Indian state and civil society often intervenes to rescue Kashmiri women and other marginalized groups from the domination of 'Kashmiri Muslim male society' which is assumed to be essentially patriarchal. In any discussion on Kashmir, the question 'but what about women, Gujjars, Pahadis, Shias, Buddhists, Dogras, Pandits . . .?' invariably comes up. The Centre is able to subvert the mobilization around a particular marginality by bringing up the issue of sub-marginalities within and around the claimant group. In turn, the mobilization around the dominant discourse tries to suppress or ignore the discrimination within or around itself in response to this subversion. In the case of Kashmir, the demand for the right to self-determination is hostage to the question of what happens to the women, Gujjars, Shias, Pandits, Hindus of Jammu, and Buddhists of Ladakh. On the other hand, the dominant discourse around the unresolved nature of Jammu and Kashmir has subsumed other effective marginalities experienced by Kashmiris of various denominations at various other levels. These binaries are highlighted, and engineered in opposition, as though the natives cannot come to terms with such questions on their own, and a colonial state intervention is required for arbitration among the 'inherently schismatic'.

Ambivalent nature of Kashmiris

The narrative of Indian nationalism is fuelled by the 'adventures' of the Indian Army in Kashmir. It is followed by a legalistic discourse on the nature and tenability of Kashmir's accession with the Indian union. This discourse forms the backdrop against which the Kashmiris are examined and variously described: as the symbols of Indian secularism for having wilfully joined the Indian union despite their religious and geographical affinity with Pakistan; as being primordially secular, Sufi and non-violent; or being treacherous people capable of cross-border allegiance, duplicity and deceit.

This problematic status makes them unfit for democracy, and provides a good reason why Kashmiris need to be mainstreamed and denied autonomous self-definition, and a dignified independent identity. The only identities permissible to Kashmiris are the one that pass the litmus test of Indian ideals, the ideals which the Indians may themselves not have been able to uphold. If the identity proclaimed or exhibited by Kashmiris does not fit within the standards offered to other regional minorities in India, then these have to be shorn off in the interest of the 'unity' of the nation. Kashmiris are defined partially, in contradictory ways, in a diffused form, and only to the extent that it serves the political purposes of the state. And then left to deal with the schizophrenic condition on their own.

The Kashmiri counter-narrative sees the illegal accession signed on their behalf by their tormentor, Maharaja Hari Singh, and the denial of self-determination as only milestones in their long struggle for emancipation, which began much earlier and continues till date. Kashmiris subscribing to this narrative see themselves as de facto and temporary citizens of India who have been subjugated against their will.

While Kashmiris at different stages in history have bought into the discourse about the secular, peaceful compositeness of their culture, they resent its use to make them into the 'essence of Indian nationalism' and react by adopting the exact opposite stereotype. Simultaneously, the emphasis on their affinities and continuities with regions that spread beyond the de facto borders of the Indian state—that is the connection with Pakistan, Afghanistan, China, Tibet, Central Asia, Persia and beyond—provide them a lever to establish their separateness.

Self, community and the universe

In order to engage with the Kashmiri self I will begin with myself. I find myself marginalized from the community in which I was born because my intellectual and emotional trajectory pushed me to transcend my 'received self', by imbibing fragments of and influences from the exposure to other cultures and intellectual currents. In the process I hope to evolve by contrasting these fragments and make something new out of them and thus constantly manage to recreate myself.

The process, however, distances me from my community in terms of my appearance, opinions as well as associations. But since the community I come from is marginalized, if I were to become too different from it in terms of my looks or my subjectivity, I would be perceived as a betrayer. Apart from this, seeing the community under distress, I personally sense my own betrayal. I get forced to identify with the community and represent it. The struggle I am confronted with is how to retain the individual self and maintain its natural growth while at the same time not abandon my community in distress. The third commitment is to the universal whole, the affinity and commitment one feels towards the shared values and heritage of the human community.

It is hard to negotiate a commitment to self, community and universe, all at the same time. Yet this negotiation is important since a sense of justice is at stake. The luxury of being able to accord justice to all becomes difficult, as the communal sense of victimhood alters one's subjectivity in its favour. For example, when the outsiders perceive and treat Kashmiris unfavourably, it reduces my emphasis on other identities within Kashmir and the collective Kashmiri identity becomes the focus of my attention. As long as I am able to keep myself outside and inside at the same time, I might be able to maintain a fairer view of things. But in this lies the danger of blunting one's outrage and protest.

Normally, one does identify—and should be able to—with multiple marginalities at the same time. Some marginalities I embody, like Muslim, South Asian and Kashmiri. Others I may not (like gender, caste, rural, disabled) and yet I am able to identify with them. I cannot have my concerns limited to myself and my community since my own victimhood shapes my identification with other marginalities. But how exactly does one locate oneself with respect to other marginalities in real politics? How does one negotiate between strategy and idealism? When do I remain silent about a particular marginality to privilege the other? When do I maintain strategic silence about other marginalities so as to keep a certain marginality in focus? How does one combine these simultaneous movements to ensure that a particular marginality does not acquire fascistic proportions?

This negotiation has to take place in a colonial context where differential importance is given to marginalities by the state or dominant interests in order to subvert, fragment and hijack marginalities. One marginality is played up against the other. Demands are counterposed—something more general or ephemeral like 'Azadi' against something more concrete like 'bijli-sadak-pani'. It is like dangling one need before the deprived in order to wean them off the other. The choice offered is often between dignity and the basic amenities of life.

Symbolic activity can hijack the real issues around marginality. The more radical I sound, the more legitimate my voice becomes in a marginalized community. This triggers one-upmanship within the marginalized group, in the race to lay claim as real representatives of the marginal community. One has to arrive at a position between compromising oneself and being reduced to a radical rant.

In order to make the larger sense of marginality a composite of the marginalities within and a principled and strategic alliance with other marginalities without, the process of emancipation of different marginalities has to happen simultaneously. There is need for an ongoing dialogue to negotiate the genuineness of claims of marginality and to resolve conflict of interest and issues of justice in the context of different marginalities working together. There is need for democracy within the alliances of marginalities. For Kashmir, 'Azadi' has to be redefined in terms of (and achieved through) the notional and substantive emancipation of all the sub-marginalities that constitute it. Or risk being fragmented or reduced to yet another chauvinistic movement. It is only this rigorous self-definition that will facilitate principled alliances, and the synchrony with other movements and conceptions of marginality.

This article first appeared on the website http://www.risingkashmir.com, 31 January 2010.

Kashmir
Three Metaphors for the Present

Arif Ayaz Parrey

This summer, Kashmir is again flooded by freedom's terrible thirst.[1] There is blood in the streets, of children mostly, running simply, as the blood of children does.[2] There is talk, much talk; reality clashing against the machinations of propaganda, verifiable facts up against plausible but untrue theories which hover inside the offices of bureaucrats and news rooms, stone-hard truth versus manufactured bulletins. The verdicts are out, both of the courts of Delhi and the tribunal of the Kashmiris, the former declaring victory and the latter a fight till victory.

There is nothing new in these confrontations between fact and fiction. Kashmir is a conflict in which truth and lies have, in response to the efforts of the powers that be in New Delhi, Islamabad and beyond, always floated without anchor. The smaller

---

[1] From Agha Shahid Ali's poem 'After the August Wedding in Lahore, Pakistan', in *The Veiled Suite* (New Delhi: Penguin Books India, 2010), p. 241.

[2] From Pablo Neruda's poem 'I'm explaining a few things', translated by Anthony Kerrigan in *Selected Poems* (New York: Houghton Mifflin, 1990), p. 151.

truth is eaten up by bigger lies which in turn feed even larger truths which are gobbled up by even bigger lies and so on and so forth. A million metaphors find a niche in this *satisar* of free-floating meaning.[3] Our purpose here will be to examine three of them.

The mirror

The temptation is to blame it on the quirks of the human mind itself, a structural malfunction which can be kept in check by maintaining a constant vigil, but which can never be completely eradicated. I am talking of the tendency of a human mind to mirror itself in another. Whenever we are in opposition to the Other, our immediate reaction is to assume that the ideas, motives, plans and their execution of that other are the mirror image of our ideas, motives, plans and their execution. Thus, the impulsive inference is that the protests in Kashmir are guided by reasons which are the faithful reflections of the reasons which guide the Indian state and its forces, and vice versa.

In the narrative of the Indian state (I am including the Indian media within the definition of the state, for the simple reason that with regard to Kashmir, it does behave like a state instrumentality), the protests, particularly the ones with stone-pelting incidents, are well-planned and highly organized when, in fact, it is the conduct of the Indian state which is well-planned and highly organized. The Indian security forces are paid for their action and so it is presumed that the protesters must also receive money for protesting. The ordinary Indian soldier is largely indifferent to the political situation on the ground and the past and the future of Kashmir, so it is assumed that the same must be true for the protesters too.

In the narrative of the Kashmiris, because their own protests are spontaneous and without well-organized hierarchies of command and power, the brutality of the Indian foot-soldiers is taken as

---

[3]In mythology, Kashmir is a primeval lake.

spontaneous and unorganized with no chain of command and hierarchy of power and orders. The demand for self-determination, for Azadi, is, and the protests in pursuit of that end are essentially in the nature of a personal struggle for Kashmiris, in which they are involved for individual reasons; they echo it by believing that the soldiers fighting for the other side are also motivated by personal reasons.

Before we move on to examine the veracity of this *mirror effect*, we must first admit that blaming the human mind for it in Kashmir is far too simplistic. Because one of the parties, the Indian state, is not a human mind or a shambolic congregation of human minds acting impulsively, but the sum total of structures working through an organized group of human minds, expected to *act in their most rational capacities*. Yet the state machinery has regularly been reinforcing the mirrored myth, leaving no stone unturned to prove that the protests in Kashmir are organized, conducted and paid for by Pakistan, Lashkar-e-Toiba, Hurriyat leaders and even the constructed rivals National Conference (NC) and People's Democratic Party (PDP). While on the other hand, the Indian state, working through its instrumentalities (the military and paramilitary forces) is all too human, and fires bullets, pellets and tear gas, resulting in deaths and injuries, only on the spur of the moment, as human beings will do when faced with the imminent danger of the mob. This, as we shall see, is clearly an inversion of facts.

Power, like that mirror in the Borges story[4] (or the looking-glass through which Alice discovered more wonderlands), works both ways. Policies like the use of the Jammu and Kashmir (J&K) police—it's abuse you could say—for maintaining state terror, help the Indian state in lessening the burden on its dead-tired paramilitary forces, but also provides a valuable site of clarity and understanding. Being Kashmiris themselves, a majority of the

---

[4]See Jorge Luis Borges's story 'The People of the Mirror' in *The Book of Imaginary Creatures* (Buenos Aires: Penguin, 2005), pp. 18–19.

policemen share the experiences and the sentiments of the people at an individual level. By acting as a translucent window into India's statecraft vis-à-vis Kashmir, ordinary people realize that it is not the foot-soldier on the ground but the juggernaut of the Indian state which is responsible for the ruthless cruelty and the gruesome occupation. This window opens onto a wider room.

The ordinary Indian soldier is a much-maligned fellow trapped in a thankless job. Generally belonging to the poorer, marginalized sections of the society, the primary reasons for his joining the armed forces are economic in nature. Typically, he has been brought up in a milieu which is mildly communal, vaguely patriotic, faintly democratic but still perceptibly humane. His experience in 'troubled areas' quickly washes off the rudiments of '*mera bharat mahaan*' (India is great) from his persona—being part of an institution which is made to do the state's dirty work makes him realize that the hands of the state are so blood-stained that all the perfumes of Arabia cannot clean them. The deeply chauvinistic discourse built in and around the armed forces is in direct contradiction with these personal experiences, creating a surplus neurosis which exhibits itself every now and then through the violent assertion of nationalism, alternating with an equally intense assertion of humanism on other occasions. As a consequence of the experience in troubled areas, the original patriotism in him is replaced by a feeling of solidarity and brotherhood for his fellow soldiers who, like him, are instruments and victims in equal measure. Loyalty to this band of brothers becomes the new nationalism and love for it becomes the new patriotism. Faced with a mass uprising like the one in Kashmir, nothing equips these soldiers to deal with the situation humanely, their primary concern, other than following state orders, being the security and well-being of their unit in particular, and the armed forces in general.

The state recognizes this. An overwhelming majority of the soldiers have had no previous experience of living in a setting in which Hinduism is not the dominant religious discourse. So many loudspeakers blaring from so many mosques on all sides, beards and *burqas* galore, a million symbols of a religion they are taught to *tolerate*, not let dominate, rubs their mild communalism the wrong way. The state recognizes this. The realization that a language, a culture and a society about which they were schooled is an integral part of India but has nothing Indian about it is bound to not only violate their vague patriotism, but also to produce a surge of alienation in the soldiers. The state recognizes this. Coming from marginalized communities and classes, these soldiers have never had any measure of control over their immediate surroundings before being posted to the 'disturbed areas'. Thirsting for some power and control, the soldiers are tempted by the combined seductive powers of the guns (provided by the state) and the impunity provided by laws promulgated by the state (like Armed Forces Special Powers Act [AFSPA], Disturbed Areas Act [DAA], etc.), and the othering of the entire native community as the enemy lures them into the abuse of their newly found power. Killing natives in fake encounters for monetary and other benefits is one of the visible outcomes of the way this structure works, but there are a million other outcomes which are hidden under rhetoric and deceit. The state recognizes this.

Over this base of emotions and feelings, the state builds the superstructure of its command and control. The probable instruction given to the soldiers, oft-repeated in the media these days by ministers, bureaucrats, politicians and high-ranking officers of the armed forces, is to 'exercise maximum restraint in crowd control'.[5] These instructions can be broken up into three laws mirroring

---

[5]'Exercise maximum restraint, CRPF told (by the Union government).' *The Hindu*, 30 June 2010.

'Security forces are exercising maximum restraint. They are sometimes compelled to use force to protect public property and defend themselves,' he [Union Home Minister P. Chidambaram] said. He said security forces have been asked to deal with the crowds in a restrained manner. Shockingly, he revealed that armed militants were mingling with the protesting crowds.' *Time Out*, 4 August 2010.

'Omar (Abdullah) asks police to exercise maximum restraint.' *Thaindian News*, 22 November 2010.

Asimov's Laws of Robotics, because each latter law is subject to the preceding law(s):

1. Control the crowd.
2. Ensure the security of self and fellow soldiers.
3. Exercise restraint.

Even when applied to emotionless robots, these instructions would be dangerous because the primary goal is crowd control and not exercise of restraint. It is therefore natural to expect that if the crowds were motivated by such strong reasons that even the fear of imminent death would not deter and control them, it would be obligatory for the soldiers, *to carry out the instructions of the state*, to use any method necessary to disperse the crowd, including firing upon it and killing protesters.

When applied to soldiers who are human, subject to the emotions and sentiments described above, these laws become even more dangerous because in addition to the structured instructions from the state, the unstructured emotions and sentiments of the soldiers, again a construction of the state, also come into play. For example, notice that the provision of self-defence is wedged between crowd control and exercise of restraint, subject to the former but having precedence over the latter. The soldiers have instructions to control the crowd at any cost possible, even if that means putting their own lives in jeopardy. If and when the confrontation with angry protesters, who are seething with indignation at the injustices committed against them and brimming with self-righteousness because of the moral superiority of their demand for their basic human rights, puts the lives of the soldiers in peril, they will obviously (and in line with the policies of the state, courtesy the second law above) fire in self-defence, to protect themselves and their fellow soldiers. But can we ignore the fact that this need for self-defence is necessitated in the first place by the state's refusal to acknowledge the demands of the people and its insistence on using the hapless soldiers to confront the crowds? The state therefore becomes doubly culpable for the actions of its soldiers.

The human experience in the contemporary world trains most individuals to have natural empathy for the struggles of other individuals while at the same time being suspicious about the grinding, overbearing nature of structures and systems. Perhaps, this too comes through mirroring, individuals appreciating the strong inertia to resistance that people possess and how it really, really takes a lot for people to stand up and fight for something. The struggle in Kashmir is a people's movement. This gives it legitimacy. All the attempts by the state to portray it as a planned, funded and organized monstrosity, when the state itself fits that description—and the inverse attempts to prove the state to be individual, emotional and human, when the Kashmiris are all those things—are just perverse endeavours to usurp the legitimacy which belongs to the Kashmiri people.

Unable to come out of the colonial legacy it has inherited, of giving precedence to territory over people, the best the Indian state can do is to be cunning enough to use the marginalized and the poor from one part of the empire, whose energies would otherwise be spent in fighting the same oppressive, hegemonic state structures of which they are the soldiers, to control another part of the empire, where the natives are demanding Azadi and spending *their* energies fighting the soldiers.

The state thus kills two birds with one stone, without ever being labelled a stone-pelter.

The rising sun

Satyajit Ray, the Bengali film-maker and master of imagery, has created an evocative metaphor in the beginning of his film *Mahapurush*. A crook disguised as a Baba, travelling in a train with his disciple/junior partner in crime, is sitting opposite an elderly gentleman and his young daughter. It is dawn. Suddenly the fake Baba begins to mumble, pointing his two little fingers towards each other and moving them in circles. A moment later, he looks out the window, spreads his arms and starts to gesture upwards with them, intoning, '*Uth! Uth!*' (Rise! Rise!) Sure enough the sun rises, which allows the Baba to let out a guffaw and remark that he has to wake up the fellow every single morning. The show is so impressive that it convinces the elderly gentleman that the Baba is responsible for sunrise!

Why do Kashmiris protest? Why do they pelt stones, even when faced with bullets? Why do they come out in tens of thousands whenever an opportunity presents itself? Why do they observe hartals for such long periods, bleeding their own economy and ruining their own livelihood? Why does every new event, month and year make it clearer and clearer that 'these stupid Kashmiris' would rather die fighting than give up their demands? Why?

The immediate reason is the overwhelming military presence in the region. Statistics testify that there are about 7,00,000 military and paramilitary personnel in J&K. A huge number by any estimate, particularly when the government itself puts the number of active militants, the official reason for the presence of the security forces in civilian areas, at about 500. But statistics alone do not tell the whole story. The disproportionate number of security personnel and the disproportionate amount of power and impunity they wield under the AFSPA and other laws means that the everyday life of ordinary Kashmiris is turned into living hell. There is a bunker every few hundred metres and a camp for every few villages. There are so many security checks and so many orders to produce ID proofs that the whole of Kashmir is transformed into a jail for the natives. There are regular killings, rapes, molestations, beatings and an unrelenting dose of threats to life, honour, family and property, resulting in constant fear and humiliation. To an ordinary Kashmiri, even when the security forces are not indulging themselves in their privileges, the nature and the memory of the relationship the people share with the security forces is such that in a common space the former are reduced to an inferior class, further enraging the natives who see such degradation in their own land as one of the worst possible disgraces.

Underneath these apparent reasons for the militarization of civil spaces, with impunity, are buried deeper reasons akin to a political subconscious. Suppose all the security forces are removed from J&K and AFSPA and other such laws are revoked; would that end the protests in Kashmir? The probable answer is no. Why? Because what Kashmiris assert through the protests is the political right of self-determination and not just the facts of human rights abuses. They don't merely want removal of the military and withdrawal of AFSPA and other such laws; they want complete removal of India from their land and the withdrawal of the Indian Constitution. Find proof in the slogans of protesting Kashmiris: '*Hum kya chahte? Azadi*' (What do we love/want? Freedom); '*Ae zalimo ae jabiro Kashmir hamara chhod do*' (Cruel oppressors; leave our Kashmir); '*Yeh mulk hamara hai, iska faisla hum karenge*' (This country is ours; we will decide its fate); and the latest versions of these old declarations—'Quit Kashmir' and 'Go India, go back.'

The right of self-determination is a universally acknowledged principle. It is based in the belief that people are the best judge of their own good and their future. This belief may not be an absolute standard, but the truth is that all criticisms of the principle are self-contradicting and self-defeating. The logic of this belief becomes clear when you acknowledge that it is difficult to find individuals or a people who will deny self-determination to themselves. Can anyone deny it to others then? For example, Indians will say that they are the best judge of their own good and their future and British claims a century ago—that Indians had no right to choose swaraj because they were an integral part of the British empire—were laughable and absurd. Can Indians deny equivalent rights to Kashmiris? Possessing the same cognitive faculties as the rest of humanity, Kashmiris are also in love with the logic in the principle of self-determination.

The Indian state attempts to delegitimize this love, downsized to a right, primarily by creating the fiction that India is a monolith which has existed since the time of Manu and the movement for independence in Kashmir is a secessionist movement. To open the

Pandora's Box of the problems with this notion, the country Jammu and Kashmir, in its current form, was born in 1846 when the British sold it to Maharaja Gulab Singh; while the country India, in its current form, was born only in 1947. How can the struggle for ending the occupation of a country by another country which is 101 years younger to it be a secessionist movement?

Even if we take into account the definition given by Anderson,[6] that a nation is an imagined community of people who consciously visualize themselves to be a part of it, Kashmiris never imagine themselves as Indians and cannot be forcibly made to do so.

In 1947, the people of Jammu and Kashmir had already been fighting for democracy, and an end to the despotic Dogra rule, for many years. When raiders from the newly formed Pakistan invaded Kashmir, the Dogra maharaja, under duress, was made to sign the Instrument of Accession to India as a precondition for military help. The fact that the maharaja was under duress when he signed the instrument coupled with the fact that he had no legitimacy in the eyes of the common people of Kashmir raises serious questions of validity regarding the instrument. The newly formed Indian state formally recognized these questions when it promised Kashmiris plebiscite. Many may wish to, but nobody can ever erase these historical facts.

Kashmir's right of self-determination is thus not a right of secession but a right of consent. The possible accession by J&K to India was to be a contract between two sovereign parties and it is common knowledge that consent of both parties is necessary for validating any contract. In the paradigm of democracy, the Indian public needs to be asked whether they want Kashmir to be a part of India and the Kashmiri people need to be asked whether they want to be a part of India, and if either party does not consent, Kashmir cannot become a part of India.

---

[6]Benedict Anderson, *Imagined Communities: Reflections on the Origin and Spread of Nationalism* (London: Verso, 2006).

By making the will of the people central, democracy automatically reinforces and reiterates the right of self-determination. India claims to be a democracy, and the serious structural and functional problems with this claim notwithstanding, it makes it obligatory for the state to adopt a democratic discourse as its major narrative. This narrative is disseminated through the education system, media, bureaucracy, politics etc. to all territories held by the state, including Kashmir. In this manner, the very ideas of democracy promoted by the Indian state feed into the discourse of self-determination of Kashmir, thereby strengthening evermore the resolve of the Kashmiri people. However, to contain this resolve of the people the State has to behave like a colonial power and use force, coercion, propaganda and deceit to maintain control over the territory against the wishes of the people. This creates a basic contradiction in the policy of the Indian state with regards to Kashmir: promoting democracy and practising occupation. The tragedy is that common Kashmiris and the foot-soldiers of the state have to pay the price, a very heavy price, for this paradox the state has created for itself.

The history of India in Kashmir has been a story of false promises, manipulated elections, slow but systematic economic ruin resulting in dependency, decay of institutions and structures due to neglect and active curtailment, promotion of corruption by colonial policies like rewarding people for loyalty to the empire, organized violence, lies, brutality, propaganda, terror, more lies and so on and so forth. During the last twenty years, 70,000 Kashmiris have been killed, mostly by the Indian military apparatus. This year alone, at the last count, more than one hundred (I have had to update this figure many times while writing this piece) unarmed protesters, most of them in their teens, have been killed by soldiers and policemen *working under orders from the Indian state*. India has by and large been able to talk its own people—and the rest of the world—into a shaky, temporal conviction through media control and propaganda that such things do not happen in Kashmir, and even if they do, it is not responsible for all these misdeeds. But the Kashmiris know better—from first-hand experience. The memory of such a brutal occupation is a formidable force in itself. The energy of this memory propels the demand for self-determination, and like an avalanche coming down an infinite slope, each new event, killing, abuse, falsehood, and protest only adds more power to this motor of memory. The Kashmiris won't stop demanding the right of self-determination, because there is nothing wrong with this demand per se; the Indian state, as long as it wants to be a colonial occupier, will kill more Kashmiris, jail others, abuse even more and go on telling lies and broadcasting propaganda; all actions which will make Kashmiris even more determined in their struggle.

The protests in Kashmir in connection with the demand for the right of self-determination are, therefore, as natural and predictable as the cycle of day and night. Memory, history, democracy and humanity—all lead a Kashmiri to the logic of this demand. In the metaphor of the rising sun from Satyajit Ray's *Mahapurush*, the trick the fake Baba performed was to understand a natural phenomenon and its timings and to attach his own actions to it. In the theatre of Kashmir, many individuals, interests and parties hitch their wagon to the rising sun of the yearning for self-determination. This serves the Indian state well and so it actively promotes and orchestrates this harnessing of disengaged politics to the real struggle of the people.

When the protests—which, we need to remember, are always only the visible manifestation of freedom's terrible thirst—started this summer, they were summarily dismissed as being guided from Pakistan. The trick was that because the protests use a green flag and an idiom partially based in Islam; it is easy to claim that the green-flag-bearing, 'Islamic' state of Pakistan is responsible for making the sun of protests rise in Kashmir.

(The green flag and chanting of slogans like '*Naarai takbeer, Allah-hu-Akbar*' are taken as conclusive proof that Kashmiris are Muslim fanatics of a kind who would be poisoned by the very air in which a non-Muslim breathes. According to this theory, Chinese

Buddhists, when agitated, should chant, '*O Khodaya!*', Catholics '*Hai Ram!*' and Hindus '*Ya Elohim!*' in order to be considered 'moderate'.)

The protests in Srinagar and other areas where National Conference (NC) candidates had been chosen as Members of the Legislative Assembly (MLAs) were ascribed to the manoeuvrings of the People's Democratic Party (PDP). When the protests spread to south Kashmir, which has been designated a PDP bastion, the scheming NC was held responsible for them. These attributions are as correct as accrediting Communist Party of India (CPI) and Communist Party of India (Marxist) [CPI(M)] for the Maoist uprising in the eastern Ganga plains and peninsular India.

All these attempts aimed at inventing fake reasons for the sunrise are an effort to delegitimize the life and struggle of the Kashmiri people. These theories are based on the premise that Kashmiris are a headless and heartless people who can neither feel their own pain, nor think of the reasons and responsibility for, and solution to, that pain, and need external agencies to spoon-feed them a discourse.

Perhaps the most dangerous manifestation of this dehumanization and de-democratization of Kashmiris is the attribution of the protests and the demand for self-determination in Kashmir to the Hurriyat leaders and their networks. The fact is that the Hurriyat ideology gains legitimacy because among all the existing political arrangements, it is closest to the sentiments and political ideals of the people of Kashmir. The Indian state tries to prove that it is the other way round and the people derive legitimacy from Hurriyat.[7] To contest this ridiculous argument, one only needs to ask the rhetorical question(s): What will happen if all Hurriyat leaders, 'moderates' and 'hard-liners', Syed Ali Shah Geelani, Mirwaiz Umar Farooq, Yasin Malik, Masarat Alam Bhat, Asiya Andrabi, Shabir Shah and the rest come together and declare that they

---

[7]It reminds one of Bertolt Brecht's remark: 'Now that the people have failed the government, it is time for the government to dissolve the people and elect another.' From 'The Solution', c. 1953.

believe Kashmir is an integral part of India? Will Kashmiris still consider them their leaders? Will they still follow their calendars? Will that end the struggle for freedom? Will Kashmiris say 'Yes, we are a part of India'?

Sheikh Mohammed Abdullah, the tallest leader Kashmir has ever produced, the one who successfully supervised one of the greatest land redistribution schemes ever carried out in the world, a man who gave the poor Kashmiri peasants a share in their own lives, the one who gave some of the first lessons of democracy to the common people of Kashmir, the one who is still affectionately called '*Bub*' (father) and '*Toath*' (dear one) by Kashmiris, is today remembered bitterly in Kashmiri memory because of his final act of bending before the might and the guile of the Indian state. I rest my case.

The Babel

Against the backdrop of such knowledge, India's *Kashmir experts* ask: 'Oh, but what do the Kashmiris *really* want?' This is not the innocent and innocuous question it appears to be; behind it the politics of delegitimization is at work again. Because Kashmiris cannot make their demands any clearer—self-determination and Azadi—what this question implies is that Kashmiris, millions of them, are an infantile society wishing for an unattainable moon when a lollypop may well satisfy them. These Kashmir experts have been gleefully dishing out this belittling understanding of Kashmiri society for years now, oblivious to the fact that history is very unkind to the practice of patronizing.

The protesters in Kashmir are always described as 'misguided youth'. Images of middle-aged women throwing stones and old men raising their fists, which have flooded the internet, are allowed to have no effect on the tenability of this argument. At any rate, the same experts, who are otherwise so interested in 'scholarly' exegesis on Kashmir, fail to highlight how the youth are always, in every freedom struggle, at the forefront of the protests but that in no way means that older generations are indifferent to the situation. Generation after generation of Kashmiris has been protesting for the same cause through the Plebiscite Front, the Muslim United Front, the Mahaz-e-Azadi and through military methods in the 1990s, and they were always met by the most brutal face of India's power. To think that these are a people who have already surrendered terminally before India's military and strategic clout, without having expanded and passed on a culture of revolution, betrays a denial of how human societies function. Such attitudes are again informed by the processes of delegitimization and infantalization.

On these 'youths' being 'misguided', we have to go deeper and ask ourselves: What makes an idea legitimate in the paradigm of democracy? That India should be a free nation is an idea, and so is Free Kashmir. What gives the idea of free India legitimacy? The belief of a majority of Indians in it. What gives the idea of free Kashmir legitimacy? The belief of a majority of Kashmiris in it, of course. Why are Kashmiris 'misguided' for holding beliefs similar to those which make Indians 'nationalists' and 'democrats'?

When it becomes impossible to dodge the relentless bombardment by truth and reason (and stones), these experts—intellectuals, media-persons, bureaucrats, law-makers and civil society members—seek refuge in the Tower of Babel. 'Ah, but there are so many voices. There are so many shades of opinion. Whom do we listen to? Who do we talk to?'

This is followed by talk of engaging all sections of the society. More than six decades after Independence and 'democracy' in India, media-sketches of young politicians continue to be full of words like 'scion' and 'blood-line', as if the most important qualifications for being a leader was the dynasty you belonged to. India has hardly moved away from its 'republican' tradition of 'India is Indira' and its various temporal and regional variants, and politics has come to mean playing out the differences of caste, class, religion, language and region, instead of any real responsibility of the politician to the people. The phrase 'engaging all sections of the society' therefore translates into inviting a few old men, and sometimes a couple of women, to have lunch at one of the finer places in Delhi, or better still, sending envoys to Kashmir to have the same lunches and dinners on the banks of the Dal Lake. The refusal to acknowledge the aspirations of the common Kashmiri people is therefore as much a function of the process of delegitimization of Kashmiri people as a failing of democracy itself in India, where the practice of power flowing from the leader to the masses—instead of the other way round—is condoned, if not expressly ratified, by the enlightened sections of the citizenry. Why else would there be silence on the hackneyed technique of engaging the Kashmiri leadership, when a much simpler, more logical, democratic and decisive solution is available in a plebiscite?

When the people started to build the Tower of Babel in the valley of Shinar, after the Great Flood—the last metaphor we are perusing here—God remarked: 'Behold, the people is one, and they have all one language, and this they begin to do: and now nothing will be restrained from them, which they have imagined to do,' and since they intended to reach the same heights as their God he decided to confound their speech.[8] God confused the people rather than destroying them because destroying the people with the Flood hadn't taught them to be godly.[9]

In *India's Struggle for Independence* Bipin Chandra writes that when World War II broke out in September 1939, India demanded that Britain define its war aims and, since the war was being fought for democracy, gives India independence:

The British government's response was entirely negative. Linlithgow, the Viceroy, in his well-considered statement

---

[8]See Genesis 11:1–9 of the King James Version Bible.

[9]See Flavius Josephus, Book I, 4.3, from *The Works of Flavius Josephus* translated by William Whiston, A.M. Auburn and Buffalo John E. Beardsley in 1895. The likeness between the Flood and the terror unleashed on the people of Kashmir since the beginning of the last decade of the twentieth century is too obvious to be ignored.

of 17th October 1939 harped on the *differences* among Indians, tried to use Muslim League and the princes against the Congress and refused to define Britain's war aims beyond stating that Britain was *resisting aggression* ... For the future the promise was that at the end of the war the British government *would enter into consultations with 'representatives of several communities, parties and interests* in India, and with the Indian Princes' ... On 18th October, Zetland (Secretary of State for India and Burma) spoke in the House of Lords and stressed differences among Indians, especially among Hindus and Muslims. He branded the Congress as a purely Hindu organisation.[10]

So when the Indian state suddenly becomes the champion of Kashmiri Pandits, Jammu Dogras, Ladakhi Buddhists, Gujjars, Paharis and sections of the very privileged and the very unprivileged among Kashmiri Muslims, it is only following a time-tested formula of all colonial empires. Similar ventures aimed at a purely sociological explanation of the demand for Azadi, and trying to base it in poverty, in Islamic radicalization and in unemployment, are also something the world has witnessed a million times now. Efforts have been made to describe the protesters as *nouveau pauvre* who are demanding Azadi because they have lost their privileges, or unemployed frustrated youth, or plain brainwashed kids. While this may help the Indian state to buy some more time on Kashmir from the world and its own people, it at the same time fuels the indignation of the Kashmiri people, the only real stakeholders in the long run.

Self-determination works in the space of international relations and is the right of the people who inhabit a territory to decide on their sovereignty and international political status. Structures like

---

[10]Bipin Chandra, Mridula Mukerjee, Aditya Mukerjee, J.K. Pannikar and Sucheta Mahajan, *India's Struggle for Independence* (New Delhi: Penguin Books India, 1989), pp. 449 and 450. Emphasis mine.

class, caste and patriarchy work in the space of sub- and meta-national paradigms. The Dalits and the poor do not demand their separate homeland, and women do not demand their island of Lesbos, because the existing homeland is already their own, built from their blood, sweat and tears; what they demand is their rightful place in it. Kashmiris, like Indians a century ago, are asserting their unalienable right to decide on the political future of their homeland. This assertion does not flow out of the structures and critiques of class, caste and patriarchy, although they do inform its context and flow into it.

Notice, however, that when elections are held in Kashmir, the people 'vote' for none of these considerations; all of them are mysteriously unified and 'vote for India'. There are no regional divides, caste divides, religious, ethnic and lingual divides at that time. Abracadabra. So if all the election commissioners and their staff are members of the Bharatiya Janata Party (BJP), all the paramilitary forces deployed to ensure 'free and fair' elections are BJP workers, the candidates, too, all belong to the BJP, no prizes for guessing who will win the elections. India is a party to the Kashmir dispute, and any primer on democracy informs us that no entity can organize and preside over an election in which it is a party.

This in no way means that what is known as the state of J&K is a monolith. There is a wide variety of linguistic, ethnic, religious and cultural groups within J&K. People are as discriminating and patriarchal as anywhere else. However, the presence of India in J&K is not going to solve this problem. When India has not been able to solve these problems in its core territories, as a matter of fact only worsening them over the years, how will it solve them in J&K?

The very presence of an occupying force accentuates the existing differences between natives. For example, the differential experience of Indian state terror in various parts of J&K has created a divide on the basis of experience among the people. The valley of Kashmir and the adjacent areas of the erstwhile Doda district and Poonch and Rajouri, having faced the brunt of this terror, show the most urgency in the demand for self-determination when compared to the areas around Jammu and Leh. Those Kashmiri Pandits who were forced into exile have no experience of the brutalities of the last two decades, having lived in Jammu, Delhi and beyond; many of them therefore do not share the immediacy of the conflict with their brethren—Muslim, Pandit and Sikh— who have been living in Kashmir over these years. The younger generations among these exiled Kashmiris have never had the full experience of Kashmir's very unique cultural heritage, long history and distinct identity. In turn, those who did not migrate do not share the awful experience of living in exile. (Is this the reason why the Indian state infinitely procrastinates their return?)

When these different groups, sections of Kashmir Pandits, Jammu Dogras and Ladakhi Buddhists, are made to reject Azadi what they are actually rejecting is a most extreme version of what independent Kashmir *might become*. India is made; it has a Constitution in place, laws, institutions, establishments, practices and a million other structures. Kashmir, on the other hand, is a work in progress. In this lies the greatest hope and the darkest fear. In Kashmir the struggle for freedom has put the paradigm of democracy right side up on two very important counts—one, people are setting the agenda and the leaders are just representing it; two, people have realized the viciousness and wickedness of denying outrightly to others the same rights which one claims for oneself, or setting conditions that they exercise it in a manner not chosen by them. It remains to be seen whether people will extend the application of this real concept of democracy to other aspects of life and society. In case all the people of J&K realize that they have as much power to shape the future of their country as everybody else, the Kashmir which finally emerges will be a vibrant democratic society in the true sense of the words. If, on the other hand, the struggle for freedom and the decisions about the future are left to a few representatives of the majority, everybody will suffer on account of the monolith that will emerge.

It is important to mention that India wrote its Constitution after independence from the British. This is a natural course of such political events. Is it, therefore, justifiable to expect that Kashmiris should come up with their draft constitution, or a complete vision for the future, before a decision on their future can be taken by India? The weight of state hegemony and the institutionalization of fear have rendered the making of a free choice by Kashmiris impossible in the present circumstances. Once India stops obfuscations, recognizes the true nature of the problem, demilitarizes the territory and discourses in J&K and sets a time-frame for the exercise of the right of self-determination, then it will be reasonable to expect Kashmiris to come forward with a programme for the future. Only then will people and territories within the present state of J&K have a choice between the Indian Constitution, the Pakistani Constitution (whatever version is applicable at that moment) and the Kashmiri manifesto; and if some of them choose India, who, in the name of democracy, will stop them?

The right to choose must reverberate from the lowest to the highest columns of this Babel, because an echo is the death of a false God.

Beyond the metaphors

Kashmiris need to use the Indian occupation as a mirror to judge themselves. Everything that is structurally wrong with the Indian version of democracy (Constitution, other laws, institutions and so on) and functionally (the way structures are implemented) needs to be identified and avoided in the vision of the future of Kashmir. The democratic spaces created by the struggle for freedom need to be widened and strengthened. The position of women and various ethnic, religious, cultural and linguistic groups, the poor and the underprivileged have to be re-charted in a fundamental way. In this regard, the debates generated by the period between 1930 and 1947 need to be restored in the collective consciousness of the people of J&K.

This should also hasten the making of a choice by the common people of India, between being blacklisted in history as a people who supported, or through their silence allowed, a fascist-style regime to operate, like Germans of the Nazi era. Instead of standing in a queue to get a visa for the odd trip some of them make to Kashmir once in their entire lifetime.

India's Kashmir project is doomed, because it requires nullifying the memory of the people of Kashmir, their culture, language, folklore and society, it requires falsifying Kashmir's history of the countless centuries before 1947, it requires wiping out the events which have taken place since 1947, it requires hiding permanently the brutality of the last twenty years, it requires perverting democracy and democratic ideals, it requires contesting humanity itself by negating human emotions, experiences and responses. It thus requires preventing each new generation of Kashmiris from becoming Kashmiris, democrats, human. It thus requires attempting to convince every new generation of Indians and the people of the world through lies, propaganda, misinformation, media control, and more lies and more lies and more lies that Kashmir is an integral part of India. It requires making these mammoth efforts generation after generation after generation till eternity.

Kashmiris: they just need to make the avalanche of truth and justice, coming down the infinite slope of history and memory, gather enough mass.

This article first appeared in the *Economic and Political Weekly*, 20 November 2010.

Making a Part Inalienable
Folding Kashmir into India's Imagination

Mridu Rai

Like the vanishing cheshire cat

Kashmir to Kanyakumari
Timbuktu to Kalamazoo

As evocations of space go, both have a nice ring to them. The logic
of their connection derives partly from neat linguistic tricks: a
shared initial in one instance and a rhymed ending in the other.
Of course, some niggling sorts will point out that the second pair
of names conjures up an imaginary space while the first is real. But
is that true? Timbuktu and Kalamazoo are both real places, as are
the people, cities, towns, villages, mountains, rivers, lakes, one
ocean, coasts, one desert, fields and forests that lie between them;
they just happen not to be connected within the sorts of entities
modern humans have devised to circumscribe expanses on the
globe. If the space encompassed by Kashmir and Kanyakumari is
real, as common sense will have it, one might still ask whether that
space can be demarcated only through these particularly chosen
markers? Neither place is intrinsically a more accurate sign of any
geo-political limit to the exclusion of another pairing. In fact, why

be a slave to a north–south axis? Why not celebrate the idea of India from east to west, or west to east? 'Jorhat to Jaisalmer', 'Dwarika to Kohima'. These evanescent end-points and boundaries of earthly spaces are like the vanishing and reappearing Cheshire cat, its lingering smile suspended mid-air long enough to mock the rigidities of our human imaginations.

Possessive maps

A physical map of India available on the internet carries a familiar disclaimer—a requisite doffing of the cap to the lawyers of sovereign nation-states who keep strict vigil lest an inch of land or a drop of water be wrongly attributed to a rival claimant—that while 'all efforts have been made to make th[e] image accurate . . . Compare Infobase Limited and its directors do not own any responsibility for the correctness or authenticity of the same.'[1] The caveat having been duly inscribed, the mapmakers proceed to fix the meaning of this image. 'India the land of diversity, is endowed with variety of physical features [sic]. The country has almost every type of physical feature. Whether it is the lofty Himalayas or the plains of Ganges or sweltering hot deserts of Rajasthan or the rain abound coastal plains, the country has it all [sic]'. Maps such as these are ostensibly depictions of 'pure' signs of physicality in a space that is presumed to have existed *a priori* its demarcation. However, this is far from a neutral representation; continuing a colonial practice, this act of visualization is intended to claim

---

[1] Physical map of India showing major rivers, hills, plateaus, plains, beaches, deltas and deserts. http://www.mapsofindia.com/maps/india/physical-map.html. Last accessed on 14 November 2010. Lest anyone doubt the existence of these national vigilantes, they should speak to publishers and booksellers and the fate of books that have included 'inaccurate' maps of India. There is probably an employee somewhere in the halls of India's many ministries whose task it is to pound a stamped imprint on every copy of each such offending map.

ownership of what is shown. The claim here is made on behalf of the nation-state. As such, this map goes beyond depiction to laud India as a territory uniquely 'endowed', and its physical diversity here celebrated stands in also for the similar virtues of its variegated people. Importantly, what is being fêted is not a diversity of elements with fluid links of free connections, but one that is eternally bound within the lines of the map. And this is a map that wants you to even sense that India.

Then there are maps that invite you to worship her. In her pictorial history of Mother India, Sumathi Ramaswamy points out the irony that 'a nation striving to be secular, diverse, and modern [sh]ould also resort to the time-worn figure of a Hindu goddess in its yearning for form.'[2] These images of a 'new deity', Bharat Mata, which began to appear in the early twentieth century presented her anthropomorphic female shape as the cartographic rendition of India and was intended to cultivate 'devotion toward a territory called India'. Abanindranath Tagore's famous and much-reproduced 1905 painting of an ethereal ascetic titled Bharat Mata—representing the artist's patriotic response to the viceroy Lord Curzon's decision to partition his home province of Bengal in the same year—may have inspired some later depictions of the mapped deity. But Tagore's image itself, in fact first named Banga Mata (Mother Bengal), had no pretentions to be either a 'goddess of the nation' or the draped goddess inhabiting its cartographic space.[3] A new generation of more fiercely assertive and martial depictions of the feminized Bharat would be both. For instance, Subramania Bharati, the poet-patriot and journalist from Madras Presidency,

---

[2]Sumathi Ramaswamy, *The Goddess and the Nation: Mapping Mother India* (Durham and London: Duke University Press, 2010), pp. 2; 11; 15–16.

[3]In fact, Ramaswamy tells us the model for the painting was the 'everyday Bengali woman—even possibly the young girls of the artist's aristocratic family', pp. 15–16.

provided space for visually imagining and depicting a feminized country in the pages of his Tamil newsweekly *Intiya*. One that appeared in April 1909 shows a four-armed Bharat Mata who embodies a pluralistic Indian national territory, a banner in one hand proclaiming Allah's greatness balanced by the patriotic phrase *vande mataram* proclaiming devotion to the nation as mother inscribed on the other side. However, as Ramaswamy points out, this latter 'signature salutation and slogan' was steeped in a 'nationalized Hindu sensibility'. Add to that the 'graphic subordination' in the picture of the call 'Allahu Akbar' to the words 'vande mataram' and 'Bharat Mata' and we have 'a visual reminder that twentieth-century India's vaunted pluralism rarely escape[d] entirely from the sensibilities and aesthetics (however varied) of its numerically most dominant religious community.'[4]

The outline map served to enable a synoptic possession of the whole national territory. And when the anthropomorphic form of Bharat Mata as mother-goddess came to inhabit that outline map, it became the synoptic depiction of a sacralized territory. The exit from it could only be accomplished through the profane act of vivisection[5], which was also a defilement of the geo-body of the Mother. When the great vivisections of 1947 did happen, Kashmir became disputed territory; its geographical space and imagination tugged at by the two nation-states born of the cutting up of the motherland. A vivid visual rendering of the unseemly political drama of Partition comes from the Hindu nationalist weekly, *Organiser*, an unlikely quarter from which to hear any condemnation on this count given that history records that the Hindu Mahasabha had made the first call for the partition of Bengal and Punjab in March 1947. On 14 August 1947 the *Organiser* carried a cartoon titled 'The Wise Pandit' showing a cartographed Bharat Mata in

---

[4]Ramaswamy, pp. 20–21.

[5]When medical schools were first established in colonial India vivisection was considered so polluting and impure it could only be performed by lower castes.

agony as her prone figure is stretched across the yet unpartitioned subcontinent. The two villains of this vivisection, as the cartoon showed it, are 'The Wise Pandit' Nehru and Mohammed Ali Jinnah. Jinnah, or rather his head tenuously attached to what are hints of a scaled body, growls and snarls as Nehru wields a sword to mercilessly slice off Mother India's right arm extended over the territory of Pakistan. And all the while Nehru's left arm snatches painfully at her hair where it shrouds the territory of Kashmir, the opening salvo in the ongoing battle to possess the Valley.[6]

How do Kashmiris find themselves in this cartographic imagination? For Hindus, Bharat Mata's crown, her halo or her flowing tresses may have folded them comfortingly into her form until a few decades ago. But after the departure of large numbers of the community from the Valley in the wake of the insurgency that began in 1989, there is a feeling among some of betrayal, perhaps of having been cast outside the protecting drapes of Bharat Mata. At the same time, however, they also express the desire, indeed the right, of belonging. For the vast majority who were Muslim, however, neither could they worship a nation deified as goddess, whether or not in image form, nor have they been able to substitute it with their own cartographic artefacts of patriotic belonging.[7]

---

[6]Ramaswamy, pp. 231–33.

[7]An idea may be had of the sort of cartographic imagination that had prevailed in the Valley before its displacement by that of the nation from one early nineteenth century map now kept in the British Library. Following a most un-Mercatorian logic, this is an extraordinary riot of colour-coded demarcations of different physical features and scribbled over with abundant identifying text as it 'draws' the habitation of both the spiritual wealth and the agrarian economy of the Valley. Drawn by one Abdur Rahim of Bukhara, the invitation is to open a carefully folded package, peeling away first the mountain ranges painted all along the four edges of a very large piece of cloth to find nestling within them the Valley

(Contd.)

The contours of India and Pakistan shifted soon after Sir Cyril Radcliffe surmised them[8] in 1947, and those of Kashmir were dragged in their tow. By October, within months of the announcement of the Radcliffe Award in August 1947, the two newly formed states went to war over Kashmir. When the United Nations brokered an end to hostilities in January 1949, a ceasefire line reallocated one third of the state of Jammu and Kashmir to Pakistan's control, leaving the rest in Indian control. Following a third war fought in 1971 between the rival neighbours, Pakistan's national contours were truncated when its majority Bengali citizens won independence and reshaped lines to the east of India around the new nation-state of Bangladesh. In the northwest of India, the Simla Accord of 1972 rechristened the ceasefire line of 1949 into what is still known as the Line of Control, the capitalized initials emphasizing its extraordinariness; that it is neither frontier nor porous boundary, but a legacy of a rushed and incomplete decolonization, a marker of an unresolved dispute, the scene of potential future wars, keeping Kashmiris divided, as well as the two nation-states that hold their future hostage. And within these split Kashmirs, there would be internal shape-shifting of national

---

(Contd.)

with its streams, rivers, lakes, groves, towns, parganas, fields, an oversized Srinagar and its surroundings, its famous Mughal gardens, the fort on the Hari Parbat, temples, mosques and shrines and the roads, some with travellers painted in on them, that connected all these elements of the natural, material and spiritual assets of the land. *Map of the Vale*, attributed to Abdur Rahim of Bukhara, probably early nineteenth century. Ink & watercolour on cloth. Size of the original: 408 x 226 cm. British Library, London (B.L. Maps S.T.K.).

[8]Cyril Radcliffe worked in cloistered privacy, but still under considerable political pressure from the contending nationalist leadership of the two nations he was charged with dividing and a far from impartial viceroy of India. Vastly bedevilling his task was the poor material made available to him such as outdated censuses and maps on the basis of which to determine those fateful lines known as the Partition map of India.

imaginations, too. The year 1989 witnessed one such in the Indian-administered portion of Kashmir when an overwhelming number of the Kashmiri Pandits, left their home—or, as some of them tell it, were driven out—to seek refuge in India in the wake of a popular insurgency against the Indian state that began then, and continues twenty years later.

Several organizations claiming to represent the demands of Kashmiri Pandit 'refugees' based in the cities of India[9] have adopted the cartographic logic of the nation-state to demand territorial fulfilment of their political and cultural aspirations. By and large, their understandings fold seamlessly within an imagined India, the rupture of their departure expressed as a rupture within the fragment, while the wider homeland of India remains intact and beyond History. Thus, many of the Pandits who left their homes to cross the Pir Panjal range, speak of belonging to a 'this-side-Kashmir' and a 'that-side-Kashmir'.[10] The cultural content of the India that encompasses it is constructed as static and, like the 'invented traditions' that the historian Eric J. Hobsbawm has written about, it is 'quite unspecific and vague as to the nature of the values, rights and obligations of the group membership' inculcated.[11] India becomes a loose bag of ritual practices, deities,

---

[9]Some of these Kashmiri Pandits' Organizations are the All India Kashmiri Samaj (AIKS), Kashmiri Pandit Sabha Ambphalla (KPS), Jammu Kashmir Nationalist Movement (JKNM), Roots in Kashmir (RIK), Kashmiri Hindu Council (KHC), Jammu Kashmir National United Front (JKNUF), United Kashmiri Pandit Youth Forum (UKPYF), All Displaced Co-ordination Committee (ADCC) and Vitasta Sewa Samaj (Nagrota). *Ground Report.* URL: http://www.groundreport.com/World/Displaced-Kashmiri-Pandits-jointly-hail-20-June-as_1/2924975. Last accessed on 30 January 2011.

[10]Ananya Jahanara Kabir, *Territory of Desire: Representing the Valley of Kashmir* (Minneapolis: University of Minnesota Press, 2009), p. 163.

[11]Eric Hobsbawm, 'Introduction: Inventing Traditions', in Eric Hobsbawm and Terence Ranger, eds. *The Invention of Tradition* (Cambridge: Cambridge University Press, 1989) p. 10.

or philosophical traditions, held together in their broadest commonality. A generalized reference to unchanging Hindu cultural and religious traditions and practices has provided safe mooring when needed in the face of local challenges in the regions for communities across India, including Kashmir's Hindus.

More radical groups among them, such as *Panun Kashmir* (Our Own Kashmir), demand a homeland to be scooped out of segments of the Valley.[12] The map that Panun Kashmir's website carries only

---

[12]The Panun Kashmir movement was founded by Pandit émigrés or, as they prefer to be called, 'refugees' now living in various parts of India. It has not been possible for me to determine with any precision the size of the following Panun Kashmir enjoys among Kashmiri Pandits and others. My guess would be that its formal membership is minuscule. However, their significance is derived from other arenas. First, they find a sympathetic endorsement of at least some of their demands by other Kashmiri Pandits or even agreement with part of their narratives of expulsion, their reading of Kashmiri Pandit history, and their rhetoric of suffering and victimhood. Second, what trumps the numerical size of the Panun Kashmir organizations is the support it is given by Hindu supremacist parties in India. For this see also footnote 16 below. Panun Kashmir has recently acquired an activist youth wing, so to speak, in the shape of the body 'Roots in Kashmir', which is a separate organization but broadly in consonance with the aims of Panun Kashmir. Its recent public manifestations have been in the shape of organized disruptions of seminars and other events discussing questions with which the group does not find itself in sympathy. See a discussion of the group's activities in an article of which the title none-too-subtly exonerates its actions. Kaveree Bamzai, 'Jammu and Kashmir: Revenge of the Lambs', *India Today*, 6 November 2010. URL: http://indiatoday.intoday.in/site/article/jammu-and-kashmir-revenge-of-the-lambs/1/119075.html. Last accessed on 30 January 2011.

Finally, as with Hindu chauvinist groups in India, common cause is made with a wider global conservative alliance against the War on Terror. Tellingly, a 'Kashmiris in Exile' blogspot helpfully provides a link to the 'Terrorism Awareness Project' (http://www.terrorismawareness.org/) based in the United States and formed in the aftermath of the 9/11 attacks on the United States.

delineates the territory to which they lay claim, that homeland otherwise apparently hanging suspended in a void. However, reading this map alongside their stated goals and aims fills that empty space. The struggle of the Panun Kashmir movement, as its website declares, is to '*Save Kashmiri Pandits to Save Kashmir to Save India*' and a 'struggle to reconquer that Kashmir which is almost lost' from the grip of 'Islamic religious fundamentalists in the valley of Kashmir [who] took to armed subversion and terrorism and drove them out of their centuries-old habitat'. They see themselves as stepping in to ward off dangers that even Indians have not fathomed: 'Today, Kashmir is on the brink of being separated from India. It is the beginning of a comprehensive plan to bring about the total disintegration of India—a fact not realized by most of the Indians'.[13] Kashmiri Pandits emerge here as an interesting mix both of victims and warriors of their community and soldiers of Bharat Mata whose cause they identify fully as their own.[14] This is an unusual embracing of a martial identity for a community that has long taken pride in its scholarly refinements. Perhaps nationalism makes all its votaries speak the language of soldiers. Although the community and the homeland they are 'fighting' for are not marked by religion, the explicit identification of those against whom it wants to protect the integrity of India

---

[13]Panun Kashmir website: http://www.panunkashmir.org/. Emphasis in the original.

[14]This intermeshing of identification as victim and soldiers is common to other communities staking their claims in the aftermath of dislocation. Thus Sikhs produced numerous retellings of the riots that accompanied the Partition of India in which they emerge not just victims of violence but also as the defenders of the nation who made greater sacrifices than any other community and so deserved particular consideration for their claims in the modern Indian nation. This legacy was frequently invoked in the wake of the politically engineered pogrom in Delhi in 1984, in which thousands of Sikhs were killed ostensibly in revenge for the assassination of Prime Minister Indira Gandhi.

makes this unnecessary. Furthermore, when the cause is aligned with political parties in India that also espouse the cause of a Hindu religious nationalism, no matter how thinly disguised as cultural identity, the religiously exclusionary nature of Panun Kashmir's claimed homeland becomes evident.[15] Similarly, the blank vastness around the cartographed Panun Kashmir does not need to be named, the implied encompassing by India being obvious. Its border is at best a dotted line that marks the territory from which 'Islamic religious fundamentalist' usurpers must be expelled. Its outline is a *cordon sanitaire* around an infected part of the otherwise unbreakable, embodied nation that must be sterilized, sutured and strengthened. Maps such as that of Panun Kashmir are fashioned to enable easy pleating into that of India, the status quo power in the Valley.

This is not very different from the mapped belonging imagined by religio-political groups like the Jamat-e-Islami of Kashmir that, drawing together people in broadly common religious unity, seeks enswathing within that of Pakistan. However, there is one essential point in which the Jamat's separatist/assimilationist map cannot be drawn as easily as that of the Hindu nationalists of India or Panun Kashmir's of Kashmir-in-India. It requires a violation of Islamic norms even as it makes Islam the thread that binds Kashmiris to Pakistan. The place of Islam even in Pakistan and in the public life of its citizens has never been precisely established or been beyond

---

[15]A recent reminder of the links sought by certain groups of Kashmiri Pandits, both in India and abroad, with the Bharatiya Janata Party (BJP) and other Hindu right-wing parties came in the form of a conference call organized by the 'Overseas Friends of BJP, USA,' on 30 January 2011 and attended by 405 participants including Kashmiri Pandits worldwide. Here, members had an opportunity to speak with Nitin Gadkari, the president of the BJP. Identifying themselves as 'the aboriginals of Kashmir' now 'living in exile in [their] own Independent India for more than two decades', they appealed of the BJP to launch a nationwide campaign to 'Save Kashmiri Pandits from extinction' and to 'prompt BJP-ruled states to pass a resolution in their respective assemblies to support this campaign'.

challenge. As events after 1947 demonstrated, it could not provide the adhesive to hold together Muslims dispersed in territories separated by over a thousand miles of India, speaking different tongues, worshipping in different landscapes and eating different foods. Oddly, even the party today associated with the demand for an Islamic dispensation in Pakistan, the Jamat-e-Islami founded by Maulana Abul Ala Maududi in 1941, had been vehemently opposed to the state's very formation until it was presented as a *fait accompli* in 1947. Maududi's opposition stemmed from normative Muslim thought that 'decried affinity to territory' represented in nation-states as undermining the more proper 'identification with a non-territorially defined *ummah*', an ideological conception of the community with global reach.[16] Of course, Muslims inhabited not only spiritual but also temporal worlds and, in their various environments, have needed to negotiate between the local and the trans-local, the lived everyday experience and the ideal of the ummah. But what it does mean is that any envisioning of a Muslim nation can fit only awkwardly within bounded territories, and mapped representations remain open to challenges on the grounds of religious (non)conformity.

As for including Kashmir within Pakistan, Jinnah had discovered even during his visit to Kashmir in 1944 that the separate homeland for Muslims he allegedly desired had takers among only disappointingly small numbers, mostly confined to elite Kashmiri Muslims led by the relatively orthodox Mirwaiz of the Jama Masjid or to the Muslim Conference—a breakaway faction of the secular National Conference—dominated by urban Jammu Muslims.[17] If the Jamat-e-Islami's proposed future for India's

---

[16]Ayesha Jalal, *Self and Sovereignty: Individual and Community in South Asian Islam Since 1850* (New Delhi: Oxford University Press, 2001), pp. 10–11.

[17]Rai, *Hindu Rulers, Muslim Subjects*, p. 280. In any case, Jinnah, no matter how he came to be interpreted by his contemporaries, was at heart as much a secular liberal as was Nehru, the other contender for Kashmiri hearts and minds.

Muslims challenged the Muslim League's quest before 1947, there was no reconciliation after either. Indeed, the territorial Partition of 1947 even brought about a split within the Jamat that ironically followed national boundaries with the formation in 1948 of the Jamat-e-Islami-e-Hind. But within Indian territory the Jamat-e-Islami of Kashmir retained its separate organization from the latter largely politically inactive umbrella organization.[18] As parties representing the same religiously defined interest, it is remarkable how webbed their existence is within territorially defined nations. How does one fold a web and what does one fold it into?

Of the secularist parties in Kashmir, the National Conference party's understanding of the proper boundaries of the state have varied over time along with their political demands, only briefly hinting at the possibility of excision of the territories of the state from both India and Pakistan when Sheikh Mohammed Abdullah made that demand in 1953 and was promptly jailed for it. It otherwise accepts the boundaries demarcated following the first Indo-Pakistani war of 1947–49. At most, demands for greater autonomy weakly issued from these quarters might require a shading of the state in slightly different tints than the other constituent units of the Indian union. Their cartographic imagining of the nation would fit within that of India without much discomfort, so long as that India is as ostensibly secular as is the state of Jammu and Kashmir.

Such encasing does not come easily for those in Kashmir who demand independence. Their renderings of the nation challenge current geo-political reality and so the spaces of India and Pakistan must remain as deeply marked in their imaginations as the entity

---

[18]As if the picture were not complicated enough, the Jamat in Kashmir was split in 1997 over the decision by its then chief Ghulam Mohammad Bhat that the organization would sever its links with all militant groups including the Hizb-ul-Mujahidin. This decision was immediately repudiated by Syed Ali Shah Geelani, the more hardline pro-Pakistan figure within the Jamat.

for which they seek a new future. Therefore it may seem surprising that these political organizations would find equal utility in presenting their demands in as totalizing territorial terms as the nation-states they resist or wish integration with. On the other hand, it may be the only way to get the ear of nations and the rigidly territorial presentation of the nation may be 'strategic essentialization' requisite to make claims in an age of nation-states. Thus secularist parties like the Jammu and Kashmiri Liberation Front (JKLF) seek 'independence' for a state whose frontiers were those of the princely state ruled until 1947 by Dogra-Hindu dynasts from Jammu. This cartographic reshaping for a new nation-state bears the burden of negating two partitions, the one that created India and Pakistan in August 1947 and the second that split Jammu and Kashmir along the ceasefire line of 1949. But paradoxically, if unsurprisingly, it is a demand that has set off, in turn, calls for 'partitions' or 'secessions' within.[19] This mapped nation for which the JKLF and others seek independence encloses a multitude of different religious, linguistic and cultural groups deriving their unity only from having formerly been subjects of a princely state constructed to suit British geo-political interests in their Indian empire. Then there are also transhumant groups such as the Gujjars and Bakarwals whose annual circuits in search of pasturage in high mountain meadows defy all borders. Justifying why the boundaries of the princely state that was challenged from within the Valley before 1947 should be privileged any more than those of the nation-states of India and Pakistan—that Kashmiris have resisted after 1947—can only be as simple as squaring the circle.

---

[19]Among these are demands made by Hindu right-wing parties for a 'trifurcation' of the state into Jammu, Kashmir and Ladakh, with the first and last remaining with India. Groups within Ladakh have autonomy within their sub-region and would in all likelihood choose to remain with India. There is, of course, also the demand for a Panun Kashmir discussed above.

But here the latter have an advantage: over sixty-three years of living within the lines ordained in 1947 has given the mapped myths of the nations then created at least a tenuous reality, which in turn has allowed them to arrogate to themselves the mandate, defended by powerful armies, to determine which other national aspirations they will consider legitimate. Alternative representations of nation-states' boundaries even by outsiders with no interventionist political agendas are treated almost like contraband. As an article by Umar Ahmad in the Kashmiri daily *Rising Kashmir* recently pointed out, India has joined eleven other countries since January 2009 in banning or censoring issues of the British newsmagazine *The Economist*. In fact, 'having censored 31 issues of the weekly' for publishing a map of Kashmir that does not accord with the government's version, India leads a group that includes countries like China, Libya and Saudi Arabia.

Despite all the evidence of the obduracy of such national boundaries, in the name of whose inviolability governments permit themselves to oppress defiant citizens, the modern cartographic representations of Kashmiri nationhood outlined above replicate those of the nation-states they seek to exit or merge with. Marking their terrains also in territorial terms, the people that fill them are formed by an imagination that seeks convenient homogeneities. Map first, its world conjured after; a map's nation. Recalling Carroll once more, this dissociation between representation and reality could well have been what Alice meant in her remark that while she knew of cats that do not grin, '. . . a grin without a cat!' was the 'most curious thing' she had ever seen.' In the end, cartographic challenges to cartographically defined entities are like endless reflections in a hall of mirrors of the same absurd conundrum of maps that seek to define people. Not only can such maps not fully encircle the plural groups within them but every effort to do so sharpens the angularity of their imaginations bearing down both internally and vis-à-vis the surrounding nation-states.

World(s) before possessive maps

Power, authority and sovereignty in pre-colonial polities, thought of as layered and shared, could never have been accommodated within the strait-jacketing of modern nation-states and their frontiers. And yet modern nation-states nearly all claim very ancient existence. The historical reality in India is that the territorializing of sovereignty began only in the nineteenth century and, moreover, it represented no native or indigenous impulse but was the preferred political arrangement of a colonial power. In the specific case of Kashmir, for instance, the disjuncture in the pre-colonial state system came with the Treaty of Amritsar signed on 16 March 1846. This treaty had followed on the first Anglo-Sikh war fought to a draw earlier that year, and in which the Dogra ruler had helped the Company by remaining neutral rather than intervening on the side of the Sikh ruler, until then his overlord. The reward was that the British made Gulab Singh the maharaja of the new princely state of Jammu and Kashmir. Article I of the Treaty of Amritsar transferred 'forever' and into his 'independent possession' and of his male heirs 'all the hilly or mountainous country' east of the River Indus and west of the Ravee' until then governed by Lahore. These came to include the territories of Jammu, Kashmir, Ladakh, Hunza, Nagar and Gilgit. In return for this bountiful yield of territory, Gulab Singh agreed to pay to the British government the sum of Rs 75,00,000 (a significant proportion of the compensation demanded earlier from the Sikhs). In many ways, business appeared as usual. The Company's expansion in the preceding decades had proceeded through similar treaties with a variety of Indian rulers. Also, this was evidently not the first time Kashmir had been held by 'outsiders' having passed from Mughal (1586), to Afghan (1751) and, finally into Sikh (1819) hands. However, what was altered critically at the same time as Kashmir was handed to the Dogras was the nature of the political world.

The British understood the Treaty of Amritsar to transfer the rights, titles and interests the Sikh government had possessed in the territories concerned into their own hands. These were then handed over, along with territory, 'completely and absolutely' to Maharaja Gulab Singh.[20] Before this novel intervention, however, rights and interests had never been possessed absolutely and exclusively, nor considered transferable in the manner understood by the British. Instead, they had been arranged along a hierarchy that recognized superior and inferior rights established and maintained as relational entities through accommodative and negotiated processes. Power at all levels was held by mutual recognition and this pattern of mutuality protected against the complete subsumption of the rights of subordinate levels. As wielders of localized power viewed it, the superior authority of an overlord was not only compatible with their own authority but was necessary to establishing their own influence and prestige. Furthermore, sovereignty in pre-colonial India had operated in overlapping polities in which the primary political exercise had been one of winning over people rather than territory.[21] This vertical and horizontal architecture of power, authority and sovereignty had ensured fluidity in both the content and the boundaries of kingships.

The Treaty of Amritsar drew the curtains on this world of 'nested authority'. Partly driven by concerns for stability on its crucial northwestern frontier,[22] and wishing therefore to strengthen the hands of its new ally, the structure of relations between

---

[20]Frederick Currie's judgement dated 12 May 1848 cited in K.M. Panikkar, *The Founding of the Kashmir State* (Allen & Unwin, 1953) pp. 121–23.

[21]See Andre Wink, *Land and Sovereignty in India: Agrarian Society and Politics under the Eighteenth Century Maratha Swarajya* (Cambridge: Cambridge University Press, 1986).

[22]The north-western frontier formed part of the arena of the Great Game and the region's sensitivity derived from British imperial concerns of preventing inroads by the Russian empire through that route.

superior and subordinate levels of the polity was taken apart after 1846 and power held in localized niches yielded up to the Dogra maharaja. Within the state, the British vested solely in the person of the new maharaja, a lesser version of its own sovereignty, the latter viewed as paramount and monolithic in the imperial arena. And in 1858 the right to wage war and make peace was removed from the princely domain, a prerogative of sovereignty appropriated in perpetuity by the colonial state. This meant that the Indian 'circle of kings' would remain forever frozen. And, concerned to tidy up the clutter left behind from an earlier seamless terrain of overlapping sovereignties the colonial state inaugurated notions, new to India, of a subordinate 'native' sovereignty circumscribed by rigidly demarcated territorial frontiers.

The land of Kashmir is Hindu

While their sovereignty may have been territorially circumscribed and relegated to a subordinate level, the Dogra rulers turned aspects of this transformation to their own advantage and increased their control over their subjects. From the second maharaja Ranbir Singh's perspective, as a recognized ruler of his state, he was given a territory, whose frontiers could not err into British domains. At the same time, he was assured of his legitimacy, founded on his being a 'traditional' Rajput-Hindu ruler, to claim this territory and its populace. Within these parameters, Ranbir Singh's efforts were directed towards matching the political dominion allowed him and the religious identity assigned to him within the territories marked for him.

By the time Ranbir Singh died in 1885, the religious boundaries of the Hindu faith united the provinces of Jammu and Kashmir in a state that not only had a Hindu ruler but that also witnessed new degrees of control over a territorialized Hindu religious arena of patronage and worship. Indeed, the Dogra re-invention of their religio-political landscape as Hindu had registered so widely that the eminent civil servant Walter Lawrence could declare in 1931 that Kashmir was 'holy ground to *all* the Hindus of India'.[23] But such firm Dogra control also meant that the fluidity and competitive nature of pre-colonial patterns of patronage that had ensured a measure of deference to the Muslim religious domain in Kashmir had disappeared. And with this went the erasure of the vast proportion of Muslims in the state.[24] However, this is not to suggest that Kashmiri Muslims were left out of the power-sharing arrangements of the Dogra state simply because they were Muslims. The Dogras were neither particularly bigoted rulers nor did bigotry have anything to do with it. The marginalization of the Kashmiri Muslims became possible only because they became peripheral to the legitimating devices installed by the Dogras and their British overlords. The British guarantee of Dogra sovereignty vis-à-vis his subjects obviated the need for the ruler to seek legitimacy through the time-honoured practice of granting patronage to the religious and cultural sites of his diverse subject population. This meant that Muslim shrines and cultural symbols suffered the withering cold of neglect, while the Dogras in the later nineteenth century set about conjuring the ceremonial trappings of a specifically Hindu sovereignty derived from outside the territorial confines of their fiefdom and enacted within it.

There are echoes of this Hinduization of territory in Panun Kashmir's map, discussed earlier, which depicts a valley denuded of any references to the faith of its majority population, Islam, while being plentifully speckled with the markers of that of its

---

[23]Mss.Eur.F.143, Walter Lawrence Collection, copy of a letter from Walter Lawrence to Sir Samuel, 6 October 1931, IOL. Emphasis mine. Lawrence went further to suggest that should the colonial government permit cow slaughter in Kashmir, as individuals he does not identify had been suggesting, it 'would infuriate the Hindus throughout India, and it would, further alienate all the Hindu princes of India . . .'

[24]Constraints of space prevent me from discussing fully this very important aspect of the history of Kashmir. For elaboration see Rai, *Hindu Rulers, Muslim Subjects*.

minuscule Hindu population—including inter alia the
Shankaracharya hill[25], Mattan, Tulamula and Amarnath. Indeed,
one might be forgiven for thinking this a map of Kashmir dating
from the thirteenth century, before, as the story is told, the Sufi
divine Bulbul Shah's melodious singing of the *fajar azan* made a
Muslim of Rinchen Shah, the prince of Kashgar and Ladakh and
the rescuer of Kashmir from Tatar depredations. This expunging
of Muslims' sites of religious and cultural affinity is a necessary
step in underwriting Panun Kashmir's separatist demand, which it
makes by contradicting overwhelming evidence that the land of
the Valley has many equally legitimate claimants.[26]

Claims to the ground of Kashmir have been made by many
through the centuries—by rulers and traders, poets and craftsmen,
those who worked its fertile soils and those who plucked its fruits,
those who made ambrosia from its purple saffron flowers, those
who brought gentle thoughts of God in its temples, springs,
mosques and shrines. All these jostled with each other, sometimes
settling into peaceful coexistence and shared spaces, at others
borrowing parts or whole from each other and at yet others
ousting rivals. But the age of nations brought ideas and claims of
a different kind and that sought more permanent habitation. They
spoke of all time past and all time to come.

C.A. Bayly has described the rise of new eighteenth-century
Indian states in which rulers established their sovereignty through
links with powerful symbols of their own faiths. They were still
based notably on traditions of 'religious compromise' as Hindu,
Muslim and Sikh rulers 'insisted not on the exclusiveness but on

---

[25]There are many sites in Kashmir that have names with Hindu as well
as Muslim associations, so the choice of appellations is a marker of
religious identity. One such site is the Shankaracharya hill in Srinagar,
which was also known widely as the Takht-e-Suleiman (Solomon's seat/
throne). Similarly the town of Anantnag also came to be known as
Islamabad.

[26]http://www.panunkashmir.org/images/PK_map2.jpg

the primacy (or merely the equality) of their own form of worship' and a subject's belonging to a different faith did not preclude access to power.[27] The state of Jammu and Kashmir founded in the mid-nineteenth century, however, was of a different order. Created to meet imperial requirements of securing the north-western frontier of India, the British were also keen to ensure that this largely arbitrary feat of state construction be seen as legitimate. Given the newness of Dogra rule in Kashmir, this legitimacy was sought largely extra-territorially by fashioning the Dogras into 'traditional' Hindu rulers generically identified as 'original' Indian sovereigns. As Eric Hobsbawm has pointed out, 'invented traditions' did not necessarily break with the past but could tap into 'ancient materials' to establish new traditions for 'novel purposes'.[28] The Dogras were concerned with mining in rather general ways 'older' stores of Hindu symbolism. Thus, they became regular visitors to and patrons of worship at Haridwar and Benares, the great Hindu sacred centres of northern India. The promotion of Sanskrit learning similarly provided access to a prestigious 'Hindu' symbol. This was reinforced when eminent European linguists explained the break in a tradition of Sanskrit scholarship in Kashmir as the result of 'Mahommedan oppression' interrupting the rule of 'native kings'.[29] Renewed princely sponsorship would therefore signal the revival of 'indigenous' Hindu rule. But by the end of the nineteenth century, the Kashmiri political landscape had not only been re-imagined as Hindu but also as having always been Hindu, justifying British intervention through the Dogras as an act of legitimate restoration.

It was not until the aftermath of Hindu–Muslim riots in 1931, that the certitude of Hindu claims to Kashmir's land would be challenged. The British-appointed B.J. Glancy Commission was given the task of examining a wide array of economic and political

---

[27]Bayly, *Origins of Nationality*, pp. 45, 214–21.

[28]Hobsbawm, 'Introduction', pp. 4–6.

[29]Buhler, 'Detailed Report of a Tour', p. 25.

grievances believed to have caused the disturbances. Its report of 1932 included a criticism of the Kashmir durbar's partisan functioning in favour of its Hindu subjects to the neglect of Muslims. This was in reference, among others, to the work of the state's archaeological and research department. The report stated bluntly that upholding Pandit claims to 'a large number of buildings . . . at one time temples' but later transformed into Muslim places of worship was 'impracticable' and 'out of the question'. In light of 'mass conversions' to Islam, as had occurred in Kashmir, it was 'only natural that a number of sacred buildings devoted to the observances of one particular faith should have converted to the use of another religion'.[30] Strikingly, the report had invalidated the principle of 'first peoples' on the basis of which the Dogras and Pandits had re-imagined Kashmir as 'originally' Hindu. Drawing attention to mass conversions re-inscribed Muslims into their history and region. And, perhaps unconsciously, it also redefined the contemporary territory of Kashmir—no matter what lay beneath its historical layers—as Muslim.

However, this recognition of the claims of Muslims to Kashmir's territory was soon drowned out by the assertion of Indian nationalism's sole claim to the territory of the subcontinent from Kashmir to Kanyakumari. Indeed, since independence in India, there has been a steady recycling and circulation of the rhetoric of vivisection derived from Partition narratives, of memories of the bloodbath that accompanied that division, of hyperbolically expressed fears of another partition/balkanization and of a 'total disintegration of India' as hinted at by Panun Kashmir. These have served to reinforce dramatically both the image of the nation as geo-body and of its parts as '*atoot ang*' (inalienable, integral or, literally, unbreakable part).[31] And when Kashmiris who happen

---

[30]Glancy, *Report*, p. 4.

[31]Ironically, given the constant reminder of the threat of break-up that sustains supremacist or hyper-nationalist political agendas, one might

(Contd.)

also to be Muslim demand freedom from this sanctified oppressive entity, their demand is doubly delegitimized for being both 'communal' and 'secessionist'. However, such condemnation is doled out selectively. While Panun Kashmir opposes demands for Azadi as an illegitimate demand of 'Islamic separatists', their own territorial claims are no less 'separatist'. Yet neither these nor the proposals of Hindu chauvinists from India for 'trifurcating' the territory of Jammu and Kashmir are greeted with the same nationalist opprobrium. These calls can be readily braided into the imaginations of India's Hindu majority; apparently unlike those of Kashmir's Muslims.

A Hindu exodus from a Hindu land?

There is a wide-ranging nomenclature Pandits access to describe themselves today that represents their understanding of the events of 1989 and their experiences within them. Some call their departure from the Valley an 'exodus', others an 'exile', and still others an expulsion disputing the voluntariness of their exit. Many of those who have made new lives in India, or those others living in limbo in overcrowded camps while still awaiting resettlement two decades after their departure, speak of themselves as 'refugees' or 'refugees in their own country'. This reference is an indictment of the Indian state first for not protecting them within their homeland and then for neglecting them outside it, challenging at the same time its euphemistic description of them as 'migrants'. Other radically disposed individuals describe their community as

---

(Contd.)

suggest that their purpose is, in fact, better served by highlighting possible fragmentation than by emphasizing the integrity of the parts of the nation. In a curious twist then, those who speak about the inalienability of India's parts seem in fact to rely more than or at least as much as their opponents on drawing attention to the various challenges to its integrity.

victims of 'genocide', 'ethnic cleansing' or a 'holocaust'.[32] All these terms meld departure, movement, expulsion, displacement, settlement, and homeland into a narrative of common victimhood suffered by a purportedly homogeneous community of Kashmir's Pandits.

In a convention held in Jammu in December 1991, Panun Kashmir had defined its demands in a 'Homeland Resolution' in terms that would be familiar and unexceptional to many patriotic peoples. These included the 'establishment of a Homeland for the Kashmiri Pandits in the Kashmir Valley' referred to earlier and the demand for its full integration with India through a common constitution and, administratively, as a union territory governed by the central government in Delhi. Additionally, the Resolution asked for the return and equitable resettlement of the 'seven hundred thousand Kashmiri Pandits, which includes those who have been driven out of Kashmir in the past and yearn to return to their homeland and those who were forced to leave on account of the terrorist violence in Kashmir.'[33] The number of 7,00,000 Kashmiri exiles is intriguing. More neutral estimates have suggested a population of 1,40,000 Kashmiri Pandits in the Valley of which a dramatically high proportion of 1,00,000 were said to have left in 1989 and in the months after.[34] Some of these departures are

---

[32]On 20 June 2010, several Kashmiri Pandit organizations joined together to protest in front of the United Nations Military Observatory Group (UNMOG)'s office in Sainik Colony, Jammu, 'against the apartheid, human rights violations and apathetic approach of Govt. towards displaced Kashmiri Pandits.' They also demanded that 'Kashmiri Pandits living in Exile be given the proper nomenclature of Internally Displaced Persons and all facilities recommended for this category of refugees be provided to them.' Cited in *Ground Report*. URL: http://www.groundreport.com/World/Displaced-Kashmiri-Pandits-jointly-hail-20-June-as_1/2924975. Last accessed on 30 January 2011.

[33]http://www.panunkashmir.org/resolution.html

[34]Sumantra Bose, *The Challenge in Kashmir: Democracy, Self-Determination and a Just Peace* (New Delhi and London: Sage and Thousand Oaks, 1997) p. 71.

attributed to the machinations of the Indian government specifically through Jagmohan, its appointed governor in Kashmir at the time, who allegedly encouraged the non-Muslim population of Kashmir to leave, making arrangements for their exit, so as to clear the ground for military action against 'terrorists'. At the same time, there are also accounts of calls issued from mosques and of posters and pamphlets distributed widely by Islamist groups who threatened with death those non-Muslims who would not leave the Valley. While the reasons for their departure will remain mired in controversy until there can be a careful sifting through competing narratives, disputed facts and memories at variance, that so many Pandits left so quickly belies speculations that this 'exodus' was undertaken entirely out of a free choice. Notwithstanding the difficulty of either establishing or disproving the suggestions of direct threats by unnamed 'Islamist' groups or of engineering at government hands as a factor, it seems reasonable to propose that large numbers of Pandits left in response to a sense, at the very least, that they, their families, their property and their futures were no longer as secure in Kashmir as they might be outside it.

The figure of 7,00,000 does not enumerate the exiles of 1989 and after. It refers, as the resolution states, to a much larger collection of Pandits who had departed at different times over the centuries. Given that there is no census of such migration available, it must be read as a rhetorical reference and the number an impressionistically gathered one, preserved in and circulated as collective memory. Kashmiris, both Hindu and Muslim, have a long history of leaving the Valley and the reasons for this have been various. Many left temporarily to seek work and a livelihood in the cities and towns of Hindustan, or to trade their widely sought after handicrafts, their shawls and carpets and brassware and carved walnut goods. Others left to serve in armies in the kingdoms and empires that surrounded their mountain- encompassed home. Still others traded their calligraphic skills, working as administrators and scribes in these foreign polities, and others writing exquisitely illustrated religious texts and biographies for wealthy families in Hindustan with money to spare and the aspiration to patronize.

And then there were those drawn out of the vale in search of protection from the hardships of famine, failed harvests, and other natural disasters. Finally, political and religious persecution drove some to seek freer climes.

Many Pandits today, speaking of their contemporary migration, recall memories of Sultan Sikandar (r. 1389–1413), also known as *but-shikan* (the idol-breaker), who, living up to his moniker, is said to have persecuted Hindus mercilessly and forced large numbers to leave Kashmir. However, this association across centuries is untenable for being anachronistic. The migration of Pandits today is, of course, not analogous with those of the late fourteenth to early fifteenth centuries. Sultan Sikandar may have indeed persecuted Kashmiri Pandits, but he did so from a position of power. The present insurgency in the Valley is overwhelmingly the protest of the powerless. And until the causes of the modern Pandits' departures after 1989 and the identity of those who are reported to have issued threats to the Hindus to instigate it can be ascertained, even the numerical preponderance of the Muslims of the Valley does not make their insurgency the arbitrary act of the powerful bearing down on a religiously defined minority. In much current Pandit discourse, however, there is an unspoken suggestion that the Valley's Muslims were somehow complicit in the threats issued to them, creating the impression that they were all assailants and Hindus the only victims. This allusion is fortified through the absence in Pandit narratives of exile of any acknowledgment that many Muslims, too, have left the Valley over the centuries, coerced by similar circumstances of poverty, natural calamity, and oppression. Such partial narration suggests that Kashmir's Muslims today are unaffected by the disruptions of life in the Valley and threats to their lives, family and property, whether from the state or indeed from elements espousing political and religious ideologies inimical to theirs.[35] The silence about these other victims of

---

[35]And it puts the full burden of correction on Kashmiri Muslims. Only such a blinkered understanding of suffering in the Valley can justify the

(Contd.)

contemporary conditions implicates the many Kashmiri Muslims in the actions of a few aggressors.

Azadi for a Nizam-e-Mustafa?

A twenty-year-old insurgency in the Valley rose to a dramatic crescendo in this past summer of 2010 when thousands came out onto the streets of Kashmir to protest the killing by Indian security forces of young Kashmiris, some as young as eight or twelve, for throwing stones at them. This summer was the culmination of a militancy growing over the last two years in which Kashmiris have challenged the Indian government's writ in the Valley largely through non-violent protest. Not insignificantly, agitation in summer 2008 was triggered by rival claims to Kashmir's land. The state government's decision to transfer ninety-nine acres of forest land to the Shri Amarnathji Shrine Board in the Kashmir Valley to set up temporary shelters and facilities for the annual Hindu pilgrimage to the shrine drew widespread resistance, one demonstration drawing more than 5,00,000 protesters at a single rally. But even this peaceful mode of civil disobedience could not exempt it from an older pattern of delegitimation used by the Indian government and even liberal Indians with regard to the challenge in Kashmir. The protests in 2008 and those in the two

---

(Contd.)

suggestion by Sanjay K. Tickoo in a memorandum written on behalf of the Kashmiri Pandit Sangharsh Samiti and submitted in Srinagar to the United Nations Special Rapporteur on Human Rights Defenders on 19 January 2011, that unless the Valley's majority community acknowledges the 'victimization and subsequent forced exodus of Kashmiri Pandits in 1989 and 1990 which is still going on' there can be no 'dialogue of reconciliation'. Indeed, 'a true closure will not occur until all important Valley leaders, regardless of their party affiliation or political inclinations, show sincerity in recognizing the origins of pain and wounds inflicted on Kashmiri Pandits and *viz-a-viz* to majority community' [sic].

summers that followed have been dismissed as the work of 'Islamic terrorists' and of that other nefarious group of Muslims, the 'separatists'. Through a remarkable feat of rhetorical short-circuiting, the fact that the majority of the demonstrators are Muslim is sufficient to mark them as illegitimate Islamicist demonstrations. That the slogans of Muslims are inflected in the religio-cultural idiom of Muslims only serves as proof-positive of terrorist and Islamist motivations driving these summer processions for Azadi.

This selective condemnation of Kashmiri Muslim actions is justified through wilfully ignoring a history that explains not only contemporary but also much older traditions of protest in the religious mode. It is conveniently forgotten that if the Dogra rulers could borrow symbols of sovereignty and legitimacy from elsewhere to make Kashmir 'Hindu', there was nothing to prevent their subjects from welcoming extra-territorial bonds of solidarity such as those available from affiliation with Islam. Given the nature of this state, in which the religious affiliation of the ruler was explicitly tied to his legitimacy to govern, it is hardly surprising that an emerging political assertion by Kashmir's Muslims from the turn of the twentieth century should have also embodied a religious sensibility. This remains true of a largely popular insurgency in the Valley of Kashmir begun in late 1989 and continuing to this day. Indeed, the stage was set more than a hundred years ago for a regional people to register their protest in a religious idiom against an equally religiously identified princely autocracy buttressed by colonial paramountcy.

Instances of the religious basis of national or regional identities are not peculiar to South Asia. By contrast, in the view of one strand of anti-colonial Indian national ideology which rose to dominance at the moment state power was captured, religion was theoretically castigated as a false, because a politically divisive, creed. Yet, paradoxically post-1947 Indian secular nationalism has played no small role in keeping alive a sense of the regional and religious particularity of Kashmir, at the same time as it has worked towards effacing it. In 1947, at the moment of independence and also the Partition of the subcontinent along religious lines, India claimed Muslim-majority Kashmir as its prize; a vindication of its secular credentials and a repudiation of Muslim Pakistan's 'communal' politics. In the rhetoric accompanying this incorporation, the Indian nation valorized its achievement precisely by stressing the Muslim nature of Kashmir and Kashmiris. The accrediting of an Islamic identity to the Kashmiris was related to yet another purpose they were to serve in the secular nation-state. They were the nation's security blanket with which to reassure an even more critical constituency in the aftermath of the traumas of Partition: the Muslim minority that had remained in India either by choice or by force of circumstance. However, the thrust of nationalist rhetoric has moved gradually towards erasing Muslim-ness especially since, in light of the new militant mood of Kashmiri self-assertion, it can no longer remain safely part of a secularist state's project of a controlled ascription of religious identities. It now conveniently wants Kashmiri Muslims, to quote the line of the pro-Khilafat and non-cooperation leader, Mohammed Ali, written in his paper *Comrade* in 1912, 'to shuffle off [their] individuality and become completely Hinduized'. To become secular is essentially to be Hindu in an Indian nation that has not acknowledged the tenuous nature of its own secular credentials.

For their part, while Kashmiri Muslims have resisted appropriation by 'secular' nationalist ideologies since 1947, they have similarly defied assimilation within an Islamic rhetoric that fails to recognize their regional specificities. The reference to religion in the political mobilization of Kashmiris has been, for the most part, free from markers generically or stereotypically associated with a process of Islamicization. Thus, barring a few relatively marginal militant groups active in current-day Kashmir, few in Kashmir have ever demanded the application of the Sharia' (Islamic law) or the veiling of women. Above all, the clamour by Kashmir's Muslims is for a legitimate government. It is the helplessness in which they were placed first by their Dogra rulers and then by Indian politicians, each neglecting to negotiate their legitimacy with the popular constituency of Kashmir that has provoked a militant response and the demand for 'Azadi'.

This history is drowned out by the recently amplified rhetoric of protecting from amputation a nation conceptualized as sanctified body. Perhaps the most effective response to those who wish to possess Kashmir as an integral part came in a recent meeting with members of the Indian all-party delegation deputed to Kashmir in September 2010. Gathered in the town of Tangmarg several Kashmiris 'expressed their frustration that India insists Kashmir is a part of India but suspects Kashmiris of being Pakistani agents and uses that suspicion as justification for its security tactics.' Which Indian defender of national integrity will answer the question that a Kashmiri in Tangmarg asked: 'Why don't you feel our pain if we are a part of your body?'[36]

---

[36]Jyoti Thottam 'Does India Have an Endgame in Kashmir? *Time*, New Delhi Friday, 24 September 2010 [http://www.time.com/time/world/article/0,8599,2021259,00.html].

A Letter to Fellow Kashmiris

Mohamad Junaid

Dear fellow Kashmiris,
I'm writing this letter from New York, a place far away, yet so close to everything.

This city can make you forget, by filching reality away from you. But it also reminds you perpetually, by bringing you close to a different reality, through the pain and suffering of others. There are exiled specimens from all over the world here (yes, mostly those permitted to come to the US). There are Irish and Greeks, escapees from famines and wars. There are Jews from Germany and Germans from Russia, the ones who survived persecution. There are Latinos from El Salvador, Peru, Guatemala and Bolivia, who fled Western-backed dictatorial regimes in their countries in the 1970s and 80s. There are Africans who narrowly missed genocide in Southern Sudan. There are Kurds from Turkey and Berber from North Africa, driven out of their lands by years of conflict. And, then there are African Americans, who were forcibly brought hundreds of years before to slave for their White masters, and who, despite recent claims of the dawning of an age of 'post-racial America', are still grovelling at the bottom of the socio-economic heap. The stories come to a similar conclusion: the world is shrinking for small nationalities and powerless minorities.

In their desire for control over more territory—and the unchallenged right to inflict violence—large and powerful nations run roughshod over legitimate rights of smaller and weaker peoples. Those who claim a permanent 'state of exception' have shred international law, which is supposed to guarantee the right of self-determination of nations both 'big and small', to pieces. Persecution of minorities all over the world continues in spite of numerous declarations to uphold human rights. Powerful countries use these declarations selectively, and instrumentally, to pursue their parochial goals. Europe, which has been claiming to be the flag-bearer of universal human civilization for centuries, is again in the grip of hatred, readying itself for yet another sacrificial genocide; so is America, whose citizens are being whipped into frenzy by racist, xenophobic and ignorant politicians. Meanwhile, the Muslim world is hurtled from one crisis to another. Already an object of global misunderstanding and hatred, it continues to fail to produce an enlightened, effective and coherent response. It either produces nihilistic violence of extremist groups like Al-Qaeda, or builds examples par excellence of vulgar exploitation like Dubai; both based in one way or other on a bastardized, logical extreme of Western rationality, and both far from the lived experience of most Muslims, and the spirit of their faith.

Amidst all this, where do the founts of hope lie? As Kashmiris, one of these numerous, struggling, small nationalities, caught in the whirlpool of forces of imperialist domination and religious-nationalist chauvinisms of recently formed states—while the grinding machine of military oppression keeps adding to the long history of our suffering—where must we situate ourselves? How must we imagine, think and plan a new life?

First, let me say this: the continued existence, persistence and resilience of Kashmiris, and of other oppressed peoples around the world, is itself indicative of the fact that the struggle is on: between the coercive, militarized reality and the power of free imagination, between the drudgery of dominating others and the beauty of resistance, between the technologies of power and the critical practices of the subject, between calculation and compassion, between the patriarchal, paternalistic hatred and the love for justice, between national fascism and national liberation, between metal and heart, bullet and wound, between the shadow of death and the canopy of life. The hope first springs from the existence of this struggle; and this struggle, let's keep in mind, is happening not between nations, cultures, or civilizations, but within them.

Given this, I would suggest then that we rethink our struggle, and posit it not in terms of Kashmir and India—as territorial entities, with settled national identities (and obviously not in terms of Muslim and non-Muslim, or for that matter, East and West), but as between the opaque rationale that leads to militarized brutalization of the other, and the moral reasoning that necessitates resistance. This reconstitution of our struggle opens us up comprehensively: it leads to openness towards the unknown, and the unknowable others, to radical new ideas and life, to an un-predetermined future. It evokes the obligation to build alliances of solidarity with those others whose suffering is invisible to us, and whose tortured voices we are unable to listen to. It demands that the plan for a new life not be based on, or become, a model. The un-predetermined future, however, does not mean an unplanned, chaotic path into the future either. It would be logically challenging (and useless), in any case, to plan an unplanned, chaotic path. What it means is that the future free and independent Kashmir, to continue to remain free and independent, and to continuously live the moment of freedom, should not replicate any socio-economic blueprints (especially the ones handed out by institutions of the hegemonic global economic order), nor should it accept the kind of modular democracy a tragicomic version of which Indian government makes us Kashmiris suffer every few years.

It also means that we challenge those who vacuously exhort us towards setting up of an 'Islamic state'. We must renounce their historically and logically unsound claims, and constructively dislodge the formalistic aspects of their thinking, while, if possible, retrieve the (deeply buried and often turned-insignificant) ethical core of

Islam,[1] which calls for universal solidarity and social justice. Instead of seeking to build a state based on religious ideology (which in essence would not look much different from India, Pakistan, Iran, Israel or the US and would always be exclusivist) we must build an independent, free society based on faith—faith and trust in each other. This confidence in each other would mean getting rid of the fear of the other, and of mutual suspicion. And in consequence it would mean a society that doesn't feel a need to keep an eye on each other, which renounces surveillance and its

---

[1]Although a majority of people in Kashmir follow Islam and may look to its politico-legal traditions to found the new society, in my view we must not restrict ourselves to what we find in Islam, while at the same time take as much as we can. The reasons for this 'selective appropriation' are multiple. I only mention a few here:

First, I don't see Islam as a 'coherent system of thought' (as an ideology, a tightly bound whole) and find plurality, contradictions and logical paradoxes within its traditions and essential texts, many of which are surely a result of the historical/geographical differences for and across which Islam has been sought to be 'interpreted'. I must clarify that many of these interpretations are quite productive, evidence for which are the varied sects, schools of thought, theologies, philosophies and social movements that are associated with Islam.

Second, to even begin to 'interpret Islam,' as some suggest we should, would be to see it as some sort of a coherent, seamless text, where Islam as lived reality is an ensemble of practices, traditions, beliefs, hopes and fears, often mixed in plural ways with many other traditions and beliefs. It goes back to the same old argument: 'Whose Islam?' That is why I speak of Islam only with regard to some of its ethical dimensions, which I see as full of potential for reinforcing the moral foundations for a just human coexistence.

Third, the sort of society I envision for Kashmir pre- and post-independence is guided by a concern and a hope. The ideal of Azadi must not draw its force and spirit from one tradition alone, but from as many as possible, which is not a political imperative but an ethical duty: to remain open to others' traditions as well. An inclusive society 'is owned by none, but it belongs to everyone'.

(Contd.)

executing spies. We must keep in mind though that this mutual confidence cannot be grounded in our sameness, but in the unreservedly given acceptance to the uniqueness of our separate beings as individuals and cultural groups, brought together through a freely chosen fellowship, as full and meaningful participants in the society that is always fluid and becoming. We must not think like the Indian nationalists do: that we are one as Kashmiris; that there is something called 'Kashmiriness' which—like some sort of genetic or chemical substance, or blood—we all have in our bodies. Instead of oneness, we must think in terms of togetherness.

The basis of our togetherness is freedom, democracy and dignity. I often think of the three ideas together: there can be no democracy without freedom and dignity, nor can there be freedom without democracy and dignity, and obviously freedom and democracy is dignity. Only such society which freely allows and appreciates criticism, and not in an empty, meaningless fashion, as is the trend in the West these days, but keeps itself open to progressive transformation through critique (progressive: what continuously expands the horizon of freedom and rights), is worthy of being called truly democratic. And dignity arises from freedom from suspicion and stereotype, and therefore, from a positive trust that the society places in its fellow citizens and cultural groups. When I think of Azadi I see freedom, democracy and dignity as its inseparable core.

(Contd.)

In the end, the question we are faced with is: What sort of society will oblige its non-religious members to be respectful towards those who profess religion, and oblige its religion-professing members to be respectful towards those who are not religious or not of their religion? These concerns become an issue in the context of places where claims to religion/religious authority are used as licenses to silence others, a feature not so different from places where exclusive claims to 'Rationality' and 'Science' are used to vilify those who follow religion. We have to find a way to foster this reciprocal obligation in the spirit of radical openness.

You and I know that we have been regularly asked, both by those who oppose us and those who support us, to explicitly state what we mean when we 'demand' Azadi. We have often articulated it only in formal terms: that we want independence from India— a freedom from its illegitimate sovereignty over our lives (and yes, those who sit at the helm of coercive power, have refused even to hear this clear statement of our Azadi). But we know that Azadi goes far beyond this voluntary separation from a forced union. It touches upon the core of what it means to live as a small, but dignified nationality in a world where the global leviathan of big capital and its associated uneven crises meets, in a violent orgy, the international space saturated with muscular, bellicose, (often nuclear-armed) nation-states. Our search for Azadi is in reality the only choice left in this din. Not that we can compete with big nations in their pursuit of dominance (I see desire for dominance as a sort of death-wish, madness—a mutually assured destruction), but we truly don't want to, even if we could. We don't demand to create just another state in the world; that wouldn't make any sense. Our demand for Azadi is a clear need and aspiration—and a last, desperate wish, if you will; so that when the big states would have mutually assured our collective destruction, we could know that we at least lived a better life, and it will be sweeter because we would have done it without brawn, bruises or too much money. That is what we mean when we say we have a right to decide our own future (path, if not destination). Big bully states have decided their and our future, and we can't escape the moment when it all vanishes—this Utopia that things will always remain the same— but we demand that till that time is upon us, let's find our own way in this world. We will go down with you, but we can't be forced to walk along with you all the way to that final burial ground.

My fellow Kashmiris, we have borne the wounds of our collective suffering on our bodies. And yes, for the Azadi that we talk about, it is a price absolutely worth paying. Our bodies are testament enough that we deserve Azadi. We, however, don't demand only our own Azadi, but Azadi for all the suffering, small nations and minorities with whom we stand in moral solidarity—a principle we derive equally from Islam and other faiths, and from the universal norm of a just coexistence that underlie our collective life on planet earth.

If our Azadi has the moral content that it has, it would not be so difficult to answer the questions that will unquestionably face us in the future, after (and before) our inevitable independence. Since we can't deny that we live in that coercive, real world which we want to cast off to build a new Kashmiri society, we will have to engage with it, but on our own terms, in the spirit of Azadi— Azadi as a living principle. What will be our relationship with the states of India, Pakistan or China? And, what will be our relationship with the peoples of these countries and the world? Azadi demands unconditional friendship with our neighbours. We must offer this unconditional friendship, an offer that will never be withdrawn, to both the big and small states in our neighbourhood. It would mean never to harm them, or their mutual relations, but to actively foster healthy relations in South and Greater Asia, to infuse in them a spirit of mutual cooperation. For the peoples of these neighbouring, and other countries, it would mean unrestricted access to Kashmir and its sites of pilgrimage; except for those whose visits are proven to have a violent intent: that would lead to violence against humans and nature. In the same spirit of Azadi, wouldn't Kashmiris happily accept the presence of those whose safety is threatened in their own countries of origin for speaking for justice and truth? Who wouldn't offer with gratitude Arundhati Roy a Kashmiri citizenship?

Over many years, and perhaps centuries now, Kashmir's Muslims have had a fractured relationship with Kashmir's Hindus. The relationship between Muslims and Sikhs, if not so laden with power, coercion and retribution, has remained fraught with potential violence. The same has been the case within Kashmir's various Muslim communities and social groups. I don't suggest that all these fractures can be easily sutured, but it is incumbent upon all of us, and comparatively easier, to remove violence from these relationships. A new life deserves a chance. History must not be allowed to come in the way of building a shared future. Within Kashmir our society requires gestures of friendship not only between communities that will constitute the Kashmiri nation, but also among individuals, from within their own and other groups. It is much more an obligation upon Kashmir's Muslim majority to extend a hand of true and everlasting friendship to Kashmir's minorities.[2]

Our Azadi, the basis of our new life as a nation and society, is deeply connected with Kashmir as a place. This place, however, is a place of generosity and hospitality, and not of exclusion or hostility. Our ties to Kashmir are not natural, but of nature. And

---

[2]Over the last twenty years Muslim Kashmiris and Hindu Kashmiris have not only grown apart physically—out of each others' daily lives, but also they tell different stories about this separation. These stories have their own plots, conspiracy theories and main actors. They use different tropes, from unrequited love to great betrayal, while imputing clear motives where, perhaps, it is very hard to determine them. However, there are more than two neat stories. A plurality of stories collides with each other creating doubt and better wisdom. Once juxtaposed with stories about past harmony (or conflict), they create a contested ethico-political space that has potential for unsettling dominant and domineering narratives, and preventing exclusionary politics. It gets complicated once one begins to see 'interests' of Hindu and Muslim (and of other communities) as mutually exclusive. In my view, that is not the case. But it is a judgment that is better left for the future to make. My belief is that Muslim Kashmiris and other communities must welcome their Hindu compatriots unconditionally, and Hindus must return unconditionally; which means Muslim Kashmiris must not demand that Hindus necessarily have to support (or even understand) Kashmiri struggle for freedom, while Hindus must not demand that they will return only if Kashmiris give up the struggle for freedom. This is not to say that Muslim Kashmiris don't have a right to oppose the struggle for independence, or Hindu Kashmiris can't join the movement for Azadi. They can, and they have. The Indian government connects the return of Hindus to the return of 'normalcy'— which they define as giving up of the struggle for Azadi. We must not fall into this either/or false dichotomy.

by that, my friends, I mean we have a strong obligation as grateful residents of Kashmir to prevent relations of exploitation between humans and nature. Nature is not a natural resource. It is a collective gift, which has to be judiciously shared with, and protected for, humans and non-human forms of life, now and for the future. What would Azadi be worth for Kashmir if its trees were gone; if its rivers and lakes dried out and its mountains were dug up; if its air was polluted and the soil was full of chemicals; if its bears and snow leopards, those other proud residents of Kashmir, were forced to come down, or hunted out of their natural habitats? What forms would our sources of sustenance— our economy—take in terms of an Azadi that is in a respectful relationship with nature? What would we produce, and how would we consume? How would a balance be struck between production and consumption, which is in ethical alignment with our obligation towards nature as well as our principles of justified needs? Must we not do away with economic rationalism, industrial overproduction and runaway consumerism? And how would we exchange our goods and services? Shouldn't small-scale business become a principle and normative mode of exchange in our society, one that will remain ever watchful against predatory corporatization?

My friends, our journey towards freedom began the day we realized that we need to be free. As time has gone by, more and more of us have understood that it is only by struggling and achieving freedom for Kashmir and its residents that we can truly and authentically live our lives. Our work of construction has, accordingly, long begun, and it will require an extraordinary effort of will and tremendous endurance to create a sort of society that is really worth living in. We wouldn't have succeeded in achieving our true freedom if we don't expunge from our hearts and minds the last traces of hatred and violent anger toward others, including those who oppress us. We must remember that we are fighting against ideologies and processes that legitimize, and lead to, the domination of others, not those who execute it, especially not the foot soldiers of occupation. We must become what we want to be, not what our oppressor wants to turn us into. I don't advocate sterile processes of 'dialogue' as an alternative to the methods we adopt in our everyday resistance—especially the 'dialogue' where one side is backed by military power. Dialogue can happen only in a free and fair atmosphere of mutual comprehension. What sort of a dialogue can take place when one side denies the other the right to be free? What sort of a meeting place can there be between justice and injustice? We must, however, not close our ears and eyes to what the other is saying or showing us. Listening is a great gesture of friendship. We must politely refuse to accept what is fundamentally unjust.

In this moment of suffering, our fundamental duty is towards our own people, towards those who are hit the most every time our society protests, the poor and the weak. My thoughts go to that one Kashmiri mother, in a picture I saw recently, who was being violently pushed around by a cop, an ignorant man, who could be her neighbour. And I still can't get the image of a little boy weeping over the body of his dead brother out of my head. His scream of pain, draining all the blood from his face, cut through the picture and hit me like a shell. No freedom is worth an innocent life. Our occupiers tell us the same, while they continue to feed innocent Kashmiri lives to the fires of occupation. Our occupiers tell us to send our children to schools, where they could learn how Bhagat Singh and Subhash Chandra Bose fought for India's freedom, but they don't want our children to learn about their own long overdue freedoms, far from enjoying them. They urge, and even force, us to vote in their form of democracy, a democracy stripped down to the barren and inconsequential act of voting, a democracy designed not to empower our voice but to inflate turnouts.

My friends, we are through with all that. Our imagination is more powerful than their military. They have been proven wrong over and over again. We must keep the spirit of Azadi alive, because that is the only way it can be. That is the only way we can be.

This article first appeared on the website http://kashmir solidarity.wordpress.com, 6 November 2010.

Timeline

1846

After being ruled by the Mughals, the Sikhs and eventually the British, Kashmir finally comes under the Dogra dynasty. The ruler, Maharaja Gulab Singh, had bought the Kashmir Valley from the East India Company, and formed the new state of Jammu and Kashmir under the Treaty of Amritsar. With Dogra rule, a new phase of oppression begins for the Kashmiris.

1931

Widespread protests against Maharaja Hari Singh erupt all over Kashmir, and the revolt is brutally suppressed by the maharaja's constabulary. The uprising was attributed to the fact that the predominantly Muslim population was kept poor, illiterate and was not allowed representation in the state's administrative apparatus.

1932

Sheikh Muhammed Abdullah launches the All Jammu & Kashmir Muslim Conference (MC) with a manifesto to fight for the liberation of the Kashmiri people. Maharaja Hari Singh's subsequent efforts to redress the grievances of the masses, first by appointing the Glancy Commission and then by constituting a legislative assembly, turn out to be hollow.

1939

Muslim Conference splits due to differences between its leaders. Sheikh Abdullah launches an independent party, the Jammu & Kashmir National Conference (NC).

1944

National Conference adopts the Naya Kashmir (New Kashmir) resolution, which calls for radical socio-economic transformation and full citizenship rights for the people of Jammu and Kashmir.

1946

The 'Quit Kashmir' movement is launched by the NC against the monarchy, calling for the sovereignty of the Kashmiri people. Sheikh Abdullah is taken into custody.

1947

Following Independence, and the Partition of British India into India and Pakistan, a grave dispute arose over the question of which nation Kashmir should accede to. Based on geographical and religious factors, Kashmir was expected to go to Pakistan.

Aug: there is heightened unrest in the wake of the revolt in Poonch against the maharaja's taxation policy—leading to an exodus of over 60,000 Muslim refugees.

Sep: there follows a chilling massacre of Muslims in Jammu. Long hidden, this carnage saw more than 50,000 people slaughtered in the streets.

Oct: Tribal fighters from Mirpur invade Kashmir, said to be incensed by the atrocities against fellow Muslims in Poonch and Jammu. The tribesmen engage in looting and killing along the way. Fearful for his safety, Maharaja Hari Singh asks India for help.

26 Oct: having fled to Jammu, the maharaja signs the 'Instrument of Accession' integrating the state of J&K into the Indian Union in return for support against invaders. The clauses in the Instrument of Accession give India control over defence, communication, foreign affairs and ancillary items. Sheikh Abdullah, after his release from prison in September, is a willing partner in the deal.

27 Oct: The Indian Army enters Kashmir. Pakistan subsequently disputes the accession as illegal and the first war over Kashmir breaks out.

1948

India takes the case of Kashmir to the United Nations. The world over, Kashmir is officially recognized as a disputed territory. The United Nations Commission for India and Pakistan (UNCIP) passes a resolution providing for (i) Ceasefire (ii) Withdrawal of Pakistani troops and tribals, followed by Indian troops and (iii) Plebiscite.

1949

Ceasefire is proclaimed under UN auspices.

1950

The Constitution of India comes into effect. Article 1 proclaims the entire state of J&K as a part of the territory of India, and Article 370 gives a special status to the state of J&K, corresponding to the terms of the Instrument of Accession.

1951

The first post-Independence elections are held in the state. The UN passes a resolution to the effect that such elections do not substitute a plebiscite, because a plebiscite offers the option of choosing between India and Pakistan. Sheikh Abdullah wins, mostly unopposed, and rumours of election-rigging emerge. Such charges continue to plague most subsequent elections in J&K.

1952–54

Sheikh Abdullah begins to repeatedly shift positions between endorsing Kashmir's accession to India and supporting the right of self-determination for Kashmiris. He signs the Delhi Agreement in 1952, but later procrastinates in confirming the accession of Kashmir to India. He is dismissed and arrested. Bakshi Ghulam Mohammed is installed in power—he gets the accession formally ratified in 1954.

Formation of Plebiscite Front

1956–57

The J&K Constituent Assembly adopts a fresh constitution for Kashmir, declaring it an integral part of the Indian Union. The UN passes another resolution stating that such actions would not constitute a final disposition of the state. India resists plebiscite efforts. Kashmiri activists continue to insist on the promised self-determination.

1963–64

Mass agitation erupts in the Kashmir Valley when a holy relic—a strand of hair from the Prophet's beard—is found missing from the Hazratbal shrine in Srinagar; the lost relic is later recovered on 4 January 1964.

Protest demonstrations occur against the implementation of Articles 356 and 357 of the Indian Constitution, by virtue of which the Centre can exercise its authority over legislative powers in Kashmir. The special status accorded to the state under Article 370 continues to get eroded.

1965

Indo-Pakistan war breaks out after Pakistan sends infiltrators across the ceasefire line in August. The war ends in a ceasefire on 23 September.

1966

India and Pakistan sign the Tashkent Declaration. Although a peace agreement, it does not contain a no-war pact or any measures to reduce guerilla warfare in Kashmir.

1971

Maqbool Bhat and others form the Jammu Kashmir National Liberation Front (a precursor to the Jammu and Kashmir Liberation Front or JKLF), which calls for complete independence of J&K from India and Pakistan. The Indo-Pakistan War of 1971 takes place, resulting in the secession of East Pakistan, and the creation of the new state of Bangladesh.

1972

India and Pakistan recognize the ceasefire line as the Line of Control (LoC). In July both countries sign the Simla Agreement, which has a clause that the final settlement of Kashmir will be decided bilaterally in the future and that both the sides shall respect the LoC.

1977–83

NC wins back to back elections in 1977 and 1983. International watchdogs accuse India of rigging elections again. Sheikh Abdullah dies.

In 1979, USSR invades Afghanistan. The US and Pakistan are involved in training, recruiting, arming, and unleashing the mujahedin in Afghanistan.

1984

The Indian Army takes the Siachen Glacier region of Kashmir. Maqbool Bhat hanged in Tihar Jail.

1987–89

Farooq Abdullah wins the elections and forms a coalition government with the Indian National Congress. The Muslim United Front (MUF) says that the elections have been rigged. The rigging of 1987 elections provides a boost to the demand for self-determination. The insurgency in the Valley gains momentum from this point on.

The end of the Soviet occupation of Afghanistan in 1988 releases vast numbers of militants and weapons into Kashmir. Pakistan provides arms and training to militants in Kashmir, fuelling the discontent already smouldering in the Valley. Massive protests start in Kashmir in 1989. JKLF declares armed struggle against Indian rule.

1990

Jan: Farooq Abdullah resigns as CM. Jagmohan—a bureaucrat with pronounced right-wing Hindu leanings—is appointed as the Governor of Kashmir. All powers are invested in the Central rule. An estimated 100 unarmed protesters are killed by Indian troops at the Gawakadal bridge. People blame the administrators for this massacre. The armed movement gains widespread popularity. A number of other massacres take place. The government puts a strict curfew in place which lasts for several months, leading to widespread misery. With the rise of new militant groups, warnings, anonymous posters and the unexplained killings of innocent members of the Kashmiri Pandit community contribute to an atmosphere of insecurity for them. Governor Jagmohan's administration actively discourages any reconciliation between members of the Hindu and Muslim communities. By March most of the estimated 1,62,500 Hindus in the Valley, including almost the entire Kashmiri Pandit community, flee the Valley.

Mar: An estimated one million take to the streets in protests. More than forty people are killed in police firing.

May: Over two million people attend the funeral march of the slain spiritual leader, Mirwaiz Maulvi Muhammad Farooq; over 100 mourners are shot dead. The armed movement continues to gain momentum. Girish Saxena, a former Intelligence officer, replaces Jagmohan as governor. From this point onwards, throughout the 1990s, indigenous and foreign militant groups proliferate, with an estimated half a million Indian security forces deployed in the Kashmir Valley during this period. There is increasing violence and human rights violations by all sides, leading to tens of thousands of civilian casualties.

1993

All Parties Hurriyiat Conference (APHC) is formed to promote the cause of Kashmiri nationalism.

Major incidents of state-sponsored violence take place in Kashmir. An entire neighbourhood in the northern town of Sopore in burned down by paramilitary troopers, while more than a hundred are brutally massacred.

In the southern town of Bijbehara, Border Security Forces fire upon a Friday procession in which fifty-five are killed.

1994–98

Counter-insurgency reaches a peak. Specialist Indian troops with the aid of 'Ikhwanis', former militants-turned-India-loyalists, crush the armed movement. Human rights violations reach an all time high.

Between the angry protests on the streets of Kashmir and the uneasy silence of Kashmiris in exile, comes a work of immense significance: Agha Shahid Ali's *The Country Without a Post Office*.

1999

Following the infiltration of Pakistani soldiers and Kashmiri militants into positions on the Indian side of the LoC, the Kargil War breaks out. The first 'live' war in South Asia, the conflict is given detailed media coverage, and becomes a propaganda war. Tensions between both countries flare up, and Kashmir once again is caught in the crossfire. By July, international pressure compels Pakistan to withdraw its forces.

2000

Mar: A day before US President Clinton's visit to India, thirty-five Sikhs are killed by unidentified gunmen in the village of Chittisinghpura in Kashmir. The government blames militants, but in Kashmir people suspect government agencies. Possible involvement of the government is endorsed by prominent Sikh leaders. A few days later, in an encounter at Panchalthan village in south Kashmir, security forces claim to have killed all five responsible for the massacre. Locals, however, are convinced that the killed 'foreign militants' are in fact local civilians picked randomly, shot, and their bodies mutilated. A protest demonstration is fired upon by Indian security forces in Anantnag, leading to the death of another nine civilians. Subsequent DNA tests of the corpses will prove that the five killed were civilians, and that the state government tried to fudge the DNA samples. Till date, no judicial inquiry has been conducted on the massacre.

2001

Jul: India and Pakistan, under the leadership of Prime Minister A.B.Vajpayee and President Musharraf, fail to arrive at a settlement on the Kashmir issue, despite five long arduous one-on-one meetings. Plans on Kashmir include free trade, demilitarization, shared autonomy but they fail to take off.

Sep: In the wake of the attacks on the World Trade Center in the USA, Indian PM Vajpayee urges President Bush to extend his War on Terror to Kashmir as well. President Musharraf accuses India of exploiting the situation to harm Pakistan's strategic assets and 'the Kashmir cause'. There is growing agitation in Kashmir over the US invasion of Afghanistan.

2002

May: Moderate separatist leader, Abdul Ghani Lone, is assassinated by unidentified gunmen. Thousands attend his funeral prayers. Several theories of pro-government gunmen or the role of foreign militants have been rumoured, but no investigation has been carried out till date.

2008

May: A controversial land deal, wherein the state government gives a hundred acres of land in the Valley to a Hindu shrine board, causes a furore.

Jun: Muslims in Kashmir take to the streets to protest against the land deal, waving Islamic flags, hurling stones and bricks. The ensuing months witness further instances of protest as well as a brutal reprisal by the state—over a hundred people are killed in a short span of two months, including eminent separatist leader, Sheikh Aziz. This provides a renewed basis for demanding self-determination, and against the Indian state. Although the agitation is eventually crushed, many liberal political commentators and intellectuals from India begin to articulate their anguish over the turmoil in Kashmir.

2009

May–Jun: The rape and murder of two women in Shopian lead to widespread protests across Kashmir. Kashmiris and independent investigations suggest the hand of government forces, but the government claims the two have drowned and closes the investigation.

2010

Kashmir witnesses the most explosive political atmosphere for over a decade.

Jun: The death of sixteen-year-old Tufail Ahmad Matoo after being hit by a tear-gas shell provides a charged catalyst in reincarnating the crushed agitation of 2008. Protesters shout anti-India slogans and processions continue even till late night. People burn government buildings, defy curfew, attack Indian forces in the bunkers, and demand complete demilitarization of Kashmir. Citing human rights abuses, separatist leaders organize protest calendars which last for over four months, paralysing local life. Over 110 people get killed. The Indian government, after witnessing the intensity of upheaval, recommends autonomy proposals, assurances of employment generation and compensation to victims. These developments are all rejected outright by people in Kashmir. The government announces the appointment of three interlocutors to mediate the Kashmir dispute.

Notes on Contributors

Aijaz Hussain lives in Srinagar, Kashmir, where he is correspondent for the Associated Press (AP). His reportage frequently appears in many publications, including the *Huffington Post*, *Guardian*, *Los Angeles Times*, *New York Times*, and the *Washington Post*. He also writes for the weekly news magazine *India Today*.

Aaliya Anjum was born and bred in Kashmir, and has been Commonwealth Scholar at the School of Oriental & African Studies, London. She has been involved with human rights advocacy in Kashmir with the Human Rights Law Network, and as a consultant with the J&K State Commission for Women. She currently teaches public international law and human rights at Vitasta School of Law, University of Kashmir.

Angana P. Chatterji is professor of social and cultural anthropology at the California Institute of Integral Studies in San Francisco, and co-convener of the International People's Tribunal on Human Rights and Justice in Indian-administered Kashmir. She is the author of *Violent Gods: Hindu Nationalism in India's Present* (2009), and co-author of the report, *Buried Evidence: Unknown, Unmarked, and Mass Graves in Indian-administered Kashmir* (2009).

Arif Ayaz Parrey is a conflict activist by circumstance and a fiction writer by choice. He was born and brought up in Anantnag/Islamabad and studied law at Aligarh Muslim University. He could be the second cousin of both Hamlet and Gregor Samsa. He is currently stuck somewhere in the middle of his first collection of short stories, thus mirroring his subject, Kashmir.

Basharat Peer was born in Kashmir in 1977, and studied politics and journalism at Aligarh Muslim University and Columbia University. He has worked as a reporter in India and as an editor with Foreign Affairs magazine in New York. His first book, *Curfewed Night*, an account of the Kashmir conflict won the Vodaphone Crossword Award for Non-fiction. His work has appeared in *Granta, Financial Times, Guardian, N+1, The Caravan, Open,* and *Outlook* magazines.

Dilnaz Boga is a Mumbai based journalist, who also works for the Srinagar-based website Kashmir Dispatch. She has worked as chief copy editor on the international desk of the *Hindustan Times*, Mumbai. She has an MA in peace and conflict studies from the University of Sydney, where her dissertation was on the psychological impact of human rights violations on children in Kashmir. It became the basis of the documentary film *Invisible Kashmir: The Other Side of Jannat.*

Gautam Navlakha is a democratic rights activist, member of Peoples Union for Democratic Rights, a writer, and an editorial consultant to the *Economic and Political Weekly.*

Gowhar Fazili is a researcher at the Department of Sociology, University of Delhi. He has been a socio-cultural and ecological activist in Kashmir, as a part of initiatives like Green Kashmir Environmental Trust, SPACE (Students Platform for Acquiring and Consolidating Experience), Aman Trust, Delhi, and Amnesty International, India. He has also taught political science to students at a graduate level in Kashmir. Between other mundane activities, he writes, paints, photographs, designs, travels and cooks.

Hilal Ahmad Mir was born in Nawab Bazar, in old Srinagar, in 1974. After an MA in mass communications and journalism from Kashmir University in 2001, he worked at *Greater Kashmir*, the Valley's largest circulated newspaper, and as a stringer for Associated Press. He is currently an assistant editor with the *Hindustan Times*, New Delhi.

Malik Sajad grew up in Srinagar where he learned his drawing skills from his father, an embroidery designer. At seventeen he began work as the editorial cartoonist for the newspaper *Greater Kashmir*. For eight years now he has been engaging with issues of urgency to Kashmiris, through these cartoons, as well as illustrations, photographs, animation and graphic novels. His work has appeared in *Tehelka* and *The Caravan*. The website www.kashmirblackandwhite.com features more than 300 artworks by him.

MC Kash Represents A Kashmiri Struggle. A Struggle To Speak An' To Get Heard. Straight From The Heart Of Kashmir, Srinagar, MC Kash Has Witnessed 'Nuff To Put It Down In his Rhymes An' Keep Marchin' Forward. Real Name, Roushan Illahi, Born In Da Era Of Massacres An' Armed Struggle (1990), Has A Hope Of Influencin' Those Who Support Reality An' Truth.

Mohamad Junaid grew up in Islamabad, Kashmir, in the 1990s, witness to the rise of the resistance against Indian rule, and its suppression: the humiliation of military crackdowns, the physical and verbal abuses of random frisking and house searches, the marches to protest the killings of close and unknown friends. Educated in Kashmir, at the Aligarh Muslim University, and the Jawaharlal Nehru University, Delhi, he is currently a graduate student at City University of New York, where he training as an anthropologist.

Mridu Rai is the author of *Hindu Rulers, Muslim Subjects: Islam, Rights and the History of Kashmir*. She teaches South Asian history at Trinity College, Dublin.

Najeeb Mubarki was born in Srinagar, went to school there, and later studied at the Universities of Delhi, at Jawaharlal Nehru University, and the School of Oriental and African Studies, London. He now works on the edit page of the *Economic Times*, New Delhi. He has earlier worked for the newsmagazine *Outlook*, and briefly taught literature to post-graduate students in Srinagar.

Nawaz Gul Qanungo is a Srinagar-based journalist. He was earlier based in New Delhi with the newspaper *Business Standard*, and his work has also appeared in *Tehelka*, *Down To Earth*, Rediff.com, the *Kashmir Times*, Tamil *Dinamalar* and several other newspapers and websites.

Nitasha Kaul is a perpetually homeless Kashmiri novelist, academic and artist. She has a doctorate in economics and philosophy from the UK, and was earlier a professor of economics in Bristol, a fellow in politics at Westminster in London, and most recently an associate professor of creative writing in Bhutan. She has authored numerous articles on the themes of identity, economy, gender, social theory, technology and democracy. Her as-yet-unpublished debut novel *Residue*, about Kashmiris in exile, was shortlisted for the Man Asian Literary Prize in 2009.

Parvaiz Bukhari was born and educated in Srinagar, and since 2004 has been working there as an independent journalist. He has been reporting for over fifteen years in both print and TV, on Indian politics, foreign affairs and conflict, including the post 9/11 US-led international coalition military campaigns in Afghanistan and Iraq. He has contributed articles to Indian as well as international publications including the *Times of India*, *Outlook*, *Tehelka*, *Mail Today*, *Time*, *AsiaTimes* and the *Nation*.

Ravi Nessman is the Associated Press's South Asia chief of bureau, and has reported for more than a decade on conflicts across Africa, the Middle East and Asia for them. He was in Afghanistan in 2001 and embedded with the US marines when they rode into Baghdad in 2003. He reported on the crisis in Zimbabwe, the second Palestinian intifadeh and Israel's pullout from the Gaza Strip. He was in Islamabad when Benazir Bhutto was assassinated, in Mumbai during the 26/11 attacks and in Sri Lanka for the end of the civil war with the Tamil Tigers.

Saiba Varma is currently writing her PhD anthropology thesis on psychiatry, trauma and healing in Kashmir, and has recently completed fourteen months of fieldwork in Srinagar. She is also an eager *hak* aficionado.

Sameer Bhat lives in Dubai and Delhi, and is one of Kashmir's earliest and most widely read bloggers. A journalist by day (and a raconteur at night) his short stories and satirical writings have appeared in leading English dailies in Kashmir. He is also a contributor to *Counter Punch*, USA, and has done fleeting stints in NDTV, *Hindustan Times* and the *Financial Times*. He is currently working on a book of fiction set in Kashmir.

Sanjay Kak is a documentary film-maker whose work includes *Jashn-e-Azadi* (How We Celebrate Freedom, 2007), a feature-length film about Kashmir. Based in New Delhi, he has been actively involved in the documentary cinema movement, and in the Campaign Against Censorship. He writes occasional commentaries, usually about Kashmir, and reviews books he is passionate about.

Shuddhabrata Sengupta is an artist and writer with the Raqs Media Collective. He is a co-founder of the Sarai Programme at the Centre for the Study of Developing Societies, Delhi, and a member of the editorial collective of the Sarai Reader Series. Sengupta occasionally contributes to the group blog Kafila.org.

Suvaid Yaseen was born and brought up in Srinagar, Kashmir. His undergraduate degree at Delhi University was in political science, where he is currently finishing a masters programme.

Suvir Kaul teaches literature at the University of Pennsylvania, visits his ancestral home in Srinagar when he can, and worries about the nature and quality of life he sees around him in Kashmir. He hopes for a future in which both Kashmiris and Indians can live at peace with themselves and their neighbours.

Tim Sullivan is senior Asia correspondent with the Associated Press. As a foreign correspondent for more than a decade, he has worked mostly in South Asia and West Africa, and covered stories ranging from India's economic rise to the civil war in Liberia. Sullivan grew up in Boiling Springs, Pennsylvania, is a graduate of Georgetown University and was a Nieman Fellow at Harvard University in 2001–02. He lives in New Delhi with his wife, Michele Caputo, and their two sons.

Wasim Bhat is a sociologist based in Srinagar. Educated by the multiform presence of Sufi *Tariqas*, which the city of Srinagar has for long been a centre of, his writing and research has meandered around the city for a considerable time, much like waters of the Jhelum. He is currently researching a book that attempts to straddle the multilayered history of the city, a retelling through modes of social history and poetry, juxtaposing mythological and contemporary narratives in a context where two millennia of a civilizational space have been reduced in two decades to a bunker.

Yirvun Kreel, literally meaning 'an insect that floats on water', is an anonymous activist who operates via Facebook. The quotes attributed to him in this book have been taken from his Facebook status updates.

Acknowledgements

The unhesitating support of our contributors suggests that they might find gratitude unnecessary, but their solidarity is warmly acknowledged here.

Some individual names must still be taken:

Basharat Peer, Dilnaz Boga, Hilal Mir, Najeeb Mubarki, Nawaz Gul Qanungo and Parvaiz Bukhari, for reassuring us that journalists can always exceed the limitations of their editors.

Aaliya Anjum, Saiba Verma, Angana Chatterji, Gowhar Fazili, Mohammad Junaid, Nitasha Kaul, Sameer Bhat, Shuddhabrata Sengupta, Suvaid Yaseen and Suvir Kaul for letting us share in their intense preoccupation with Kashmir's present.

Malik Sajad, for making this the print debut of his graphic novel, a work in progress that we await with excitement; Arif Ayaz Parrey and Aijaz Hussain for letting us dip into their growing hoard of stories; and MC Kash for generously sharing his song—and incidentally gifting the volume a title.

Gautam Navlakha, Mridu Rai, and Wasim Bhat were persuaded to turn their commitment, understanding and scholarship into pieces written specially for this volume: honoured.

Satish Sharma and Yasin Dar, Associated Press, New Delhi.

At Penguin India, Ravi Singh unhesitatingly supported the idea of this book; his colleagues, R. Sivapriya and Ambar Sahil Chatterjee, with their keen antennae, and a lightness of touch, helped transform the text into a book. Bena Sareen, designer, didn't forget an old debt of tea and coffee.

Agha Shahid Ali, for his presence, and for the extract used in my introduction, taken from 'A Pastoral', *The Country Without a Post Office* (W.W. Norton & Company, Inc., 1998).

And Arundhati Roy. Always.